Black Male Success in Higher Education

Black Male Success in Higher Education

How the Mathematical Brotherhood Empowers a Collegiate Community to Thrive

Christopher C. Jett

Foreword by Duane Cooper
Afterword by Erica N. Walker

TEACHERS COLLEGE PRESS

TEACHERS COLLEGE | COLUMBIA UNIVERSITY
NEW YORK AND LONDON

Published by Teachers College Press,® 1234 Amsterdam Avenue, New York, NY 10027

Front cover design by Edwin Kuo. Photos (clockwise from top left) by: mavo, XArtProduction, and Hryshchyshen Serhii, all via Shutterstock.

Library of Congress Cataloging-in-Publication Data is available at loc.gov

ISBN 978-0-8077-6740-5 (paper)
ISBN 978-0-8077-6741-2 (hardcover)
ISBN 978-0-8077-8125-8 (ebook)

Printed on acid-free paper
Manufactured in the United States of America

Dedicated to

. . . Auntie Precious
. . . Marshall Latimore
. . . Dr. Karen King
. . . Dr. Rudy Horne
. . . Dr. Jacqueline Rouse

Thank you all for faithfully supporting and encouraging me. I wish that you all would have been here to see this book come to fruition. Continue to rest in peace.

Contents

Foreword

In a sense *Black Male Success in Higher Education: How the Mathematical Brotherhood Empowers a Collegiate Community to Thrive* has its roots in a telephone conversation in the late 1980s or early 1990s between me and Henry Gore. I was a mathematics PhD candidate at the University of California, Berkeley, and he was professor and chair of Morehouse College's Department of Mathematics. Furthermore, "Doc" was a hero to me and to generations of Morehouse Men—he was a marvelous teacher, leader, and mentor; he inspired passion and dedication in others for learning, broadly, and for mathematics, specifically.

In that conversation, I remember Doc telling me that Morehouse's mathematics department does a great deal of good and impactful work but that much of it goes without notice or renown because we don't write it up. From my undergraduate years there I could recall elements of this good and impactful work, such as challenging assignments and high expectations, enriching projects and presentations, and dedicated faculty commitment and time. Doc went on to explain that the work of the Morehouse mathematics faculty was all-consuming and that documenting and disseminating their work and ways they develop the students had gone undone.

When I joined Morehouse's mathematics faculty in 2002, I remembered Doc's words. I was committed to continuing the department's work of teaching and mentoring our students while also being more attentive to documentation. But very quickly I, too, became part of our team doing good and impactful work without documenting what we were doing and how.

I remember my first conversation with Christopher Jett. It was 2013, and he had reached out to me regarding his work with African American men successful in mathematics and his hopes of interviewing some high-achieving mathematics majors at Morehouse. I assured him that, indeed, we had high-achieving mathematics students and that I could help him identify interview subjects. I also described for him our work in the mathematics department, of which I served as chair, our excitement with a then-promising senior class of majors, and the long-held desire—discussed by me and Doc—to document our work. It was fortuitous that Dr. Jett, with his expertise and research agenda, could bring an external lens upon us and capture the Morehouse Mathematics experience specifically through our majors' eyes, based on his extensive interviews and observations of them. His investigation identifies a number of elements of our success in developing Black mathematics majors while helping us to assess and improve our efforts. His research provides us an opportunity for introspection about the work that we do and our students' perceptions of that work. Dr. Jett's qualitative study, culminating in this book, is a contribution to us at Morehouse and, more broadly, to mathematics and mathematics education.

Morehouse College has a very proud history and reputation as a prestigious liberal arts institution educating Black men—Morehouse Men!—and we in Mathematics are very proud of our students and alumni. Our alumni are accomplished in various careers in industry, government, and academia, and our department has been recognized for launching dozens of alumni toward PhDs in the mathematical sciences over decades. The pillars of our student development are instruction, exposure, and community. Specifically, we have a committed faculty that invests extensive time in the ongoing work of successfully conveying curriculum content. We help develop the students mathematically and otherwise, informing and inspiring them to possibilities in and beyond mathematics. And we foster the development of a community of hard-working men who find satisfaction and success in mathematics, who support one another while immersed in a culture of high expectations. In 2016, the American Mathematical Society honored us with its Mathematics Programs that Make a Difference award in recognition of our strong academic results.

Black Male Success in Higher Education: How the Mathematical Brotherhood Empowers a Collegiate Community to Thrive is a valuable vehicle for sharing our story beyond the walls of Morehouse. This book has potential for broad impact, as the insights about these men's development can be useful to educators in grade schools, colleges, and universities and can be replicable toward the development of Black boys and men in mathematics, where we remain sorely underrepresented.

—Duane Cooper
Associate Professor of Mathematics
Morehouse College

Prelude

One writes out of one thing only—one's own experience.

—James Baldwin

I was always a bit of a whiz kid in mathematics. In kindergarten, I was considered smart because of my mathematical prowess, and this identifying quality traveled with me throughout my school experiences (and arguably into my professional experiences as a math educator). My dad tells stories of how he taught me the basics such as addition and subtraction before I enrolled in school, so I will bestow upon him the title of my first math teacher. My mom recalls incidents where I would diligently play school with my little toys (of course, I would be at the helm as the teacher). She also mentions my excitement and fascination with the books she would bring home from her many visits to yard sales, solidifying my love for reading.

My 1st-grade teacher was a hater. What I mean is that she did not see my academic potential and even recommended that I be placed in special education, allegedly for my hyperactive behavior. When did being hyper become perceived as having lower intelligence or needing an educational intervention? Actually, this energetic behavior was largely influenced by my upbringing in a high-spirited home and community coupled with my regular attendance at a sanctified church. Yes, she was a White woman, and I perceived that she was racist based on the preferential treatment she provided to her White students in comparison to her Black students. However, because of my math performance on some standardized test, I did not fall victim to the special education trap. Writing this text might not have been possible had I been funneled through that route.

Conversely, my 6th-grade teacher, who was also a White woman, was fond of me because of my interest in math. She awarded me a certificate for earning all 100s on my math assessments during one of the 6-week grading periods, something that had not been done before during her stint as a classroom teacher. Grappling with these vastly different experiences opened my eyes to the markedly different ideologies White women could have concerning Black male students. More plainly, I perceived that some saw us as troublemakers, and some saw us as scholars. I started to wrestle with these issues during my adolescence. I am still perplexed why so many Black boys are largely negatively stereotyped in mathematics spaces, indeed in all educational spaces.

While growing up, my North Memphis community (or "North North" as Memphis rapper Project Pat calls it) embraced my academic talents. My Aunt Minnie was one person who did so unceasingly. Although she is not my aunt in the traditional sense (i.e., through familial affiliation), she "became" my aunt, as she lived next door throughout my childhood years. She gave me the childhood nickname "Professor" because of the exceptional job I did with tutoring her son and getting him up to speed with his math skills. Undoubtedly, my younger brother and sister were my first math guinea pigs, but helping someone outside of my immediate household in such a profound manner carried a different meaning. Ironically, Aunt Minnie still calls me "professor" and that name has stuck with me. During a recent visit to Memphis, she lovingly reminded me that she was the one who called it from the beginning (that I would become a professor) and jokingly asserted that I needed to give her a cut for speaking it into existence.

In junior high, I attended a math competition at Rhodes College. This competition signaled to me that I was among the math "elite," given that my competitors consisted of mostly Asian and White adolescent boys. My line of thinking was being shaped concerning what racial groups were considered mathematically talented and what gendered groups were excluded from the math table altogether. Thank God for growth in this domain, especially after I uncovered the many hidden truths concerning the mathematical brilliance of scores of Black women and men. However, being selected to attend this math competition allowed me to truly live up to my nickname among my junior high school peers—Urkel.

For college, I attended a historically Black college/university (HBCU), Tennessee State University (TSU), which was a racially affirming space. TSU gets bonus points in the HBCU community given that it was founded on Juneteenth! My dad says my love for HBCU culture was solidified when he took me to the first-ever Southern Heritage Classic—an exuberant HBCU football classic primarily featuring rivals Jackson State University and TSU. He also attended an HBCU, LeMoyne-Owen College, so the HBCU experience has had a significant impact on my academic trajectory.

In college, I majored in math. Dr. Jeanetta Jackson served as my academic advisor; she was a staunch math education advocate. As a Black woman, she was and remains an exceptional math pedagogue. To soak in this expertise, I worked with her for two summers during my undergraduate years as her teacher's assistant for the Packard Science Institute (PSI), a 6-week summer program for entering science and math majors at TSU. I also had participated in PSI the summer before my freshman year. As a college student, I took every class that she taught. I remember enrolling in an evening math course she was teaching, which was reserved for the nontraditional students and the traditional students who registered after all of the other math courses were filled. I diligently studied her craft, and my mathematics pedagogical practices resemble and pay homage to her dynamic teaching style.

Given my racialized and gendered designation as a Black man, I am deeply concerned about the mathematical needs, ambitions, circumstances, and experiences of Black male students. In this ethnographic study with 16 Black male participants, my insider status as a Black man enhanced relatability. Of course, their stories triggered some of my own mathematical memories. I resembled the participants in many respects, and our shared language patterns and general cultural understandings assisted their engagement in this study. Thus, this book project is simultaneously one of the head (i.e., a research-driven intellectual endeavor), of the heart (i.e., driven by an earnest desire to ameliorate the math experiences of Black male students), and of the heritage (i.e., determined to unearth some of the commonalities found within Black culture; see King & Swartz, 2018, for an African-centered perspective on heritage knowledge in the curriculum).

In this prelude, I have offered only a fraction of my K–16 mathematics story. In previous work, I have expounded on my math experiences (see Jett, 2016a, 2019b). What I wish to stress here is that my village affirmed my mathematical gifts in unique ways, and my experiences have heightened my desire to advance this work. I also wish to emphasize that Black male students have extraordinary mathematics potential, as evidenced by the narratives of this cohort of 16 math majors. This book is a singular testament regarding the emergent math potential among this cohort of Black men, and my story complements this book's contents. In the end, I hope this text inspires a new resolve to support Black male students in math.

Acknowledgments

First and foremost, I thank God for ordering my steps in my personal and professional life. I am deeply humbled and truly blessed to have undertaken such a timely and worthwhile project. Moreover, I am deeply indebted to my foremothers and forefathers whose profound sacrifices paved the way for this work. I appreciate the love and support from the entire Jett family—mom, dad, sister, brother, nephews, aunts, uncles, and a host of cousins.

A ginormous thank you goes to Duane Cooper and Erica Walker who cheerfully gave time and expertise whenever I needed it. You two were extremely instrumental from the project's conception until the completion of this book. A special thank you is extended to you both for contributing the foreword and afterword, respectively. I send my heartfelt thanks to my CAREER Advisory Board—Duane Cooper, Jacqueline Leonard, Robert Palmer, Christine Thomas, and Erica Walker—for their substantive guidance and genuine support of my scholarly pursuits. I also appreciate the phenomenal support from my Program Officers at the National Science Foundation, Claudia Rankins and Tori Smith.

This book was strengthened by discussions and feedback from Nathaniel Bryan, Erika Bullock, Jarvis Carter, Mario Hairston, Alison Hamilton, Julie Hawk, Mona Matthews, Angela Pashia, and Shelby Wilson. I also benefited from the advice given by Derrick Brooms and Ebony McGee about the book-writing process. I acknowledge the contributions of the following amazing research assistants: Joseph Dean, Josephine Exantus, Danielle Gorman, Bre'Ahn Heard, and Daniel Lin. Also, thank you to Janetta Brewer, Charles E. Flowers, Alesia Thompson, and Bernard Williamson for the consistent encouragement y'all provided.

My sincere thanks goes to Sarah Biondello and the production and marketing teams at Teachers College Press. I must acknowledge Robert Berry, Dianne Foster, Sandra Holt, Johnny Houston, Jeanetta Jackson, Joyce E. King, Danny Martin, Jannetta McIntyre, Chris Rasmussen, Celia Rousseau Anderson, David Stinson, and Bill Tate, who have had a significant impact on my scholastic journey. There are also tons of other collaborators, colleagues, church members, friends, and math sisters and brothers. To name you all individually would be a book by itself. Please know that I love and appreciate you all!

Last, but certainly not least, I would like to give a huge shout-out to the 16 math majors who graciously participated in this study in such honest, powerful, and liberating ways. Your intellect is astounding, and I know that you all are going to continue to do amazing things. Y'all are some bad brothers! Thank you again for welcoming me into your community and being so forthcoming with your stories. This book only captures a snippet of your story and capabilities, and please know that any errors contained herein are my own. Peace and blessings as you journey on as mathematically talented Black men!!!

FUNDING SUPPORT

Funding to support this project was provided by the University of West Georgia's President's Development Award and the National Science Foundation's CAREER (Award #1553379) program. Any opinions, findings, and conclusions or recommendations expressed in this material are mine and do not necessarily reflect the views of the National Science Foundation.

Black Male Success in Higher Education

Introduction

I think we kind of turned this department into a fraternity kind of thing.

—Epsilon

This quote is from Epsilon, a Black[1] male participant[2] who is one of the 16 graduating senior mathematics majors at Morehouse College, the historically Black college/university (HBCU) that was the research site for this ethnographic study. Epsilon is a self-selected pseudonym, as are all 16 pseudonyms. In mathematics, epsilon is a small quantity often used in epsilon-delta limit proofs (Borowski & Borwein, 1991), so this pseudonym demonstrates his passion for the subject. Equally, his use of the word *fraternity* demonstrates the brotherly connections established among the cohort through their shared undergraduate mathematics experiences, and it serves as the baseline for their story. Thus, this snippet foreshadows what this text explores—a cohort of majors that formed a fraternal, brotherly bond in Morehouse's mathematics learning community.

Black Male Success in Higher Education: How the Mathematical Brotherhood Empowers a Collegiate Community to Thrive examines the experiences of a contemporary cohort of majors. Using Black masculinity and Critical Race Theory (CRT; see Appendix A for theoretical notes), this yearlong ethnographic study explored the mathematical and racial contexts of these African American male students who were (1) persistent in the major and (2) knowledgeable of the institution given their prolonged time at Morehouse. Importantly, this book employs a strengths-based approach regarding this cohort of mathematically astute Black men and adds to the growing body of discipline-based education research (DBER).

The present environment of racial contention in the United States has shown us that, despite increased efforts to address justice, diversity, equity, and inclusion in all facets of life, racial hostility and inequity persist. In the response to the murders of Black people at the hands of police and others who assume police-like authority, the Black Lives Matter Movement has made anti-Blackness part of the U.S. lexicon. Higher education is not exempt from its effects (Dancy et al., 2018; Dumas & ross, 2016). Efforts to ban what has been called CRT[3] have forestalled some efforts centered on advancing racial equity in most institutions. Education has been a central part of the discussion regarding banning CRT, however misplaced that discussion may be. Central to these debates are questions about what version of history is appropriate for students to learn and if race should be a topic of conversation in educational institutions at all levels.

At the same time, there has been increased attention on HBCUs and their storied success with Black college students. This book is timely and necessary because of the broad interest in Black boys' and men's academic outcomes. In these discussions, math is often portrayed as an academic hurdle, which suggests that more asset-based work is needed concerning our mathematical abilities. For Black men, Morehouse leads the charge, conferring more bachelor's degrees in mathematics on this group than any other higher education institution in the nation (Owens et al., 2012). Therefore, the time is ripe for an ethnographic study of its robust mathematics learning community drawing from Black masculinity and critical race theoretical work.

The goal of this book is not to offer a magical "solution" to increasing the completion rates of Black men in undergraduate mathematics programs or to remedy their disengagement in these programs. In fact, Black men's undergraduate mathematics experiences are complex and require multiple context-specific solutions. Rather, I draw ideas from this study, the research literature, and my experiences. I hope an enlarged understanding of these men's experiences will suggest paths toward building more robust mathematics learning communities outside the rarefied Morehouse circle, and spur further research into programs and systems that can support Black men in math.

This introduction outlines the big ideas presented in this book. First, I address the discipline driving the study, mathematics. Next, I discuss Black men specifically, operationalize mathematical brotherhood, and situate it through a fraternal lens. After that, I talk about the culture epitomized at many HBCUs and delve into the scholarship on mathematics at HBCUs. I close by providing an overview of this book.

WHY MATHEMATICS?

Mathematics elicits dichotomous feelings of either love or hate for most people. Those who love it are often deemed as smart, geeky, or nerdish. They might enjoy the popular meme positioning MATH—*Making Amazing Things Happen*—in a positive light. Conversely, those who dislike the subject often have horrifying childhood memories about not stating their multiplication facts with speed, miscalculating arithmetic operations with fractions, or not seeing the relevance of textbook word problems. For those who consider math the bane of their existence, the mere sight of the quadratic formula, $x = \dfrac{-b \pm \sqrt{b^2 - 4ac}}{2a}$, or the sheer thought of integrating by parts might be fear-inducing and cause them to avoid math at all costs. The competing acronym MATH—Mental *Abuse* *To* *Humans*—has circulated in social media outlets and received thousands of likes, shares, and retweets, demonstrating the comfort many feel with expressing their painful relationship with math. There are also those in the middle of the spectrum who experience mixed emotions—feelings of admiration, appreciation, anxiety, agony, and/or anguish—depending on the mathematical subfield or topic.

Mathematics in Academe and Society

Without question, math has always been an important staple for functionality in society. Celebrated every April, Mathematics Awareness Month (now called Mathematics and Statistics Awareness Month) is designed to increase the public's understanding and appreciation of math. Whether most people realize it or not, they engage in various forms of mathematical thinking on a daily basis. Examples include calculating time for the day's activities, keeping track of finances, and reading graphs and charts via weather reports, political records, and so on, especially via assorted online platforms. Moreover, math has been used to expose the flaws of voting procedures, extrapolate big data sets, and model real-world phenomena. In addition, mainstream discussions about the COVID-19 pandemic allowed phrases such as exponential growth, powers of ten, and flattening the curve, commonly referred to as math jargon, to become the order of the day.

Regarding Science, Technology, Engineering, and Mathematics (STEM) fields, mathematics is often positioned and perceived as the disciplinary anchor. That is, those who succeed in math can enter into the STEM club and those who have mathematical challenges are often onlookers to this success. Math skills and those who have majored in math are highly valued and sought after in STEM. For example, number theorists are highly sought after for cybersecurity recruitment while real analysts are sought after for positions in machine learning (National Research Council, 2013). Black-owned businesses and startups solicit mathematical talent to meet their target goals and benchmarks. Well-known companies such as Amazon, Facebook, Google, Netflix, and Uber hire mathematics graduates to assist with predictive analytics, operations research, data science, and other emerging subfields with connections to the mathematical sciences (National Research Council, 2013; O'Neil, 2016). Being mathematically savvy opens doors for career and entrepreneurial endeavors.

Math knowledge's usefulness is not limited to STEM fields, as scholars in the social sciences and humanities increasingly utilize math knowledge. Interdisciplinary fields such as computational literacy studies, mathematical anthropology, math-political science, numerical art, and quantitative psychology have emerged to amplify the importance and relevance of math to their primary disciplines. Given the widespread applicability of mathematics, all fields will continue to be presented with opportunities to embed mathematical thought into their intellectual traditions.

African Contributions to Mathematics

In her pathbreaking text, Zaslavsky (1999) stressed African contributions to mathematics. As examples, she highlighted that the Ishango bone (the oldest mathematical artifact discovered in Central Africa) included tally marks, pyramids used slope concepts, and tombs used rectangular coordinate geometry. African numeration systems have had huge influences on math; however, the discipline is often positioned as a race-evasive subject. In other words, the math world has turned a blind eye to African-centered contributions and racism. Moreover, Joseph (1990) pointed out: "The standard treatment of the history of non-European mathematics exhibits a deep-rooted historiographical bias in the selection and interpretation of facts, and . . . mathematical activity outside Europe has as a consequence been ignored, devalued, or distorted" (p. 3).

Despite having strong roots in Afrocentric culture, mathematics continues to function as an institutional space of Whiteness (Joseph, 1990; Martin, 2009). To disrupt this racial pecking order, scholars have chronicled Black mathematicians' lives and contributions (Kenschaft, 2005; Walker, 2014). In formative work, mathematics education researchers placed a laser focus on African American students' math achievement outcomes, highlighting the disparate learning opportunities for this racialized group (Malloy, 1997; Stiff & Harvey, 1988; Strutchens, 2000; Tate, 1995). Contemporary work has debunked the racelessness of math by examining its racial lineage and elucidating how many national mathematics education reform efforts, policies, and professional organizations have failed African American children (Berry et al., 2014; Bullock, 2019; Martin, 2019; McKittrick, 2014). Researchers have also highlighted how African Americans were denied entry into math lectures, excluded from professional conferences, and provided limited job opportunities due to blatant racial discrimination (Houston, 2019; Parshall, 2016). In short, mathematics has some serious issues as it pertains to African American inclusivity (Falconer, 1996; Johnson, 1984; Lorch, 1996).

Organizations have been established to advance African Americans' mathematical success. The National Association of Mathematicians (NAM) was designed to promote excellence in the mathematical sciences among minoritized groups, especially African Americans, while the Benjamin Banneker Association (BBA) was created to ensure the highest quality mathematics education for African American children (Houston, 2000; Leonard & Martin, 2013). Moses and Cobb (2002) maintained that math is a civil right and championed math literacy for minoritized students through the grassroots program The Algebra Project (algebra.org). The Conference for African-American Researchers in the Mathematical Sciences (CAARMS) (www.caarms.net) highlights disciplinary work by African American graduate students and researchers (Massey, 2022). There are other school and community-based programs to augment Black students' mathematical genius. These programs empower Black boys and men in math.

WHY BROTHERS?

Brothers represents the collective tribe of Black boys and men who are deeply committed to the uplift and empowerment of Black people, Black knowledge, Black institutions, and the Black community. Brothers are intellectual powerhouses. Brothers are creative artists. Brothers are innovative thinkers. Brothers are stalwart leaders. Brothers are mathematical geniuses. With these strengths, brothers' contributions to society are extraordinary. In the classroom, brothers' intellectual prowess invigorates the environment. Drawing upon their personal and academic experiences, especially in Morehouse's mathematics learning community, the 16 brothers in this study are experts on their lives as Black boys and men.

Brotherhood

Brotherhood refers to a responsive kinship among Black men. In his text on manhood and masculinity among African American male college students, Dancy (2012) defined brotherhood as "a term of endearment and affirmation *from* African American men *to* African American men regardless of, and even strengthened by, an oppressor's repudiation" (p. 1). Brooms (2017a) explored brotherhood among Black male college students in a Black Male Initiative program and suggested that brotherhood bonding fosters a supportive learning environment. Brotherhood affirms Black men and fosters belonging to Black male culture. A brotherhood allows Black men to come together to share accomplishments, voice concerns, and strategize action items in a safe and trusting environment.

Black manhood is exhibited through the motifs of Black masculinity (Pelzer, 2016). Interactions between Black men such as the fist bump, handshake, and head nod are reified Black masculine behaviors. Black masculinist ideology dictates what it entails to be manly (i.e., provider, protector, etc.) and elicits robust identities (Pelzer, 2016; Richardson,

2007). However, Black masculinist thought has been critiqued for upholding hegemonic masculinity and patriarchy (Collins, 2000; hooks, 2004; White & Peretz, 2010). In light of this, Black masculinity theory aims to expand the notion of Black manhood in ways that honor women, children, and other minoritized groups.

To expand the conceptualization of Black masculinity, some scholars use Black masculinities in the plural form to represent the multiple forms of masculinity that Black men embody (Harris & Harper, 2014; Mutua, 2006; Neal, 2013). In addition to racial and gender identities, Black masculinities encompass much more, including Black men's sexual, religious, linguistic, mental/physical abilities and socioeconomic identities. In this study, I use and operationalize Black masculinity theory to systematically focus on the participants' racial and gender identities. This emphasis is not intended to suggest a one-dimensional aspect of Black manhood, as other identities were apparent during the research process. However, this meticulously defined view is operationalized in this book to concentrate on mathematics among Black men.

At the collegiate level, brothers are often depicted in less than desirable ways even though we embody positive math identities. While it is true that math is a male-dominated major (feminists and critical scholars rightly critique the masculinist nature of the discipline), these programs are not densely saturated with Black men (Hottinger, 2016; Jett, 2022b; Leyva, 2021). In fact, Black men's mathematics degree attainment is not proportional to our representation in society. For example, during the 2017–2018 academic year, Black men accounted for approximately 2.37% of the total 18,297 undergraduate mathematics degrees awarded nationally, while accounting for 6.37% of people in society (U.S. Department of Education, 2019). Such data are used to form hypotheses concerning our potential in the field. Unfortunately, these hypotheses conjure and seek to position Black men as anti-mathematical. To counter these ideological threats, a Black masculinist frame is used to highlight our mathematical strengths.

Mathematical Brotherhood

Mathematical brotherhood is a Black masculinist, CRT-informed concept that describes how Black men as a collective persist in a learning community and within the profession. Mathematics learning communities are empowering, additive spaces where students engage in and take ownership of their math education (Walker, 2012; Zhao & Kuh, 2004). In doing so, brothers improve their group- and self-efficacy, form study groups (to learn and assist others), organize disciplinary events, and ultimately strengthen their math identities. This comradeship with brothers with shared interests in math fosters an alliance and motivates brothers to achieve their math-related goals. Like any brotherhood, a mathematical brotherhood comes with both its successes and challenges, as this text will show. Building on these theoretical underpinnings, this text composes a portrait of how a mathematical brotherhood empowers Black men to thrive in a collegiate community.

As Epsilon's statement at the beginning of this chapter expresses, this cohort's mathematical brotherhood is reminiscent of a fraternity. A fraternity is an example of a brotherhood that manifests masculinity (Harper & Harris, 2006). Black fraternal organizations have positively contributed to "racial identity development, leadership development, practical competence, and cognitive development" (p. 149) for Black men. As such, fraternities are often viewed as a respectable form of Black manhood. Pledging is a process that facilitates brotherhood (Parks & Brown, 2005). Pledging has a rich history, and the social dynamics throughout the process cause brothers to bond (Parks & Brown, 2005). In this study, majoring in math is likened to pledging a fraternity.

Hence, this conceptualization of mathematical brotherhood is influenced by the distinctive culture of Black Greek-Letter Organizations (BGLOs). BGLOs include five fraternities (Alpha Phi Alpha Fraternity, Inc.; Kappa Alpha Psi Fraternity, Inc.; Omega Psi Phi Fraternity, Inc.; Phi Beta Sigma Fraternity, Inc.; and Iota Phi Theta Fraternity, Inc.) and four sororities (Alpha Kappa Alpha Sorority, Inc.; Delta Sigma Theta Sorority, Inc.; Zeta Phi Beta Sorority, Inc.; and Sigma Gamma Rho, Sorority, Inc.), and they are referred to collectively as the Divine Nine (Ross, 2000). As the first historically Black fraternity, Alpha Phi Alpha Fraternity, Inc. began as a study and support group for Black men at Cornell University. Similarly, Kappa Alpha Psi Fraternity, Inc. was founded at Indiana University to counteract the exclusion of African American students from the campus community. Originally, the fraternity's name was Kappa Alpha Nu, but it was changed because White students referred to a fraternity brother as a member of "Kappa Alpha Nig." Both fraternities dealt with racial discrimination, and the organizations turned to mutual support within the Black community to withstand the challenges Black people endured as a result of systemic racism. The three remaining fraternities were founded at HBCUs, as were three of the four sororities. The Divine Nine have extensive histories, and the Black women and men in BGLOs have been at the forefront of the fight for racial justice and the upliftment of the Black community.

To connect mathematics to the fraternal structure, this book includes language associated with BGLOs (see Appendix C for a list of the terms used). This language is included in boxed form the first time used in the text. As a point of illustration, the *line* could represent the new members of a fraternal organization. With this study, the *line* consists of the entire cohort—the 16 majors in this graduating class, collectively referred to as the mathematical brotherhood. In this fashion, this text borrows from that rich language to illustrate the brotherly bond between the participants, emphasize this mathematics learning community's special characteristics, and paint a picture of the mathematical unity personified among the majors.

> *line*: the new members of a fraternal organization that could develop into lifelong brothers or friends

Drawing upon Black fraternal language, this book helps to tell a more complete story about brothers' math abilities, experiences, and competencies. This project is in parallel to the corpus of work that highlights Black girls' and women's fortitude within mathematics education contexts (Borum & Walker, 2012; Gholson, 2016; Inniss, 2015; Joseph et al., 2017; Leyva, 2021). In addition, this book builds on the strengths-based scholarship that paints Black boys' and men's math experiences with a radiant brush (Berry, 2008; Davis et al., 2019; Jett et al., 2021; McGee & Martin, 2011; Noble, 2011; Stinson, 2013; Urschel & Thomas, 2019). In so doing, this text brings much needed attention to the asset-based orientation that operates at HBCUs.

HBCUs

For more than 175 years, HBCUs have played a significant role in educating Black students. HBCUs were designed to provide higher education opportunities for African American students, and they have a founding mission to uplift the race by fostering Black leadership and activism (Favors, 2019). HBCUs are applauded for the supportive environments they provide for African American students, and their curricula both academically and racially empower Black students. Prominent leaders such as Dr. Mary McLeod Bethune (founder of Bethune-Cookman University and cofounder of the United Negro College Fund) are heralded in the HBCU community for their deep commitment to Black students' education (McCluskey, 1989). Among the supporters of HBCUs and other Black educational institutions were White philanthropists; Watkins, in his study of them (2001), called them the "White architects of Black education." These courageous leaders possessed great power and wealth, and they were instrumental in funding, cocreating, and refining Black educational institutions. While a comprehensive overview of HBCUs' history and contributions are beyond this book's purview, this section provides contextual information about HBCUs.

HBCUs have a distinct culture, one that has been beautifully portrayed in the television show *A Different World*, movies such as *School Daze*, *Drumline*, and *The Great Debaters*, and Beyoncé's *Homecoming* documentary. HBCUs have exemplary honors programs, meritorious debate teams, spirit-filled gospel choirs, and other extracurricular activities that celebrate and bring joy to Black life. HBCUs have sports teams and host sporting events such as football classics that bring Black culture to big-time arenas

(Greenlee, 2012). Another prominent distinction is HBCU homecomings, each a Black family reunion of sorts. Essential characteristics of HBCU homecomings include parades, street vendors, one-of-a-kind outfits, and tailgates with great music and food. Of course, the main ingredients are the exhilarating football game, distinctive HBCU band, dynamic majorette dance team, and lively cheering squad. The highly anticipated halftime show, along with "fifth-quarter" performances among the HCBU bands, also highlight the rich culture established at HBCUs.

The Atlanta University Center (AUC), like most HBCUs, is located in the southeast. The AUC consortium consists of six institutions: Clark Atlanta University (CAU), Morehouse College, Morehouse School of Medicine, Morris Brown College, Spelman College (an all-women's college and sister institution[4] to Morehouse), and the Interdenominational Theological Center (ITC). The AUC is the largest consortium among HBCUs and exposes students to multifaceted disciplines and perspectives (AUC, n.d.). As a result of this exposure, students in the AUC's undergraduate institutions, CAU, Morehouse, Morris Brown, and Spelman, can cross-register to take courses at other AUC campuses. This collaborative venture allows students to leverage the academic resources at the consortium institutions. And at the heart of the AUC is the Robert W. Woodruff Library, affectionately known as the "center of the Center," which contains archival knowledge of Black institutions, people, and events.

Gasman and colleagues (2017) pointed out that "HBCUs are often treated as a single, homogenous community" (p. 188); however, this is not the case. Among the 105 public and private HBCUs, there are tons of distinguishing characteristics (Elliott et al., 2019; Favors, 2019). Even within the AUC, the institutions are distinct. Toldson (2019) emphasized that HBCUs "must relinquish the posture of defending their relevance and get in the stance of asserting their excellence" (p. 168). His argument challenged and encouraged HBCUs to achieve greatness in light of the "fair and unfair scrutiny from education consumers, policymakers, cultural critics, and social commentators" (p. 161). Whatever criticism they receive, HBCUs remain nationally celebrated for the production of Black college graduates.

National HBCU Week is celebrated every second week in September to further publicize their all-around excellence. *HBCU Buzz*, *HBCU Digest*, and *HBCUstory* provide and preserve HBCU-related news. Virginia Union University has launched the only national Center for the Study of HBCUs to advance scholarship on these institutions (Roberson, 2021). Contemporary political firsts have brought the exceptionalism of HBCU graduates to the fore. These HBCU alumni include Kamala Harris (Howard University), the first minoritized woman Vice President of the United States; Stacey Abrams (Spelman College), the first African American woman to secure a major-party gubernatorial nomination; and Raphael Warnock (Morehouse College), the first Black senator from Georgia. HBCUs have always been promoters of Black excellence, and this excellence extends to the discipline of mathematics.

SCHOLARSHIP ON MATHEMATICS AT HBCUs

Across several generations, HBCUs have supported Black students in mathematics. HBCUs represent approximately 2.5% of higher education institutions, but they produce about 47% of Black math graduates (Owens et al., 2012). Added to that, HBCUs serve as incubators that lead a large number of African American math graduates to go on to earn doctorates in the field (Inniss, 2015; Walker, 2014).

Historical giants at HBCUs have influenced the increase of present-day Black mathematicians. One noteworthy example is Dr. Clarence F. Stephens, who served on the math faculty at Morgan State College (now University) from 1947–1962 (Megginson, 2003). Prior to his arrival, no student had gone on to earn a graduate degree in mathematics. There, he established an Undergraduate Honors Mathematics Program to expose students to graduate mathematics coursework and raised the expectations for what students could accomplish. This became known as the Morgan State/Potsdam model (referred to as the "Potsdam Miracle" because of the continuous successes he experienced with math majors at the State University of New York at Potsdam from 1969–1987). His teaching methods have inspired many in the field, including Dr. Uri Treisman's Mathematics Workshop Program (MWP), which included some of these miraculous techniques (Williams, 1997).

Dr. Abdulalim Abdullah Shabazz was one of the primary anchors of Black mathematical doctoral degree recipients. He served as chair of Atlanta University's (now CAU) Mathematics Department from 1957–1963; when he started, "it was only a graduate school . . . and there were only two students in mathematics" (Kenschaft, 2005, p. 100). Under his leadership, 109 students earned master's degrees in mathematics. Many of these students went on to earn doctorates in mathematics and mathematics education, and more than half of the country's African American mathematicians were either directly or indirectly influenced by Dr. Shabazz's students.[5] His outstanding legacy was the inspiration behind the Presidential Award for Excellence in Science, Mathematics, and Engineering Mentoring (PAESMEM; Malcom, 2021).

Fittingly, scholarship has highlighted the robust math traditions at HBCUs (Inniss, 2015; Jett, 2013b; Walker, 2014). Several other HBCUs have thriving mathematics learning communities, and researchers have paid particular attention to Morgan State University (Dr. Clarence F. Stephens earned his undergraduate mathematics degree at Johnson C. Smith University) and Spelman College (Dr. Etta Falconer earned her undergraduate mathematics degree at Fisk University) as these institutions have sent several Black students to graduate mathematics programs[6] (Borum et al., 2016; Walker, 2014). Kurepa (2019) reported on North Carolina Agricultural and Technical State University's mathematics program via a scholarship funded by the National Science Foundation (NSF). In this program, a formal mathematics learning community was established to entice, support, and ensure that students complete their undergraduate and graduate mathematics programs.

Morgan State University's faculty participated in the Student Engagement in Mathematics through an Institutional Network for Active Learning (SEMINAL) project (Ellington et al., 2021). Funded by the NSF, SEMINAL is a national collaborative initiative designed to support and research departmental and institutional change on active learning in undergraduate mathematics courses (Smith et al., 2021). Morgan State University's team implemented culturally responsive practices in an effort to seamlessly integrate active learning strategies in an accelerated Pre-Calculus course (Ellington et al., 2021). Examples of culturally responsive teaching included "course problems relating trigonometric functions and identities to applications of music, blood flow, circadian rhythms, physical therapy movement study, and architecture design" (p. 302). Although the faculty had some challenges shifting from traditional teaching, the team found that culturally responsive practices coupled with active learning fostered positive attitudes among the faculty. Similarly, the students reported positive experiences in the redesigned Pre-Calculus course.

Mulcahy (2017) chronicled a century of mathematical excellence at Spelman and shared inspiring stories of these Black women who have been disciplinary pioneers. Informed by a Black feminist lens, Jones Williams (2017) examined the experiences of six Black women who earned mathematics degrees from Spelman from the 1980s through the 2000s. She found that Spelman offered the participants affirming attributes (i.e., exceptional Black women faculty, peer camaraderie, and community) and challenging attributes (i.e., difficult math courses and the dual-degree program). These findings are particularly salient for this study given that we made similar findings, as will be presented later in this text. In short, this study's explicit focus on a cohort of Black male math majors extends the scholarship on mathematics at HBCUs and contributes to the DBER by employing a strengths-based approach to delve into African American men's experiences in Morehouse's mathematics learning community.

OVERVIEW OF THE BOOK

Black Male Success in Higher Education: How the Mathematical Brotherhood Empowers a Collegiate Community to Thrive has seven chapters, which center the participants' voices and promulgate their mathematical acumen. I have preserved their natural language, and the participants and

I use Black Language at times to capture "the intersections between race and language" (Baker-Bell, 2020, p. 2). Some participants' thoughts are shared more than others. My goal is not to privilege the voices of certain majors; rather, it is to highlight narratives and examples that get at the essence of their experiences. In certain cases, longer snapshots of the interview exchange are shared. In doing so, my first name is used instead of a pseudonym, since I was the researcher and sole interviewer in the study. In addition, I use mathematical concepts and objects to anonymize professors' names, institutions mentioned, and cities referenced by the participants.

Chapter 1, "Morehouse Mathematics," provides a portrait of the institutional context. It includes historical and contemporary information to set up the study. Data from the National Center for Education Statistics' (NCES) Integrated Postsecondary Education Data System (IPEDS) are shared to help make the case of Morehouse Mathematics' significance. The chapter closes with a synopsis of the current study. Chapter 2, "The Brothers' Journey to Morehouse Mathematics," introduces the participants and provides information about their families. It describes their K–12 and home-based educational experiences. Mathematics is used as the backdrop to understand how these African American men became interested in the discipline and the institution.

Chapter 3, "The Mathematical Brotherhood," provides more comprehensive information about this cohort of majors. This chapter considers within-group differences and features prominent aspects associated with this group. Chapter 4, "The Faculty," offers an overview of the faculty members' advantages and pitfalls along the pedagogical spectrum as voiced by the majors. In particular, the chapter portrays the faculty using student-generated classifications such as *superhero*, *math geniuses*, and *night shift*. Chapter 5, "Morehouse's Mathematics Learning Community," provides information about this collegiate community, which houses the Math Lab. This chapter unpacks the concept of *third floor respect* and highlights discipline-specific activities and events at this HBCU.

Chapter 6, "The Brothers' Racialized Experiences," addresses how the participants narrate, navigate, and manage ongoing racial challenges. This includes grappling with racism in school, mathematical spaces, and society. It also situates Morehouse as a racially affirming space. Chapter 7, "Moving Forward," presents the participants' career trajectories, offers implications, and concludes the study. In all, *Black Male Success in Higher Education: How the Mathematical Brotherhood Empowers a Collegiate Community to Thrive* launches a mission to create collective knowledge about Black men in Morehouse's mathematics learning community and provides insights for families, practitioners, policymakers, and researchers regarding Black boys' and men's mathematical capabilities.

CHAPTER 1

Morehouse Mathematics

I made history at Morehouse by teaching the first course in calculus ever to be given there.

—Dr. Benjamin E. Mays

Unlike the other chapters that open with a statement from a study participant, this chapter begins with a quote extracted from Benjamin E. Mays's memoir *Born to Rebel: An Autobiography* to provide some historical context (Mays, 1971/2003). Dr. Mays, an ordained minister whose PhD from the University of Chicago would be in Religion, was nevertheless first hired at Morehouse to teach math (and psychology and religious education); it was then assumed that a college graduate was qualified to teach in multiple fields. While teaching, he made such an indelible impact that then Morehouse President John Hope offered him a position as acting dean in his third year. Dr. Mays left Morehouse to pursue his graduate studies, but he later returned and had a 27-year run as its president. He is widely recognized for his influence in the Civil Rights Movement and his mentorship to Dr. Martin Luther King, Jr., and they both have schools, buildings, memorials, etc. named in their honor. On Morehouse's campus, the Dr. Benjamin E. Mays Memorial and Dr. Martin Luther King, Jr. Statue symbolize their trailblazing leadership. And for Dr. Mays, all his Morehouse leadership began with his excellence in the field we are concerned with, Mathematics.

This chapter sets the stage for Morehouse as a mathematics powerhouse for Black men and is organized as follows. First, I provide a snapshot of Morehouse to stress some of the institution's unique characteristics. Then, I share historical information about Morehouse Mathematics. Next, I share contemporary information via national IPEDS data and the present study to invoke the significance of this disciplinary space.

MOREHOUSE COLLEGE: AN INSTITUTIONAL PORTRAIT

The Augusta Institute was founded in 1867 by Rev. William J. White (who was mixed-race) in conjunction with Black ministers Rev. Richard C. Coulter, who was a formerly enslaved person, and Rev. Edmund Turney, who was founder of the National Theological Institute, at Springfield Baptist Church, Augusta, Georgia (Brawley, 1917/2009). Although it was created for the education of Negro boys and men, women also attended the Institute. The institution's name was changed to Atlanta Baptist Seminary when it moved to Atlanta in 1879. Another institutional name change, Atlanta Baptist College, occurred in 1897 when full college rights were granted. In 1913, it was renamed Morehouse College after Rev. Dr. Henry Lyman Morehouse, a White Northern minister and benefactor who donated money and advocated for grant funds to educate Black people, placing value on a "talented tenth" (Anderson, 1988; Brawley, 1917/2009).

Designated as a historically single-gender institution, Morehouse is a private, liberal arts college catering to the education of Black men, making it the only U.S. institution of its kind (Brawley, 1917/2009). Home of the Maroon Tigers and commonly referred to as "The House," Morehouse has an enrollment of approximately 2,200 students (Morehouse College, n.d.). The institution's motto—*Et Facta Est Lux*—is a Latin phrase, loosely translated as "and there was light," implying that Morehouse students are expected to become beacons of light in the world. The "Dear Old Morehouse" song is a staple among Morehouse Men, and the Glee Club has an exceptional history of musical excellence. Institutional leaders such as President John Hope, Dr. Mays, and Dr. Walter Massey helped to propel the institution into national and international prominence (Brawley, 1917/2009; Eaves, 2009; Mays, 1971/2003). Morehouse has a strong reputation within the higher education and HBCU communities.

Rovaris (2005) posits that the "Morehouse Mystique" was created during the tenure of Dr. Mays. The Morehouse Mystique is a profound, almost spiritual sense of community that exists among Morehouse Men. People recognize the Morehouse Mystique in Morehouse Men who have strong character, integrity, and intelligence. Morehouse President Robert Franklin (2007–2012) established the "Five Wells"—well-balanced, well-dressed, well-read, well-spoken, and well-traveled—to encapsulate the expectations regarding these Renaissance men (Patton, 2014). The Morehouse Mystique has been lauded as being present in notable alumni such as civil rights leader Dr. Martin Luther King, Jr.; the first Black mayor of Atlanta, Mr. Maynard Jackson; actor Mr. Samuel L. Jackson; filmmaker Mr. Spike Lee; and physician and health care administrator Dr. David Satcher, as well as scores of other successful and influential Black men (Carson, 1997; Eaves, 2006). Succinctly, Morehouse is a bastion of Black male excellence.

Within the last decade, Morehouse has garnered widespread attention. In May of 2013, America's first Black president, President Barack Obama, served as Morehouse's commencement speaker (Slack, 2013). Also, there were recognizable institutional attributes in the film *Hidden Figures*; some scenes were filmed at Morehouse in buildings from and reminiscent of the

1960s that are still intact (Rizzo, 2017). The award-winning film, based on Shetterly's (2016) phenomenal book, depicted Black women mathematicians' brilliant contributions to the space programs at the National Aeronautics and Space Administration (NASA) for over three decades. Morehouse professor the late Dr. Rudy Horne served as the mathematics consultant for the film (see Dumbaugh, 2019, for a special tribute to Dr. Horne).

In April 2019, institutional leaders approved a policy to begin admitting transgender men in 2020, which was a huge shift given the conservatism of the institution (Mobley & Hall, 2020). In May 2019, billionaire tech investor and the richest Black man in the country at that time, Mr. Robert F. Smith, pledged that he and his family would pay off the student loan debt of the entire class of 396 young men (Kline, 2019). This included the loans that parents and guardians accumulated to pay for the graduates' education. In October 2019, Oprah Winfrey added $13M to continue the existing Oprah Winfrey Scholars Program (Morehouse College, 2019). Throughout 2020, MacKenzie Scott, Reed Hastings, and Patty Quillin, who are Amazon and Netflix philanthropists, provided multimillion-dollar donations to the institution and other HBCUs.

Although Morehouse has had its successes, the institution does not come without its critiques. Researchers have studied Morehouse's high attrition rates in order to improve Black men's postsecondary matriculation rates (Lundy-Wagner & Gasman, 2011). Scholars have highlighted the heteronormative and male hegemonic culture of the institution, arguing that policies such as the Appropriate Attire Policy are homophobic and antagonistic to gender-nonconforming students (Mobley & Johnson, 2019; Patton, 2014). Furthermore, the patriarchal traditions have been critiqued for weeding out "certain types of men while endorsing and empowering others" (Grundy, 2012, p. 50). In addition, Grundy (2021) argues that sexual allegations and assaults have been swept under the rug to preserve the institution's legacy and tradition. The point is that just like all other higher education institutions, the practices and policies at Morehouse still have room for improvement as the institution continues to evolve.

While the full history of Morehouse is beyond the scope of this book, many resources cover the institution's history and many accomplishments (e.g., Brawley, 1917/2009, 2010; Eaves, 2009; Gasman & Sullivan, 2012; Rovaris, 2005). This text is also not designed to showcase Morehouse's present-day and future plans. Instead, this text reports on a study of a cohort of 16 mathematics majors. The institution's historical and contemporary contexts of Black men in mathematics justify why Morehouse is ideal for this study.

MOREHOUSE MATHEMATICS: A HISTORICAL PORTRAIT

As it stands, Morehouse has a decades-long track record of supporting Black men in math. Borrowing from a Black masculinist frame: Morehouse

Mathematics is the ideal place where Black manhood and mathematics intersect. That is, this HBCU has a historical legacy of providing African American male students with same-race and same-gender math professors, mentors, and role models to build community. In this way, students have firsthand historical and contemporary examples of Black men who have made monumental strides in the field.

A prominent figure in Morehouse's mathematical history is Professor Claude B. Dansby, affectionately known as "Pop" Dansby (Houston, n.d.). Pop Dansby walked across two Georgia counties and took a train to get to Morehouse, demonstrating his steadfast determination to get there for a college education. He graduated from Morehouse in 1922, joined the faculty that same year, and taught mathematics for more than four decades, serving approximately 40 of those years as the department chair. To honor Pop Dansby's esteemed contributions to Morehouse Mathematics, the distinguished Claude B. Dansby Lecture occurs annually.

Pop Dansby was also heavily influenced by Dr. Mays (Houston, n.d.). He was one of the three charter members of the Psi Chapter of Omega Psi Phi Fraternity, Inc., and Dr. Mays, also an Omega Man, was the sponsoring advisor. As a member of a BGLO, Pop Dansby was influenced by those fraternal lessons to establish a brotherhood culture within the department. He left Morehouse for a year to earn his master's degree in mathematics at the University of Chicago, and Dr. Mays earned his master's and doctoral degrees in religion there. He and Dr. Mays started their careers at Morehouse together, and both retired in 1967. Dansby Hall, which houses the Department of Mathematics on its third floor, and Mays Hall are neighboring campus buildings.

Dansby's nickname, Pop, conjures up the concept of *otherfathering*, "expressed as holistic care, support, parenting, and modeling" (Brooms, 2017b, p. 1). In years past, Pop Dansby served as an otherfather for Morehouse's students. Brooms explored how Black male teachers engaged in otherfathering in a single-gender high school for Black boys. He found that the Black male teachers significantly contributed to Black boys' development, provided them with guidance on being Black and male in society, and improved their critical consciousness as they learned more about themselves. Similarly, Pop Dansby's math-related pedagogical practices, care, and support evoked otherfathering. As a father figure, Pop Dansby was consistently present in the department for several decades influencing students' development and identity, so he truly served as a mathematics mensch.

Table 1.1 provides a list of the documented Black men who went on to earn a doctorate during the Dansby era (Houston, n.d.). These Black men's attainment of the highest degree in the mathematical sciences is noteworthy considering that many representatives from math departments openly declared that they would never admit or award a doctorate to an African

Table 1.1. Mathematics PhDs under Pop Danby's Tutelage

	Name	Morehouse Class	PhD Disciplinary Area	Institution
1	Dr. Rogers Newman	1948	Mathematics	University of Michigan
2	Dr. John Ewell	1948	Mathematics	University of California, Los Angeles
3	Dr. Calvin King	1949	Mathematics	Ohio State University
4	Dr. Arthur Jones	1961	Mathematical Statistics	University of Iowa
5	Dr. Melvin Heard	1962	Mathematics	Purdue University
6	Dr. Benjamin Martin	1963	Applied Mathematics	Purdue University
7	Dr. Johnny Houston	1964	Mathematics	Purdue University
8	Dr. Manuel Keepler	1965	Mathematics	University of New Mexico
9	Dr. Henry Gore	1968	Mathematics	University of Michigan
10	Dr. Curtis Clark	1970	Mathematics	University of Michigan

American (Houston, 2021). In addition to these ten Black men, scores of other Morehouse alumni went on to have incredible careers in mathematics.

Pop Dansby served as the first department chair. After that, other scholars carried the torch. Table 1.2 provides a lineage of Morehouse Mathematics departmental leadership across the last century. Over the period 2019–2021, Morehouse phased out the Department of Mathematics as a separate unit and allied it with others in the Division of Mathematics and Computational Sciences (Morehouse College, n.d.).

There are a couple more retired math faculty worth mentioning. One mathematical pioneer whose legacy continues to the present day is Dr. Harriet J. Walton. She was hired during the Mays and Dansby era in 1958 and faithfully served on the Morehouse faculty for 42 years, retiring in 2000 (Williams, 1997). She, among other Black women, also contribute significantly to Morehouse Mathematics and stretch the brotherly ecosystem. In addition to her role as a mathematics professor, Dr. Walton was a national leader within the profession, serving as one of the co-founders of NAM (Houston, 2021). In particular, she was one of the 17 minoritized mathematicians (and one of three women) at the 1969 Joint Mathematics Meeting (JMM) in New Orleans that served as the genesis of NAM.

The original NAM caucus met during JMM to discuss issues related to math (education) at Black institutions (Houston, 2000). The JMM was

Table 1.2. Mathematics Department Chairs

Department Chair	Years
Pop Dansby	1924–1963
Dr. Alan Farley	1963–1967
Dr. Louis Padulo	1967–1968
Dr. Richard Johnsonbaugh	1968–1972
Dr. Benjamin Martin	1972–1977
Dr. Henry Gore	1977–1996
Dr. Robert Bozeman	1996–2001
Dr. Masilamani Sambandham	2001–2011
Dr. Duane Cooper	2011–2019
Dr. Curtis Clark	2021–Present

a combined meeting between the American Mathematical Society (AMS) and the Mathematical Association of America (MAA). The NAM caucus felt compelled to act concerning Blacks' representation in the mathematical community, and this desire was heightened following Dr. King's assassination the year prior (Houston, 2021). Dr. Walton remained active in NAM and received an award for distinguished service earned through her tenure as secretary-treasurer (1983–1990) on NAM's Board of Directors (Houston, 2000). To reiterate, she accomplished all of this while on the faculty at Morehouse. The Harriet J. Walton Symposium on Undergraduate Mathematics Research, held annually at Morehouse, bears her name to honor her life's work in mathematics.

Another retired faculty member with ongoing influence is Dr. Robert E. Bozeman, who had 37 years of dedicated leadership and service to the institution; he served as the department chair for 5 years. The Morehouse Mathematics sweater vest, elaborated on in Chapter 5, was unveiled in May 2010 on the occasion of his retirement (Cooper, personal communication, October 1, 2021). The sweater vest represents his signature style and honors his commitment to the department. Of note, his wife, Dr. Sylvia Bozeman, taught mathematics at Spelman for 39 years, chairing the department for 10 of those years (Williams, 2018). She collaborated with Dr. Rhonda Hughes, a mathematics professor at Bryn Mawr College (another liberal arts women's college), to launch the Enhancing Diversity in Graduate Education (EDGE) program in 1998, a program to support women pursuing graduate degrees in the mathematical sciences (Bozeman & Hughes, 2004). Collectively, the Bozemans' contributions have influenced a cadre of Black men and women doctoral recipients in the mathematical sciences.

Certainly, there are other forces who have served in multiple roles and blazed trails vis-à-vis Morehouse Mathematics. Dr. Louis Padulo, who joined the department in 1966 after completing his PhD in electrical engineering at Georgia Institute of Technology, started and directed the dual-degree engineering program (DDEP) between Georgia Institute of Technology and the AUC (Pierre, 2015). Dr. Johnny Houston, Morehouse Mathematics alumnus, was selected to serve as NAM's first acting president (Houston, 2000). The accomplishments of the historical giants profiled in this chapter, and others I have not mentioned here, are vast, as these predecessors' lasting impact continues to inspire future generations of mathematicians.

MOREHOUSE MATHEMATICS: A CONTEMPORARY PORTRAIT

The 16 participants in this study comprise a single year, but they are following in the mathematical footsteps of those who have come before them. This section provides a contemporary portrait of this phenomenal track record.

The National Numbers

This book shines a spotlight on math in relation to Black men. To make sense of this issue, IPEDS data were examined, as this data set provides a comprehensive national picture of college students' declared majors by race/ethnicity, gender, and institution (U.S. Department of Education, 2019). Figure 1.1 shows that more than half of the U.S. institutions have African American male students who declare a major in math. Keep in mind that these numbers represent the total number of Black male math majors across the undergraduate years.

The examination of these data is not meant to be reductionist, as the issues surrounding Black men's mathematical representation are multilayered. The key takeaway is that there are many Black male students who initially select math as a major upon entering college. The fact that these Black male students declare and pursue math as a major at the outset of their undergraduate studies suggests that African American men have strong interests in mathematics. Table 1.3 lists the 20 U.S. institutions reporting the most declared Black male math majors.

We see that some U.S. institutions have more than 20 African American males declared math majors on campus; depending on the size and racial makeup of the total class, those 20+ might be a hefty percentage of all math majors. We might expect the number of completers to be proportional to these numbers of declared majors. Figure 1.2 presents U.S. data regarding Black male mathematics completers (U.S. Department of Education, 2019).

The national completion data in Figure 1.2, however, display a stark reality when critically examining the 2018 undergraduate mathematics

Figure 1.1. National Data on Black Male Undergraduate Math Majors in 2014

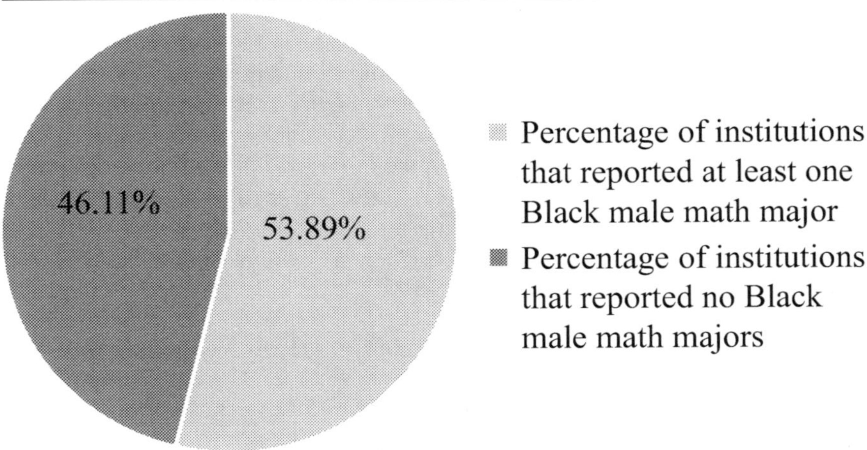

completion data. Out of the 1,221 4-year degree-granting Title IV institutions, 970 reported not having a single Black or African American man earn a mathematics degree during the 2017–2018 academic year[1] (U.S. Department of Education, 2019). To make it plain, approximately 80% of higher education institutions did not confer an undergraduate mathematics degree upon a single solitary Black male student. This is only one year, but it is representative; data across the last several years show that this is a prevalent and consistent pattern. This reality is a troubling one and casts a bright light on this national issue. IPEDS national data indicate that institutions have a difficult time *retaining* Black men in undergraduate mathematics degree programs. Where Table 1.3 shows the top 20 institutions' declared math major populations in 2014, Table 1.4 lists the top 20 institutions that conferred undergraduate mathematics degrees to African American male students 4 years later, in 2018 (U.S. Department of Education, 2019).

As Table 1.4 implies, many institutions have severe problems with getting Black male math majors across the finish line. A conspicuous exception is Morehouse, which is the continual top national producer of Black male undergraduate mathematics degree recipients (Owens et al., 2012). On a related note, HBCUs continue to produce African American male undergraduate mathematics graduates despite their meager enrollments. As a whole, institutions have some work to do to improve Black men's mathematics outcomes. And while Richards and Awokoya (2012) found that HBCUs graduate Black men at "14 percentage points higher than non-HBCUs" (p. 13) when controlling for Scholastic Aptitude Test (SAT) scores and Pell funding, these data suggest that improvements can also be made at HBCUs regarding Black men's mathematics degree completion.

Table 1.3. Top 20 Institutions with Black Men who Declared Mathematics Majors in 2014

Ranking	Institution[1]	State	Total Math Majors	Black Male Math Majors[2]	Percentage[3]
1	Morehouse College*	GA	62	58	94%
2	Georgia State University	GA	226	48	21%
3	Auburn University at Montgomery	AL	169	47	28%
4	University of South Carolina–Aiken	SC	232	41	18%
5	Oakwood University*	AL	66	40	61%
6	Alabama State University*	AL	57	33	58%
6	Allen University*	SC	54	33	61%
8	Savannah State University*	GA	74	32	43%
9	Clayton State University	GA	89	31	35%
10	Jackson State University*	MS	64	29	45%
11	CUNY New York City College of Technology	NY	96	28	29%
12	Bowie State University*	MD	53	27	51%
12	University of North Carolina at Charlotte	NC	350	27	8%
14	North Carolina Central University*	NC	51	24	47%
15	Morris College*	SC	31	23	74%
15	Stony Brook University	NY	851	23	3%
17	CUNY City College	NY	212	22	10%
17	Fort Valley State University*	GA	39	22	56%
17	Kennesaw State University	GA	301	22	7%
17	University of Maryland–Baltimore County	MD	292	22	8%

[1] Institutions marked with an asterisk (*) are HBCUs.
[2] Categories included "two or more races," "race/ethnicity unknown," and "nonresident alien." In cases where college students selected these designations, they were not counted as Black men even though there might have been some overlap (e.g., a biracial math major).
[3] These percentages are rounded to the nearest whole number.

Figure 1.2. National Data on Black Male Undergraduate Math Completers in 2018

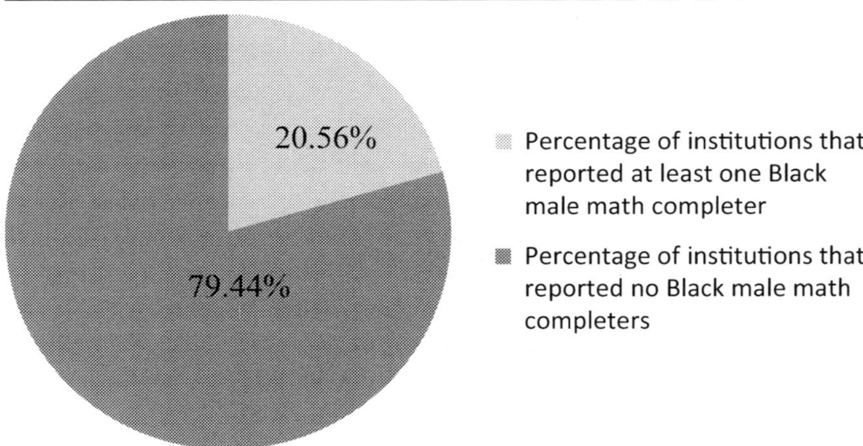

Within the 4-year time span between Tables 1.3 and 1.4 (i.e., the traditional bachelor's degree timeline, although the federal government uses 6 years to measure undergraduate degree completion), the steep decline of declared majors versus completers does not support the Black male mathematics trend noted earlier. Although these figures do not account for the underlying causes that contributed to this significant exodus during the course of 4 years, they do indicate that the retention, persistence, and completion rates of Black men in the math major is a national problem. In contrast, Morehouse's number of completers is compatible with their reported number of majors. To unpack this assertion, notice that Morehouse reported 58 Black men as math majors in 2014 and 15 Black men as mathematics completers in 2018, which is quantitatively sound. Juxtapose that with Auburn University at Montgomery, which reported 47 Black men as math majors in 2014 and no Black men as mathematics completers in 2018. Also, some of the institutions in Table 1.4 reported only one African American male mathematics completer even though they reported more than 20 Black men in their undergraduate mathematics program.

My point in highlighting these numbers is not to shame these institutions; Black male students, like other college students, change their majors throughout their college matriculation for various reasons. A crucial point is that we are losing Black men with math interests and talents who have expressed a desire to major in the discipline. In other words, something is happening between the points of major declaration to the graduation finish line that is causing these Black men to terminate their mathematics degree aspirations. Certainly we need studies asking why many Black men do not persist in the math major, but we also need to investigate why some do. My point in sharing these national numbers is to highlight Morehouse's sizeable

Table 1.4. Top 20 Undergraduate Mathematics Degree Producers of Black Men in 2018

Ranking	Institution[1]	State	Math Total Completers	Black or African American Men Math Completers
1	Morehouse College*	GA	16	15
2	Allen University*	SC	8	7
2	Kean University	NJ	55	7
2	Southern New Hampshire University	NH	145	7
2	Texas Tech University	TX	99	7
6	Mississippi Valley State University*	MS	12	5
6	University of Memphis	TN	21	5
6	University of North Carolina at Charlotte	NC	91	5
9	Alabama State University*	AL	11	4
9	Albany State University*	GA	9	4
9	Arizona State University-Tempe	AZ	121	4
9	CUNY Lehman College	NY	28	4
9	Georgia State University	GA	36	4
9	Jackson State University*	MS	10	4
9	Prairie View A&M University*	TX	7	4
9	University at Buffalo	NY	96	4
9	University of Alabama at Birmingham	AL	28	4
9	University of Arkansas at Pine Bluff*	AR	8	4
9	University of Florida	FL	90	4
9	University of Maryland-College Park	MD	169	4

[1] As with Table 1.3, institutions marked with an asterisk (*) are HBCUs.

footprint in producing African American male mathematics undergraduate degree recipients, which suggests that the Morehouse Mathematics program is doing something right. Therefore, Morehouse's mathematics learning community is a desirable space for interrogation to better understand Black men's undergraduate mathematics experiences beyond these numerical figures and serves as the crux for this book.

The Study

This ethnographic study provides a contemporary portrait of Morehouse's mathematics learning community. The study explored how a cohort of 16 Black men managed and negotiated the mathematical terrain. The field site for this study was the Department of Mathematics, which strives to provide a rigorous and balanced curriculum that serves as a solid foundation for majors' continued work in graduate programs and/or employment in career fields. Morehouse's Department of Mathematics was the sole 2016 recipient of AMS' Mathematics Programs that Make a Difference award, making it the first HBCU to receive the award (Jackson, 2016). The AMS award recognizes programs because they have achieved documentable success, are exemplary in retaining racially diverse groups, and are replicable models for other mathematics programs. This AMS award demonstrates that Morehouse is a math champion; therefore, its mathematics learning community is a distinctive one for exploring the experiences of Black men.

Black Male Success in Higher Education: How the Mathematical Brotherhood Empowers a Collegiate Community to Thrive addresses the following questions:

- How did these African American men narrate their mathematical (academic) experiences?
- What led them to attend Morehouse, declare math as a major, and persist in the major?
- How did they describe their mathematical peers, faculty, and the institutional space?
- How did they make sense of and verbalize their racialized experiences?
- What are their future plans?
- And ultimately, what might the field learn from this mathematics learning community to improve Black male students' achievement outcomes?

To address these questions, I conducted an ethnography coupled with portraiture methodology (Lawrence-Lightfoot & Davis, 1997). An *ethnography* accounts for the perspectives and behaviors of people in a community, and ethnographers embed themselves in a cultural setting to produce a rich portrait of the setting (Anderson-Levitt, 2006). *Portraiture* seeks to understand and document what works well. Because of this, portraiture has a preoccupation with "goodness," and disciplinary strengths were exemplified apropos the Black men in this study (Lawrence-Lightfoot & Davis, 1997). Voice is a hallmark of portraiture and is distinctively used to capture humans' rich experiences (Chapman, 2005). Portraiture also captures the complexities and subtleties of the human experience (Lawrence-Lightfoot & Davis, 1997).

Merging ethnography and portraiture, I conducted in-depth, face-to-face interviews with the 16 participants, had them complete a demographic survey, and observed them in their mathematics learning community (see Appendix A for methodological notes). I also held informal conversations with the participants to build rapport. The participants displayed mutual interest, as they asked me questions about my mathematics journey, the mathematics courses I teach, my research agenda, and why I was led to this area of research. These individual discussions fertilized other informal chats with the majors throughout the study. These actions, coupled with my rapport with the department chair, bolstered the participants' engagement in the study. Because the participants saw me multiple times prior to data collection, the individual interviews seemed like a dialogue between brothers as opposed to interviews for a study. This approach was particularly effective because it enhanced relatability and facilitated participants responding to data collection methods.

Throughout the data collection process, I attended the Morehouse Mathematics Alumni Conference, sat in on mathematics colloquia, and engaged in conversations with colleagues (i.e., administrators, faculty, and staff members). I also met and spoke with the majors' family members during the Morehouse Mathematics Breakfast, which was held during Commencement week (see Appendix B for related field notes). I was introduced as the "researcher" to the group, which allowed me to sit in the back corner and soak in all of the Black excellence in an unobtrusive manner. In addition, I examined historical documents and artifacts that were included within the department and the AUC Robert W. Woodruff Library. Collectively, these efforts, informed by my consistent exploration of the Black masculinity and critical race theoretical literature, influenced my analysis and research insights.

Black Male Success in Higher Education: How the Mathematical Brotherhood Empowers a Collegiate Community to Thrive examines what works well in Morehouse Mathematics, provides a portrait of a single year, and adds to Morehouse Mathematics' success story. It amplifies the participants' voices regarding their experiences, the culture of the institution, and its mathematics learning community. Readers will visualize portraits of the participants, faculty, scenarios, and so on. Looking for the strengths in these brothers' experiences and stories contributes to asset-based HBCU-related scholarship in mathematics. The next chapter depicts the contextual factors, embedded within the participants' home and schooling environments, that precipitated their matriculation through Morehouse's mathematics program.

CHAPTER 2

The Brothers' Journey to Morehouse Mathematics

I'm gifted in mathematics, and mathematics is pretty much the only thing in academia that I'm currently interested in.

—Ray

Ray's narrative shows what he believes in, ascribes to, and verbalizes about his mathematical abilities. He embraces a gifted mathematical persona as a young, gifted, and Black man, and it was why he decided to pursue this disciplinary pathway (Perry et al., 2003). He has a robust math identity, which positively influences his mathematical self-efficacy, self-esteem, and self-confidence (McGee, 2015). As expected, many of the majors in this study shared similar sentiments about the subject. These strong math identities led them on a journey to Morehouse Mathematics.

In this chapter, I share ethnographic portraits of the brothers' journeys to Morehouse Mathematics. First, I describe their family dynamics. From there, retrospective accounts of their journeys to math are shared to better understand how these African American men were ultimately intrigued by and became interested in the discipline. These accounts include school-based and out-of-school interactions, which elucidate the formation, development, and advancement of their math identities. After that, I discuss their journeys to Morehouse. I conclude the chapter by summarizing these ideas.

FAMILY DYNAMICS

Before Black boys enter formal schooling, their educational ideals and values are shaped by their family dynamics. Home life has been consistently noted as a huge influencer in Black boys' academic outcomes (Baker, 2015; Thompson, 2008). Unlike later portions of the book, this section does not match each participant with a particular family dynamic. This was deliberately done to assist with anonymity, ensure privacy and confidentiality with respect to participants' family members, and alleviate judgments based on social class dynamics and the like. My goal in this section is to provide a brief snapshot of their family dynamics that help to subsequently center their math stories.

The majors' parents' educational attainment ranged from some high school to graduate education. Their mothers' occupations included accountant, business owner, correctional officer, counselor, education administrator, human resources director, information security professional, massage therapist, librarian, nurse, physician's assistant, and substitute teacher. Their fathers' occupations included accountant, auditor, engineer, National Football League (NFL) player developer, police officer, retrovirus researcher, store manager, and teacher. A participant indicated that a mother was retired, and another indicated that a father was retired. Similarly, a participant indicated that a mother was differently abled, and another indicated that a father was. One participant reported being raised by his grandparents, and one participant reported having a deceased father.

Regarding sibling dynamics, two participants reported being an only child while the others reported having siblings who influenced their academic aspirations. Their home-based geographical regions were diverse and included rural and urban areas. In short, their different environments provided them with an expansive set of family dynamics, neighborhood configurations, and learning opportunities.

JOURNEY TO MATHEMATICS

The schooling experiences of the 16 Morehouse Men in this study were vastly different. They hailed from all over the United States. They attended public schools, private schools, and charter schools throughout their K–12 experiences. One participant attended a predominately White all-male high school.

Two participants reported being differently abled. This finding was an interesting one given the scholarship that advocates for positioning Black male K–12 students with disabilities as "vulnerable resources" instead of as students who need to be fixed through (mathematical) remediation (Proffitt, 2022). Unlike previous findings that suggest mathematical growth trajectories of students with disabilities (across race/ethnicity lines) are below that of their peers (Wei et al., 2013), the two differently abled participants in this study made substantial mathematics gains in their K–12 schooling.

First Math Interests

The participants' affinity for mathematics was recognized in different ways during their K–12 schooling. Many of the brothers participated in honors and analogous programs that nurtured their mathematical gifts. Some of them participated in mathematical olympiads while a couple participated in MATHCOUNTS, a national middle school competition designed to promote math achievement in a fun manner. Many of them received accolades for their mathematical accomplishments. One major was the valedictorian, and another was the salutatorian of their high school graduating classes. While our education system does not serve all Black boys well, the participants' K–12 experiences provided them with some rich mathematics learning opportunities.

Their attention was caught by varying aspects of grade- and high school math. Table 2.1 introduces the brothers by sharing discipline-specific information about them. Unlike other tables in this book that list the participants alphabetically, Table 2.1 presents them according to their *line number*. The *line number* is consistent with BGLO traditions as brothers are typically lined up by height; in this study, it represents the chronological order in

Table 2.1. Brothers' First Math Interests

Line #	Brother	First Math Interest	Experience
1	Andre	Grade 11	Trigonometry
2	Darius	Grade 12	Advanced Placement (AP) Calculus
3	Tony	Early Childhood	Elementary Gifted & Talented Program
4	Asa	Grade 9	Honors Math
5	Marcus	Grade 11	Algebra 2 or Geometry 2
6	Robert	Grade 8	Exposure to Algebra
7	Malik	Early Elementary School	100 Sliders
8	Epsilon	Grade 1 or 2	Loved All Math
9	John	Elementary School	Times Tables
10	Jeremiah	Early Childhood	Always Loved Math
11	Max	No Definitive First Interest	N/A
12	Michael	Early Childhood	Picked Up on Math Easily
13	Allen	Middle School	Learned about Engineering
14	Daniel	High School	Honors Math
15	Jared	Grade 2 or 3	Perfect Score on Math Portion of Standardized Test
16	Ray	6 Years Old	Math Tricks with Parents

which the participants were interviewed. The table also notes when the participants first noticed their interests in math, followed by that particular "aha" moment.

> *line number*: the number a fraternity member is assigned based on his order in the line

Math-Related Early Childhood Years

Research suggests that the early childhood years are most influential concerning African American male students' math pathways (Baker, 2015; Berry et al., 2011). Because of this, handheld devices and virtual manipulatives such as Cuisenaire rods, tangrams, and unifix cubes—along with dice, dominoes, and hundred charts—have been used to mathematically captivate students in the primary grades. As Table 2.1 demonstrates, 8 of the 16 participants noticed their first math interests during their early childhood years. For example, Ray first noticed his interest in math at the age of 6 while doing math tricks with his parents, which cultivated his disciplinary gift. He shared:

> I discovered that I was quite gifted in the field of mathematics. I'd say I'm not sure when I found out I was gifted in mathematics, but it certainly helped me when I skipped grades when I was 8. I skipped the 3rd and 4th grades.

Ray was the only participant in this study who skipped two grades. He did so at a private school, but he encountered difficulties when he later enrolled in public school. That is, he was placed in the same grade as his same-aged peers because of ironclad district policies. Therefore, he was placed below his academic ability. While this policy could be applied to all school-aged children, race exacerbates the impact of these policies. Wright and Counsell (2018) highlight how public-school practices and policies are inequitably structured to meet the needs of brilliant Black boys, and researchers have used CRT to demonstrate how school rules and policies are enacted to stall Black male advancement (Jett, 2022a; Johnson & Bryan, 2017). In doing so, school systems' policies wound the spirits of Black boys, as they grapple with racially motivated policies and roadblocks. Fortunately, Ray was able to thrive in his mathematical gift in spite of this affliction.

On a more positive note, Allen benefited in his early childhood years because of his mathematical aptitude. He acknowledged:

> I was always in the discovery class or the accelerated class starting in elementary school. I'd get pulled out of class and go to a separate class with other children, and we'd go over critical thinking exercises in math and other kind of brain teasers and puzzles.

Allen benefited from the academic support through the Discovery Program's advanced math class. The Discovery Program in Allen's school district was akin to the Talented and Gifted (TAG) program, as he was pulled out of his classroom to be challenged mathematically. In many school districts, TAG programs function whereby a gifted-credentialed teacher pulls the referred students out of the regular classroom for cognitive, critical thinking, and other creative exercises to accelerate students' learning, and Ford (2013) has shown how Black students, especially Black boys, are severely under-represented in gifted programs. Fortunately, Allen and others in this study were in these programs.

Robert was another participant who was able to take an advanced math class. He disclosed:

> In 5th grade, they gave an AP math test to kind of gauge where you are in math and if you passed the test, they will put you in a math class ahead of your grade, and so I missed the test [due to illness], but my teacher called my mother, and she wanted me to take it because she knew I would do well on it, so in 5th grade, I took that test and passed, so in 6th grade, instead of doing 6th-grade math, I started off with 7th-grade math.

In his interview, Robert shared how he became very ill and had to miss a couple of days of school when his classmates were testing for slots for an advanced math course. Although tests are customary for determining gift-edness, a single test should not determine whether students have access to these rich learning opportunities (Ford, 2013). Because his teacher recognized and believed in his mathematical capabilities, she phoned his mother to make her aware that he needed to take advantage of the opportunity to take the test. In other words, Robert's teacher advocated for him, which is typically not the case for Black boys in schools (Bryan, 2021b).

Robert described the teacher as "a White woman in her early thirties, or late twenties at that time," which is not surprising given that White women constitute about 63% of the teaching force (U.S. Bureau of Labor Statistics, 2022). His teacher's perceptions of his mathematical abilities worked in his favor, as he was able to take Algebra in Grade 8, which sparked his interest in math (as noted in Table 2.1). Prior work suggests that many teachers do not acknowledge the brilliance of Black boys like Robert, and many Black boys who are mathematically gifted are never identified as such (Wright & Counsell, 2018). Fortunately, Robert was, and his example is in sync with suggestions for teachers to identify and support Black male students' enrollment in advanced math courses (Davis et al., 2019).

Math-Related Secondary School Years

Like the early childhood years, the secondary school years are instrumental with focusing on and supporting Black male students' math identities, trajectories, and aspirations (Davis et al., 2019; Stinson, 2013). Almost half of the participants recognized their math interest during their secondary years. Even though Michael picked up on his math interest early on, his secondary years solidified his interest. He stated:

> It was just really easy for me to pick up on math; that's why it probably ended up being one of my favorite subjects. And when I got to middle school, I started to like math more just because I was on the math council, so I became the person to make students better mathematicians, and I really enjoyed that, and I was already a pretty strong mathematician by that point, compared to my peers.

As Michael shared, math has always been easy for him to understand. In his role on the mathematics council, he was entrusted with working with his middle school peers to ensure that they became better math students. He really enjoyed this experience, and this role further developed his mathematical skills. Note that he referred to himself as a mathematician, demonstrating his burgeoning mathematical acumen. Similar to other narratives, Michael's narrative shows how his math identity was formed and strengthened as a result of serving on the mathematics council (Martin, 2000).

Other participants cited similar experiences during their secondary schooling years that strengthened their math identity. Daniel expressed:

> In high school is when I really started to excel ahead of my classmates. I was put in a Calculus class with only a few others out of the whole high school, and I was able to take the AP Calculus course, and I was selected to be in the honors math courses at my high school, and that's when it dawned on me, hey, I think I have a gift here, and I don't want to be stingy with it, you know. I want to help others, and I liked it, and I enjoyed what I was doing. I can't explain it; it was something that really grasped my attention.

Daniel believed he had a special gift in math because he was selected to enroll in AP and honors courses. He mentioned not being stingy with his gift and desiring to help others, which shows a giving aspect linked to Black masculinity (Pelzer, 2016). Regarding AP Calculus, Bressoud (2021) notes that the course widens inequities across schools and is a disservice to those who do not have access to it. Students who take AP Calculus benefit significantly, as it is a positive signal of succeeding in college mathematics courses. But large racial disparities exist regarding AP Calculus, so efforts should be in place to ensure that there are more equitable opportunities for Black students to enroll in this course.

Like Daniel, several participants mentioned taking AP Calculus. Jared spoke about taking the course and exam.

> The toughest time I had was maybe Calculus in high school, took that in the 12th grade. I was in the AP course, and I ended up getting a 5 on the AP Calc exam. I think sometimes I might overcomplicate things sometimes or maybe doubt myself because at first I didn't feel like I did that well. I wasn't 100% sure, but I went with what I knew and made it happen. So when I first got my score, I was like whoa, I made a 5. I had to go to my mom and verify, like, this is a 5, right?

Jared's most challenging high school course was AP Calculus, and he experienced a bout of self-doubt when taking the exam. However, he ended up scoring a 5, the highest score possible. He went to his mother to verify that he indeed saw his score correctly, as he was in a state of disbelief that he had done so well on the challenging exam. Going to his mother for verification signaled the supportive role she played in his math education, and prior work has highlighted the central role Black mothers play in consistently encouraging their Black sons to succeed in math and science (Hrabowski et al., 1998).

Darius also spoke about his AP Calculus experience; this is when he first noticed his interest in math.

> Senior year of high school, I was in an AP Calculus class. I know it's kind of random, but I was sitting there one day while the teacher was teaching and thinking, this isn't bad. Pretty much since then I've liked it more to the point now where it's my favorite subject.

Darius reflected on his math interest while sitting in class, which suggests that something was happening pedagogically to pique his interest. The fact that he was enrolled in an AP Calculus course in the first place suggests that some mathematical seeds had been planted and were now ready to take root. As a result of the epiphany that occurred during his senior year of high school, math became his favorite subject.

The majors' secondary schooling experiences also prompted them to think about career opportunities. Ray noted:

> With the grad degree, I was thinking [of] maybe becoming a cryptographer. It started in Algebra 2 in high school. When we

learned about matrices, we also learned about cryptography, and I liked having to solve codes.

Ray was first introduced to cryptography, a math-intensive career field, as a high school student. Cryptography merges math, computer science, and electrical engineering, and is primarily concerned with data security (Paar & Pelzl, 2009). Applications of cryptography appear with software updates, with chip-based cards, and in smart buildings. Ray's example reifies the notion that secondary teachers expose students to suitable career options and sow seeds that are later nurtured in students' educational pathways, so the secondary space also holds promise for inspiring students to pursue math-related career options.

Malik was in a different situation because his developmental level was not fully considered. He pointed out:

> I felt like I was too mature for the ways they were treating me, not that I didn't joke around or get distracted, but to the sense that I don't have to do all 50 [math] problems and I don't have to turn it in. I can do the hardest problems, learn how to do the concepts, and be okay, and so the whole collecting homework, I was always in detention.

As I reported on his case elsewhere, Malik challenged the ways in which his school operated (Jett, 2016b). He viewed this homework act as neither mathematically challenging nor intellectually engaging. Because he opted not to do it, he was often empty-handed when his teacher collected homework. As a consequence, he was assigned detention quite often. Schools are structured to value conformity and compliance, and punitive consequences such as repeated detentions feed the school-to-prison pipeline for Black boys (Dancy, 2014). Fortunately, this was not Malik's fate, but this system works to the detriment of Black boys in the broader landscape. I must emphasize that Malik possessed the mathematical capabilities to complete these homework assignments, but he rejected the notion of doing what he perceived to be meaningless exercises.

Delpit (2012) made clear in *"Multiplication is for White People": Raising Expectations for Other People's Children* that Black children should practice with *worthwhile* exercises to become better mathematical thinkers. She argued:

> This discussion explains why the "basketball boy" gets better—he practices. It also explains why people get better at everything—they practice. When we encounter children in our classes who are not performing, the likely culprit is not that they do not have the innate ability or the capacity to accomplish the tasks, the reality is that they have not engaged in sufficient practice. (p. 153)

In line with this paradigm, Malik's comment suggests that students should be expected to engage in meaningful exercises that strengthen their conceptual understanding. Delpit (2012) argues for a math praxis that leads to intellectual development and challenges teachers to enact pedagogical practices that propel African American students' mathematical brilliance. Practicing relevant and challenging mathematics should be the norm in classrooms instead of schools serving as worksheet factories, where students are assigned worksheet after worksheet without any true mathematical engagement.

In another example, Epsilon was also critical of the secondary schooling space. He shared:

> Why would I sit in this World Lit class when I can teach the class? I had a good AP Calculus teacher; he was a Teach for America [TFA] teacher, so I believe in that program, so umm, when it comes to academic rigor, I wasn't prepared right there. When it came to social rigor, my school was kind of like a jail, it was a place we went to for 8 hours. If you walk through the door, you had to go through metal detectors; you couldn't walk through with book bags that weren't clear. You walk in, and it smells like pot. It was just like, you know what I'm saying? As you can tell, it wasn't an environment that was like the rest of the world.

Forthrightly, Epsilon admitted that he attended a challenging urban school. His description and this writing are not meant to perpetuate any stereotypes about urban schools; however, it is a sad reality that urban schools are often underfunded, understaffed, etc., symptomatic of the institutional and structural issues barriers embedded within a White supremacist society (Milner & Lomotey, 2021). Mentioning the World Literature class specifically, Epsilon critically questioned the need to sit in a class where he was not challenged. Taken a step further, he indicated that he could teach the class himself, demonstrating that he could either do a better job presenting the content or implying that the content was at a low bar. In his demographic survey, Epsilon indicated that his secondary schooling experiences did not adequately prepare him for college. Epsilon's experience resonates with the experiences of the Black men in Brooms's (2017a) study in which he found that many of the 40 Black collegiate men he studied did not feel that their secondary education prepared them for college, yet they maintained high educational aspirations.

As noted, Epsilon had a respectable AP Calculus teacher who was a TFA corps member. TFA's programmatic structure has been critiqued because corps members have a 2-year teaching commitment and then often pursue more lucrative careers on the backs of students in economically disadvantaged schools (Scott et al., 2016). Epsilon stressed that he believed in the program because it provided him with a math teacher who was up to the mark. In spite of his secondary schooling shortcomings and the challenges in his urban environment, Epsilon maintained his resolve to persist in math, similar to his fellow majors.

Out-of-School Math Experiences

Prior research has emphasized that mathematics participation outside of school provides African American students familiarity with mathematical ideas, increases their readiness for learning math concepts in school, and supports their cumulative math learning outcomes (Nasir, 2007; Taylor, 2013; Walker, 2016). These activities include playing board games, purchasing items from street vendors, tabulating scores via sports, and tithing or giving 10% of one's income to the church. African American students' mathematically rich out-of-school experiences shore up their disciplinary comprehension and connections across home, school, and community contexts.

The participants shared that many of the out-of-school experiences that catapulted their school math learning occurred in their homes. For example, Marcus made clear: "I had a pretty strong background in math, like I was doing math my entire life. My parents were teaching me math before I started school." This exposure to mathematical ideas in his home contributed to his exceptional performance during school. His counternarrative combats dominant narratives about Black parental involvement and coincides with prior work showing that Black parents are heavily involved in their children's education (Thompson, 2008).

Malik's out-of-school math experience was often shared with his sibling, an older brother. He relayed:

> I've always been competitive. When it came to math, I don't remember which grade exactly, probably about 4th when we first learned long division. Me and my brother would write out a real, real long division problem and race to see who finished it first. Like a billion divided by a million, and we'd check it on the calculator.

Malik prefaced his description by highlighting his competitive persona. He mentioned that he and his brother computed lengthy calculations and would use a calculator to determine if their calculations were done correctly. This home-based activity substantiated his joy associated with completing complex problems. In another point during his interview, he explained how he loved to work problems quickly when his elementary teacher would split the class into two teams to play math games. These experiences, both within and outside of school, fueled his love for math and quenched his thirst for competition.

Jared is another participant who had a strong mathematics background. He got a perfect score on the math portion of his standardized test in elementary school (an event noted in Table 2.1 as a first driver of his math enthusiasm). Recall that he also earned a 5 on the AP Calculus examination. He cited his father challenging him mathematically:

> My dad used to challenge me every once in a while. He'd do this during lunch or dinner or something and when the tab comes, "Alright, how much I can do for the tip?" Usually he'd leave a 15% tip, so you know this is when I was younger, so it was teaching different techniques. Move the decimal by 1, that's 10%, cut that in half, that's 5%, add it to the 10% you've got 15%. Just little things like that. Like, oh, "what's 25 times 3?" Just random questions just out of the blue, I used to love it when he did it; it was fun to me.

Like other members of this cohort, Jared was exposed to mathematical ideas outside of the classroom, with family in particular. In Jared's case, it was a common practice for his father to have him calculate the tip when out dining. In other cases, his father would pose spontaneous mathematical questions to him (e.g., multiplication problems) to improve his fact fluency and enhance his flexibility with numbers. Jared's repeated practice later yielded fruitful outcomes in the form of perfect scores on assessments. Consequently, this enjoyable practice solidified his math knowledge and ultimately impacted his schooling experiences.

Jared's counternarrative challenges notions about Black fathers who are supposedly absent from the lives of Black boys. CRT scholars have disrupted the positioning of Black fathers as uninvolved and unconcerned by centering them and highlighting their positive efforts regarding their children's education (Reynolds et al., 2015). Foundational research has shown how this active involvement reaps mathematical benefits for Black boys (Hrabowski et al., 1998). Also, Jared's case aligns with McGee and Spencer's (2015) finding that Black parents instill mathematical self-efficacy in their children. As opposed to placing more value on school-based channels of parenting (i.e., volunteering at the school, participating on the parent–teacher association, etc.), this home-based finding confirms prior work suggesting that Black parental involvement involves being Black children's initial mathematics supporters, advocates, and champions (Cunningham, 2021; McGee & Spencer, 2015).

Robert honed his math skills via shopping, which is an activity outside of school that has rich learning opportunities. He conveyed:

> I would say just standard currency using math and calculating how much change you should give back and when you use money to pay for things, I feel that I do those relatively quickly, or even sales,

> because I remember going to sales, I have 20% off and an additional
> 10% off, and my aunt would be like, "How much is this shirt?"
> Because when I was in middle school, she knew I loved math, but she
> would always try to keep me on my toes and try to figure things out.
> And so whenever she would go shopping and there was a sale, and a
> shirt was $20, and it says 50% off, she would have me figure out how
> much the shirt was afterwards, and it helped me build my math skills
> outside the classroom.

Robert expressed that his aunt recognized his knack for math, so she would use everyday events such as shopping to sharpen his math skills. She would challenge him to perform mental calculations involving foundational percent concepts and the like. In his interview, Robert credited his parents for being instrumental in teaching him reading and math skills and his aunt for pushing him in math specifically, thereby confirming the extremely supportive role of Black families in Black boys' education (Hrabowski et al., 1998).

Like Robert, Allen praised his aunt for pushing him mathematically outside of school.

> My aunt was a teacher, so I would visit her over the summer, and she
> would always tell me to go over my times tables, or she'd always have
> [academic] work for me to do, so I'd always practice math then.

Allen's aunt was an educator who provided him with opportunities to procure summer learning gains. He cited going over his multiplication facts, but he noted that there were other enrichment exercises to boost his academic abilities. Practicing math outside of school with his aunt positively influenced his mathematical trajectory in school. Black women, at approximately 5% of a teaching force numbering 3.672 million as of May 2021, are a significant source of educational input in Black children's lives (U.S. Bureau of Labor Statistics, 2022; also see Farinde-Wu et al., 2017). Allen was able to benefit from this Black woman educator in his family, and thus his example provides additional evidence of the supportive role of Black families.

Andre verbalized his mathematical connections, which were strongly linked to his family:

> I had a knack for and there was something that I enjoyed about math.
> And it's been told that my father, he was good with numbers. He
> was an accountant, and my grandmother, she's good with numbers. I
> honestly can't explain it. I can't put it into words.

Andre describes a familial *legacy* associated with doing math. Both his father and grandmother were good with numbers, which he believed related to how he was able to continue in that familial, mathematical tradition. This *legacy* discussion could also be attributed to some of the other majors and supports prior work highlighting the longstanding, rich heritage of Black people making significant strides in math (Kenschaft, 2005; Shetterly, 2016; Walker, 2014). The role of Black families in building math skills cannot be overstated, as we see for many participants in this study.

> *legacy*: a pledgee whose family member is a member of a BGLO

In contrast, Michael used his schooling experiences as an entry point to launch his mathematical investigations at home. He communicated:

> If I got a homework problem, I'd try to answer that homework problem and look at a lot of problems related to those homework problems, so it was more going in-depth with the coursework that I already had in school. I honestly can say, I was never really that interested in math, to where I can just go to the library and look up new problems. It was just that the teacher would introduce a new concept that I'd never seen before, and I'd use my book or just use research that I had at my house to kind of just learn more about the concepts I'd been taught.

Michael's math identity became more potent by mastering homework problems. Whereas some students might search for and conduct research on new mathematical concepts, this practice was not his modus operandi. As he shared, he would essentially go home from school, read his textbook, and conduct some research on the mathematical concepts he learned, which suggests that they piqued his curiosity. A primary takeaway is that he would take the initiative to learn more math in his home, and his example reiterates that math taught in school can serve as a precursor to mathematical ideas that students choose to investigate further at home and in other out-of-school contexts. Collectively, these Black men were on their valiant journeys to completing their undergraduate mathematics degree and had selected Morehouse to make this dream a reality.

JOURNEY TO MOREHOUSE

Choosing where to attend college is arguably one of the most important decisions that college-going students make. This life-altering decision can have a significant impact on students' successful matriculation through the degree program, higher education institution, and career path, among other things. For Black men, selecting an institution that has a supportive environment can be a huge contributing factor to this decision, given the gendered racism that exists. More and more first-generation African American male college students are matriculating at higher education institutions, and scholars have shared recommendations to support these students along their collegiate journey (Owens et al., 2010). Four of the 16 participants were first-generation college students, which is consistent with research that shows that non-first-generation African American male college students enroll in private HBCUs at a higher rate than do first-generation college students (Palmer & Wood, 2012). This section focuses on these individual Black men's decision-making to attend Morehouse.

As mentioned in Chapter 1, Morehouse has a rich history and legacy of developing Black male leaders in various fields (Brawley, 1917/2009; Eaves, 2006). John spoke about wanting to attend Morehouse because of this long-standing legacy.

> I knew when I was like in 1st grade. I did a report on Dr. Martin Luther King, Jr., when I was in elementary school. Just seeing what he did for us as a people, you know, it just really inspired me.

Data analysis revealed that John was the only participant who knew that he would attend Morehouse in elementary school. The other participants knew that they would do so in high school, with 14 of them indicating that they decided upon Morehouse as high school seniors. More to the point, this early childhood experience left a significant mark on John as it instilled a message of hope that he could attend Morehouse as well. Therefore, a key takeaway is that generating profiles of inspirational Black men during the early learning years can set a firm foundation and motivate school-aged children to be college-bound. Certainly, these reports should be inclusive of HBCU alumni to equally promote these institutions for postsecondary study for Black students.

Daniel articulated why he came to Morehouse:

> I came here because of the name and the tradition, but I feel like Morehouse offered something a lot of colleges couldn't offer, and that was just networking. Networking from alumni, from faculty, from students. It's a small college, and I felt like a small college means a smaller classroom and better interactions with the professor, and I always felt like that was better for me, you know, in my past, so I felt like why not continue that through college because I went to a small high school as well.

As demonstrated, Daniel was led to Morehouse because of the institution's prominence. He mentioned networking with institutional stakeholders and the compact student body. Daniel personalized the smaller class sizes, noting that it was reminiscent of his small high school. Many HBCUs have smaller enrollments and class sizes, and this characteristic provides Black students individualized attention, encourages participation, and builds community (Borum et al., 2016; Jett, 2013b).

While many participants wanted to attend Morehouse outright, a few of them chose to enroll at the institution after their original college plans were altered. Jared's experience captured one of those experiences. He declared:

> I played football in high school, and I wanted to go on an academic and athletic scholarship to somewhere, somewhere big. Rekenrek University was actually my first choice. I actually didn't apply to Morehouse until maybe like February, March, I literally just made the late deadline and everything. Originally, I wanted to go to Rekenrek University. I applied to Rekenrek University, and they said, they sent me to their Caliper campus, which I don't know, I guess it was more like a junior college kind of thing. Like I'd go there for 2 years, and I'd go to Rekenrek University; it's kind of like you go to Compass Community College for 2 years, and it's almost like a feeder school for a university. And I was like, I'm better than that. I'm not going to anybody's junior college; that's not going to happen.

For Jared, he thought that his academic and athletic talents would lead him to a big-name institution. As he shared, Rekenrek University was his first choice for college attendance. When he received word from the institution about his acceptance, it was on the terms that he would be granted admission into their satellite campus in Caliper as opposed to the main campus. Jared equated it to the practice of attending a community college and later transferring to a 4-year university, which is an alternative pathway to degree completion. However, enrolling as a community college student was not what Jared desired.

John, unlike all the other participants, transferred into Morehouse. He remarked:

> I transferred into Morehouse. The reason why I didn't come here originally was because of financial reasons; at least I thought I couldn't afford it. I actually could afford it, but it turns out we didn't know any better, me and my parents. I had a merit scholarship; I didn't know that financial aid would cover the rest of it, and I didn't even know I had financial aid. I turned down a Morehouse Merit Scholarship for a [state-sponsored] Presidential Scholarship, which pretty much covered everything.

Although Morehouse was his first choice, John thought that he did not have enough funds to fully cover the expenses. In actuality, his merit-based scholarship coupled with his financial aid would have covered all of his expenses. Operating under the notion that he would not have enough money, he decided to accept a presidential scholarship in his home state. John's narrative also speaks to the need to better educate Black students, parents, and caregivers about higher education's funding procedures so that all parties are adequately informed. This finding is consistent with Carey's (2019) study with five Black and Latino high school boys who needed additional information about funding their college education; he suggested that mock financial aid packages be created with counselors to demystify the financial aid process.

Other participants provided different reasons why they decided to attend Morehouse. Ray responded:

> I had the scholarship money to go. If it actually wasn't for the scholarship, I would have had trouble picking a school. When I said I didn't like statistics, I meant that both the class and I really don't want to be one.

Mathematics is often used as an overarching term to represent the mathematical sciences; statistics is its own unique field included under the mathematical sciences umbrella. In Ray's case, he jokingly referenced that he did not like his Probability and Statistics 1 class. Plus, he did not aspire to become "a statistic." By that, Ray meant that he did not hope to become a Black male college dropout, failure, or letdown. Unfortunately, Black men have to grapple with the additional layer of doom and gloom associated with being a statistic, so Ray wanted to avoid this. This belief was one of the things that kept him in college and pushed him to finish.

Even though Darius almost decided against going to Morehouse, his reason for attending the college was because he wanted a different racial environment. He voiced:

> Growing up in predominately White neighborhoods, a lot of the stereotypes they have, they kind of project them onto you as well. And a lot of the White kids would tell me that I was, like, the smart Black kid. I got kind of used to that, and I started feeling I was smart, and others weren't as smart. So being at a school with all Black people, I was like all, this gonna be sort of ratchet. I didn't know how I felt about it, but I'm glad I came here and got a different perspective.

In his case, Darius reprogramed his thinking about Black people as a result of attending this HBCU. His upbringing in predominately White settings, informed by White logics, sensitivities, and epistemologies, influenced his germinal thoughts about Black colleges, people, and intelligence. However, his matriculation at Morehouse has exposed him firsthand to Black intelligentsia and precipitated the growth in his thinking about Black people and institutions.

In one last example, Malik shared a story with enthusiasm concerning his decision to enroll at Morehouse.

> My nephew, he had gotten accepted to Morehouse College, and he had come down for the summer program, and I was at his house with his mom, my sister. He came back for the Fourth of July, and he was telling me about Morehouse, and he showed me a YouTube video of Hump Wednesday and that I just saw a solid bough of beautiful women on our campus, and he told me it happened every Wednesday, and I went, I'm going to Morehouse!

As Malik's narrative shows, he became interested in Morehouse after listening to his nephew (his older sister's son) speak enthusiastically about his experience in a summer program. Because of the significant age gap between Malik and his sister, he and his nephew are close in age. In addition to the academic component, his nephew told him about the social gatherings and explained Hump Wednesday to him. When Malik saw the video of all the beautiful Black women on the yard, his mind was made up to attend the institution.

In closing his interview, Malik shared that he "came [to Morehouse] for the women; stayed for the math." Although he originally came to Morehouse for the women (despite the fact that it is a traditionally single-gender institution), he later discovered another aspect that captured his attention and encouraged him to stay—mathematics. In other words, he came to Morehouse to live out those YouTube videos in the flesh, but he ended up staying for the math, suggesting that math became a priority along his collegiate journey.

His narrative is neither designed to reinscribe Black men as hypersexual nor objectify Black women, as these ideas have been erroneously rendered as symbols of Black masculinity (Neal, 2013). Instead, Malik's Black masculine identity and ideology became tethered to mathematics. In the end, Malik was not the only major who was incentivized by mathematics, as the next chapter shows. In this way, these Black men math majors were comparable to *neophytes* given that they were mathematical novices in the field.

> *neophyte*: a new member of a BGLO

CONCLUSION

As this chapter showed, the 16 Black men in this study had diverse family, schooling, and mathematical backgrounds; consequently, they were led to

Morehouse for different reasons. Some of the participants had parents who had college diplomas and graduate degrees, and some of their parents did not complete high school. Notwithstanding, their families positively influenced their math success. Regarding classroom teachers, some had gifted teachers and appropriate programs, while others made do with insufficient class work. Even though their formative experiences were disparate, they generally arrived at Morehouse academically prepared to thrive in the math major.

In all, this chapter revealed the ways in which their formal and informal experiences as Black boys shaped, formed, and influenced their mathematical understandings. The participants mentioned using math while playing competitive games with siblings, buying clothing items, and calculating tip amounts during casual dining outings. Moreover, their experiences in both predominately monoracial and racially diverse settings bolstered the knowledge in their repertoire, led them on paths to becoming mathematics degree completers, and contributed to their worldviews as Black men. The next chapter further delves into the participants' undergraduate experiences and divulges some particularities about the mathematical brotherhood.

CHAPTER 3

The Mathematical Brotherhood

My classmates being my brothers in Morehouse, having my back, looking
out for me when I struggled, and I for them when they struggled.

—Daniel

This extraction of Daniel's narrative gets at the core of mathematical brotherhood. First, he refers to his classmates as his brothers. He then mentions that his Morehouse brothers have his back. In other words, they look out for him when he struggles with math concepts. Reciprocating this give-and-take disciplinary relationship, he also looks out for them when they struggle mathematically. This progression unveils the hallmarks of their disciplinary union and mathematicizes the following scripture: "A man that hath friends must show himself friendly . . ." (Proverbs 18:24, King James Version).[1]

This chapter provides a portrait of this cohort's undergraduate experiences. I begin with a discussion about Morehouse's brotherhood. Then, I explore the participants' reasons for declaring math as a major followed by their narratives and experiences portrayed as the mathematical brotherhood. After that, I consider their persistence as well as their trials and tribulations in the major. I continue with a discussion regarding some division among the brothers. Finally, I wrap up the chapter by summarizing the chapter's big ideas.

MOREHOUSE'S BROTHERHOOD

Morehouse is a "brotherhood of men on a mission to lead lives of consequence" (Morehouse College, n.d.). In essence, brotherhood encapsulates the roles and responsibilities of each and every Morehouse Man to empower his fellow Morehouse brother. Thus, Morehouse becomes a part of these Black men's identities, as they join this institutionalized brotherhood. Marcus spoke about the brotherhood:

I had a little tour and people were telling me about the benefits of
Morehouse and the brotherhood. I remember I went to Harmonograph,

> and I had my Morehouse hat on, and I saw these old alums and they
> called me over like, "Is that a Morehouse Man over there?" And we
> had lunch, and we just talked, and they were like 60 years old, and they
> were like, "The brotherhood is real regardless of what age you are."

Marcus revealed that his initial visit exposed him to this unique sense of
brotherhood and was one of the reasons why he decided to enroll and matriculate at the institution. He connected this experience to a distinct visit
to a northeastern city where he came across some Morehouse Men. Even
though they were older than Marcus (referred to as *oldheads*), they had a
meal and conversed as brothers who were reared across generations. This
example leverages the bond and shows the power of the intergenerational
brotherhood that exists among Morehouse Men.

The special thing about Morehouse's brotherhood is that Black male
students get to connect, identify, and build with peers who share their racialized and gendered identity. This happens at the onset of students' collegiate journey, as Jared's example demonstrates.

> I still remember my freshman year. At the end of the parent ceremony,
> all the freshmen were supposed to go outside and stay outside and sing
> a hymn. Everybody linked arms and sang a hymn, the school song or
> whatever, and I remember it just started pouring down raining when
> we got out there, but we still sang the song; it was pretty epic.

Jared recalled attending the freshmen orientation week, which included a
parental send-off. As tradition would have it, the brothers went outside,
linked arms, and sang with their peers. The fact that they sang in the rain[2]
demonstrates their commitment to embarking upon this collegiate journey
collectively as Black men. Notable alumnus Rev. Dr. Calvin O. Butts (2006)
shared that he cried like a baby when, during his first few days at Morehouse, the Glee Club sang "Lift Every Voice and Sing." The electrifying
singing experiences encapsulate the uplifting atmosphere that is used to
usher Black men into manhood via this institutional ritual.

Tony also used language that was suggestive of a brotherhood culture.
He asserted:

> I feel as a Black man in America that this is something that every Black
> man in America ought to experience. Not just Morehouse, but any
> Black college, seeing Black people studying and collaborating together
> and moving each other forward in the real world and things like that.
> I feel like Morehouse is close-knit.

Tony used *close-knit* to describe the brotherhood culture emblematic at
Morehouse. He suggested that attending a Black college is a luxury that

each and every Black man should experience. His argument that every Black man should experience the Black intellectual regime present at HBCUs is noteworthy, and this study extends prior Black masculinist work with Black men in a single major to the HBCU space (Brooms, 2017a; Dancy, 2012). The participants also distinctively experienced Morehouse's brotherhood through the vehicle of mathematics.

MAJOR DECLARATION

Declaring a major is an important decision college students must make. Personal interests, families, peers, professors, and coursework can influence this decision. Not all 16 participants declared math as a major at the onset of college. Figure 3.1 shows their original expressed majors. One participant began college as a double major in math and physics; he is counted in the mathematics category. Two participants are reflected in the "other" category; they switched from business and history.

Five of the 16 majors initially enrolled in the dual-degree engineering program, or DDEP. DDEP students declared two majors (i.e., a science and an engineering concentration); they are counted under the "DDEP" label in Figure 3.1. Commonly referred to as the "3-2" program, the dual-degree option requires students to complete 3 years at Morehouse and 2 years at a partnering engineering institution, which leads to the attainment of two undergraduate degrees (Morehouse College, n.d.). Although this agreement

Figure 3.1. Brothers' Initial Major

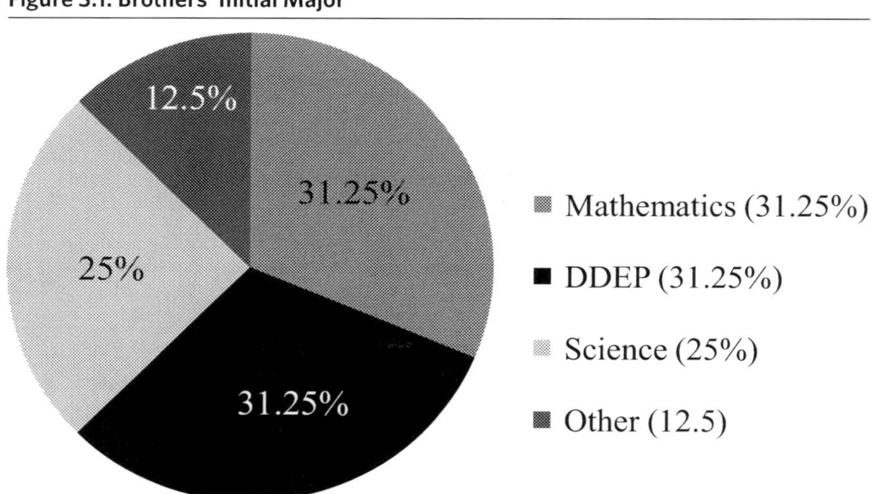

was established between the Atlanta University Center institutions and Georgia Institute of Technology, it has expanded to include other engineering institutions (Pierre, 2015). Degrees are conferred once students have successfully completed the requirements at both institutions.

Asa knew that he was going to declare math as a major at Morehouse. He revealed:

> My aunt is actually friends with Dr. Coefficient and Dr. Unbounded, so she brought me to them [when I was in high school]. I came here to study math, but also another reason was I was presented with a tuition scholarship.

Asa spoke at length about his aunt who is a math professor at another institution. Due to her position, she was able to form both collegial and cordial relationships with Morehouse's professors. Her professional relationships worked to Asa's advantage, as he was able to tour the department and get a glimpse of this space prior to making his decision about where to attend college. The scholarship he earned to study math was another incentive to attend Morehouse. Chapter 2 profiled how Black families positively influenced the participants' K–12 math education, and this example extends this influence to the collegiate sphere. That is, Asa's aunt saw something special in the Morehouse Mathematics space and played an instrumental role in facilitating his interconnection in the brotherhood bond.

Jared originally entered Morehouse seeking to earn a dual degree in computer science and computer engineering. Rationalizing why he switched out of the DDEP, he shared:

> I actually had a friend who dropped out of the dual-degree program and just went strictly computer science, you know because he was like it took too long, and it got me to start thinking about it. Yeah, if I take all these classes, I'd be here at least 5 years and that's just for one degree. I still have to go to an engineering school, and that's going to take another 2 or 3 years, because it's never just going to take 2 years, it's going to take you to overload on courses, so you know I'm not trying to do too, too much; I don't want to overload myself and end up flunking at the last minute, because then I'd be upset, wasting all this time, wasting 8 years to do two degrees, so I'm like I can do two [degrees] in 5 [years] if I just switched to math, I mean I liked math anyway.

Jared realized that completing the requirements for the DDEP would result in him being enrolled at Morehouse for several years and then at a partnering engineering institution for a minimum of 2 years, which felt excessive. Jared dropped the engineering component and switched his major to computer science and math. Prior work has highlighted the benefits of Spelman's DDEP (Sidbury et al., 2015), but Jared's counternarrative positions the DDEP as not being beneficial for some Black male STEM majors because of the additional time in college and overburden with respect to course commitments.

As mentioned, Jared's narrative uncovered some underground chatter about the DDEP's timeline to completion. Similar to Jared, other participants who were previously enrolled in the DDEP second-guessed its requirements. For instance, Marcus said, "It didn't really leave a lot of room for error." That is, the intensive program of study included full academic loads each semester without any room for mistakes. Whatever the genesis of these ambivalent thoughts about the DDEP, these brothers elected to pursue a math degree instead of the dual-degree program option.

Other participants also initially declared majors in different fields. Darius declared physics as his major. He said:

> I took Dr. Coefficient for Calculus. He would always say, "If you're a real man, then come and take Real Analysis with me." And you know, he challenged me to take it. Even though I didn't need it for the physics major, I was like, let me go ahead and take Real Analysis anyway, so I took it for fun.

Darius was challenged by the Black male department chair to enroll in Real Analysis, which signaled that he was ready for advanced mathematics. His example underscores the social construction of Black manhood being synonymous with doing mathematics (Jett, 2022b). "Real man" has been critiqued for being exclusionary to Black men who defy Black masculine norms; however, Darius used the "real man" discourse as motivation to succeed in this community. On another note, Darius's example shows how he became a math major "by induction" (Schumacher & Siegel, 2015). That is, he performed well in a Calculus course, successfully completed the Calculus sequence, and registered for another mathematics course. As a result of enrolling in the Real Analysis class and talking with some of the faculty about disciplinary opportunities, Darius decided to change his major to math.

In another example, John was a chemistry major with early aspirations to go to pharmacy school. He described how he arrived at his decision to change majors:

> I was a chem major at first. We had to take Differential Equations, Linear Algebra, and Set Theory; pretty much all the major math courses except for junior and senior year math courses, we had to take as chem majors. When I went to P. Chem [Physical Chemistry],

I realized this wasn't what I really wanted. By then, all I had left was chemistry classes. I wasn't going to change my major to sociology or something, I would have had to start from ground zero, so what majors do I have the most credit in in order to be able to get out of here in time? And mathematics was the next choice, so that's how I ended up being here.

In John's case, he decided to switch his major because it was the best option to graduate from Morehouse on time. Given that he performed considerably well in previous math courses, he decided that it was the most expedient route to a college degree instead of switching to a major that required him to begin with introductory level courses. Doing so would have prolonged his time until graduation, and he was adamant about graduating in a timely manner.

Informed by their previous experiences, these 16 men decided to major in math. Some began with math as a major and remained steadfast in that decision. Others expressed a desire to pursue the DDEP, but the timeline to degree completion seemed to be the biggest hurdle. In addition, some of them arrived at mathematics from other fields. Regardless of their reasons, all 16 of these men ended up as math majors and collectively formed the mathematical brotherhood.

THE MATHEMATICAL BROTHERHOOD

This cohort represented an outstanding group of 16 African American male scholars, and they had receipts to prove it. They made frequent appearances on the Dean's List. They were Bonner, Hopps,[3] McNair, and Vanguard Scholars. Three brothers were members of Pi Mu Epsilon national mathematics society, and three brothers were members of Phi Beta Kappa national honor society. Two brothers were members of Chi Alpha Epsilon honor society. One brother was a member of a BGLO, and one brother was a member of the Talented Tenth program and Collegiate 100, an auxiliary program of 100 Black Men of Atlanta, Inc. In addition, they served as mentors for the Boys & Girls Club, Jumpstart, and the Speak Life Foundation.

Together, these brothers have amassed several internships and have been involved with community-based programs. In some cases, they have participated in these programs together, which has strengthened their bond as a cohort. Brotherhood reflects their collective sense of community as a class of Black men with robust math identities. With BGLOs, the *pledge class* represents the group of brothers who will form a fraternal bond that could last a lifetime. In that tradition, the mathematical brotherhood represents the *pledge class* for this entire cohort of 16 African American male math majors.

> *pledge class*: a group of brothers who form a fraternal bond that could last a lifetime

The participants reported many positive aspects about the fraternal bonds in their collegiate community. Asa noticed:

> I would say it's really unique, because I heard someone a couple weeks ago from the Physics Department come into the Math Lab, and he's like, "All y'all math majors always together, talking and laughing in the Math Lab. And you know we don't have that for the physics majors," so I think that right there makes us unique, that we all decide to stay together and help each other and have this little like math brotherhood that we have.

As can be deduced from Asa's narrative, the math majors had a unique bond that was not readily apparent among majors in other disciplines. Put simply, the brothers have a sincere desire to collaborate and help the other majors accomplish their goals. This shared experience in the Math Lab, which will be discussed in Chapter 5, allows the majors to bond, fosters belonging, and so facilitates a mathematical brotherhood, similar to the process of pledging (Parks & Brown, 2005).

Jeremiah rendered his thoughts about the guys in the mathematical brotherhood.

> I've seen, more of the math majors at Morehouse, they aren't your typical math majors, as you might see on TV, nerdier and socially awkward. Most of the math majors at Morehouse have been, well, you wouldn't know they're math majors unless you heard them talking about math. Pretty much all the ones I've known have found ways to balance the math that they do with their social life.

Social, and by extension societal, constructions of mathematicians lead many people to hold stereotypical images and envision the profession as one stereotypically reserved for (Asian and White) male nerds (Picker & Berry, 2000). As Jeremiah's narrative attests, the participants challenge "traditional" notions of how a math major looks. The mathematical brotherhood consisted of Black men who did not resemble stereotypical notions associated with being a nerd—such as being socially inept, having an awkward sense of humor, and talking about math ad nauseum—thereby sending a message that the Black masculine culture belongs in math.

Epsilon shared a different perspective about the brothers:

> I have to say, they are my brothers. The math department here is my family, but with your family, there are ones that you want to hug and ones that you just want to kick in the behind, but it's only out of love. Some of them I want to kick in the behind because they can try so much harder; some of them I want to kick in the behind because they're so weird, it's like, relax!

Epsilon referred to his fellow majors as his brothers, which further supports Morehouse's brotherhood mantra. Within the context of the mathematical brotherhood, the majors might wish to encourage brothers who are demonstrating their mathematical prowess. In other cases, brothers might wish to show tough love to a brother who could do so much more to reach his true mathematical potential. Scholars have noted that showing tough love fits within a larger context of the Black educational tradition (Anderson, 1998; Siddle Walker, 1996). In sum, Epsilon's narrative demonstrates that this mathematical brotherhood represents a familial and fraternal dynamic.

Andre added to what it entails to be affiliated with the mathematical brotherhood.

> We all work toward the same thing in different ways. I would also say that some of us have stronger bonds with each other just for the simple fact that we may take more classes with each other, study with each other, or whatever it is to build that bond in whatever classes that we take. It's pretty fair.

Andre mentioned that all the brothers are working toward an undergraduate mathematics degree. Certainly, majors who have had several classes together congregate more with those with whom they have the most familiarity. However, Andre points out that this should be expected given the large number of courses they have taken together. In all, completing math courses together with fewer students resulted in getting to know their fellow majors well.

As mentioned, the mathematical brotherhood was reminiscent of the comradeship found within Black fraternal organizations. Epsilon illuminated this fraternal connection:

> Dr. Coefficient, he teaches Reals [Real Analysis] every spring semester pretty much, every spring semester that I can remember, so I crossed the Reals line in spring of [redacted], and ever since then, we always

have pledges, and we have pledges in Reals now. Once you get into the fraternity, you pass the class, it's like a haze. The line I had had eight.

This example links majoring in math to pledging a fraternity, as Epsilon's language poignantly maps these fraternal ideas onto his experience taking Real Analysis. On his math line, there were eight students who success-fully completed Real Analysis and *crossed* into the mathematical brother-hood. Additionally, Epsilon referenced *hazing*,[4] which was operationalized to mean working tirelessly through mathematical theorems and proofs to complete the challenging Real Analysis course. Stated differently, *hazing* could be perceived as a mental challenge mathematically (not to the detri-ment of their overall mental sanity), and Real Analysis served as the rite of passage course for bringing these brothers into the fold (i.e., mathematical brotherhood).

> *crossing*: process whereby a pledge goes from being on line to becoming a member of a fraternity
>
> *hazing*: the act of engaging in challenges or rituals that can be humiliating or embarrassing

In addition to the brotherhood developed through mutually surviv-ing the Real Analysis course, bonds were established among the majors by working on problem sets and attending events. These activities allowed the participants to enhance their learning and socialization, and they also facili-tated the establishment of the mathematical brotherhood. To demonstrate, Daniel shared:

> This past semester we've grown together, like, more than we have like before, but we've always been tight, just from study sessions and things of that nature that we've had together. You know who's in the department just because not a lot of people are in the math department. Just from taking courses with people and spending time outside the classroom every other day, studying things, and studying in the math department, I think it's a real bond.

Daniel noticed the *real* bond exhibited among the majors, which helped to solidify the mathematical brotherhood. He stressed that the brothers have grown more this last spring semester and that the small composition of ma-jors helps to facilitate the fraternal bond espoused in this text. He continued:

> I say that because of our senior seminar class. Yeah, so, it just seems like once you come to the end, that's when everybody really cherishes

the last moments we have together, try to spend more time conversing and talking to your classmates because you don't know when you'll be seeing each other again after this.

More precisely, Daniel attributed this bond to senior seminar. It dawned on him that their college experience was coming to an end. This compelled Daniel and others to cherish these moments because life after college would take them along many different pathways, and it was uncertain whether all 16 of these mathematically talented Black men would assemble together again.

MATHEMATICAL PERSISTENCE

Persistence was one of the noteworthy traits exhibited among the participants. In the higher education literature, there is a growing body of research in undergraduate mathematics education (RUME) examining mathematical persistence among Black students (Ellington & Frederick, 2010; Jett, 2019a; McGee, 2015). This scholarship positions Black students as resilient in the undergraduate space. In this study, the majors' persistence entailed working with their brothers to understand math concepts, coconstructing mathematical knowledge, and exerting a robust work ethic to actualize their degree aspirations. This persistence strengthened the disciplinary brotherhood when they collaborated on mathematical tasks. Tony pinpointed an instance in which they were persistent.

> We were just going over the homework and writing the proofs on the board and just going over them in our head. We were in the lab for like 6 hours. I felt confident about going to take that test. I felt I was gonna do good on it, and I did.

Tony spoke about studying with peers for approximately 6 hours. They worked diligently to learn the content to ensure success on the Real Analysis 2 exam. Persistence pushed the brothers to journey on when they encountered challenges. In previous work among four Black men, a persistent attitude was found to drive continuation with the math major despite any discipline-specific difficulties (Jett, 2019a).

Jeremiah also shared an instance of mathematical persistence fostered by his Black male professor. He stressed:

> I spent 2 weeks on a problem, maybe a little longer. My professor originally assigned the problem on the homework; I couldn't do it. I did almost all the other homework problems but that one, I didn't know what to do, so I turned in the rest of it and then my professor

was big on problems past, so like problems other people missed and did not solve, he'd give us those problems back and reassign them. So it's not just like, oh I've made it through that problem, now we're good, so it's like, problems would come back to you. So he assigned the problem again on a take-home test, but before that I had been working on it because I still didn't understand it. I'd come up to his office and you know, write up a bunch of stuff on the board and not get it. I dreamed about the problem, thought I solved it, but didn't get it. Umm, so, after about 2 weeks, I eventually solved it in a way that my professor hadn't thought about; I used mathematical induction to solve the problem when he originally wanted us to use some Cauchy-Schwarz inequality or something like that. And another reason I liked the problem so much was because my proof was written out nicely, used the lemma, and at the end of my paper he wrote Q.E.D. Cosine. [Cosine is the pseudonym for his professor's last name.]

Jeremiah worked on a problem in earnest that stumped him for a couple of weeks. In some courses, students are assigned problem sets to practice the concepts covered in class. Typically, these are not traditional math problems where students are expected to perform calculations; rather, they are problems that require more sophisticated mathematical reasoning. Jeremiah's professor's approach was to assign the most challenging problems. This problem challenged Jeremiah so much that he dreamed about it, and he was able to eventually solve it because of his persistence. The fascinating part is that he solved the problem in an unconventional way using mathematical induction, a specialized form of proof.

For Jeremiah, the icing on the cake was that this proof was sealed with the Q.E.D. Cosine written at the end of his paper. The Latin phrase *quod erat demonstrandum* ("that which was to be shown") is abbreviated Q.E.D. In math, this abbreviation is often written at the end of a proof to demonstrate that its conclusion has been reached (Borowski & Borwein, 1991). The Q.E.D. designation means that the proof has been reached with airtight precision and beauty. In the hip-hop community, the equivalent would be dropping the mic. The mic drop occurs when artists exude valiant confidence after a flawless performance. Like the mic drop, the Q.E.D. stamp can be used to signify an elegant mathematical proof.

Jeremiah shared another illustrative portrait in which he persisted in his Number Theory course with a Black woman professor.

The midterm, I didn't finish it, so I think I ended with a C at midterm. But also having that C at midterm made me hungry. And I remember the final to this day. The night before the final I didn't sleep, and I mean it probably wasn't the best idea, but I figure I didn't sleep, I'll get this coffee, and I'll be good. Even though I wasn't a coffee drinker, but you know, that's what coffee does, so actually while I was taking it, I fell asleep during the final a few times but umm, people woke me up, and so then I actually finished the final. When I came back and saw it, and so I was scared of looking at my paper. I'm a very nervous person, but as soon as I saw an A and I asked, "Is that my grade in the course or on the final?" And she said both, and then she started chastising me about my handwriting, and I was going to accept all the chastising you know because I wasn't going to argue any points as long as I had the A.

Jeremiah recounted his experience where his midterm grade of C caused him to be "hungry." He wanted to acquire the course's knowledge and pulled an all-nighter studying for the final. When he dozed off during the final, his math brothers had his back and nudged him to wake up and finish. This supportive atmosphere of Black men looking out for one another is commonplace among peer groups of Black male college students, and this supportive climate fosters a unique sense of community and brotherhood (Brooms, 2017a).

The faculty discussion will occur in Chapter 4, but Jeremiah's comment about his professor chastising his handwriting bears mention here. Jeremiah confessed that his penmanship is not the best and that it resembles "chicken scratch." He also admitted that his professor advised him to make certain that his writing is legible. He realized it was silly to argue about his handwriting when he had accomplished his goal of earning an A on the Number Theory final. Jeremiah's description of this Black woman mathematics professor resembles that of a *warm demander*, as her interpersonal relationship with him prompted care for his education (Gay, 2018). That said, her caring persona exemplified via lovingly scolding him about his scribbly handwriting also demonstrates the personable yet supportive characteristics of warm demanders.

The majors aspired to reason flexibly, construct valid proofs, and complete the required problem sets. They demonstrated both persistence and a strong work ethic. They also strengthened their bonds with their fellow majors as they often completed these tasks together. A portion of Michael's interview painted a picture of this.

Chris: What are your relationships like with your fellow mathematics majors?

Michael: Really good. So, umm, all math majors pretty much know me, and I have a pretty good relationship with all the math majors. Everyone is pretty much a friend in our department, and it's just because there's some sort of camaraderie that builds up. We, like, take these math classes and it kind of starts when you start taking your first upper-level math classes, like your Real Analysis 1,

> Abstract Algebra 1 where you're in the Math Lab till 2:30, 3:30
> working on a problem.
> *Chris:* Like 2:30, 3:30 in the morning?
> *Michael:* Yeah, sometimes. I mean I won't be the only one in here, so
> it won't be like just me, so I'd be like, "Hey, we need to work
> on this problem set, it's due in two days and we're barely getting
> through it"—because we be struggling, and that's just concepts
> that we just have a hard time understanding and just problem
> sets that we have a hard time doing and I mean, when we're all
> struggling and we're all trying to get a good grade, and always
> trying to understand the concepts with these people, and you see
> these people every day trying to get these concepts and get help,
> you develop some sort of a friendship with them.

Michael mentioned that there were some occasions when the majors studied until the wee hours of the morning, demonstrating the time, drive, and effort they put into their studies. The majors eagerly took on these long study sessions to delve deeply into the material together. As Michael acknowledged, the majors struggled on some problem sets or challenging concepts. These problem sets and other assignments precipitated putting their brains together to solve problems.

In this final example, Jared unpacked what it means to arrive at the sum total when constructing proofs.

> What it really comes down to, when you try to do something in Real
> Analysis, you have a theorem and you want to prove this theorem but
> in order to do that, you need to take this theorem, this axiom, this
> lemma and put this all together and make it work, to piece together all
> the pieces of the puzzle in order to get to the big idea.

Jared likened putting mathematical attributes (i.e., corollaries, axioms, lemmas, and theorems) together in a cohesive manner to putting the pieces of a puzzle together to form a complete picture. Earlier in the interview, he mentioned that math could get tough at times. However, when you place all of the pieces together, it becomes easier to manage. From his analogy, it can be extracted that being persistent leads to an exciting proof, puzzle, or portrait.

MATHEMATICAL TRIALS AND TRIBULATIONS

Even though the majors persisted in their studies, this persistence did not negate the fact that they had some trials and tribulations with coursework. Because Real Analysis and Abstract Algebra pose challenges to math majors, these courses have received attention in the RUME literature (Alcock &

Weber, 2005; Johnson et al., 2018; Lew et al., 2016; also see Rasmussen & Wawro, 2017). Table 3.1 lists the courses this study's participants identified as their most challenging courses.

Real Analysis was identified as one of the most prominent challenges, as it is often the first course where students engage in complex proofs that require deep, mathematical insight. At Morehouse, Real Analysis parties were thrown for the majors to come together with an explicit focus on mastering Real Analysis concepts. In prior work with minoritized students, peer study groups were found to be effective for improving students' achievement outcomes in a Calculus class (Fullilove & Treisman, 1990). In the present study, I observed the effectiveness of peer study groups among Black men in a theoretical math course. Because of its difficulty, completing Real Analysis served as a badge of honor among these Black male math students (Jett, 2022b).

Further, this finding that Real Analysis is challenging for most of the majors reinforces previous literature that identifies Real Analysis as a gatekeeper to the math major and magnifies the issues associated with moving from computational-style courses to proof-based courses (Alcock & Weber, 2005; Bressoud et al., 2015). This study confirms this finding with a cohort of Black male math majors. Tony's discussion of the mathematical challenge

Table 3.1. Brothers' Most Challenging Course(s)

Brother	Most Challenging Course(s)
Allen	Real Analysis 1
Andre	Real Analysis 2
Asa	Real Analysis 1
Daniel	Number Theory & Differential Geometry
Darius	Real Analysis 1
Epsilon	Real Analysis 1
Jared	Real Analysis 1
Jeremiah	Number Theory
John	Real Analysis 1
Malik	Real Analysis 1
Marcus	Real Analysis 1
Max	Abstract Algebra 1
Michael	Abstract Algebra 1
Ray	Probability and Statistics 1 & Real Analysis 2
Robert	Real Analysis 2
Tony	Real Analysis 1 & Real Analysis 2

he faced in taking the two-part Real Analysis course puts it clearly. He disclosed:

> When I had Real Analysis, that's when I hit a wall. That's when math started getting theoretical instead of computational. I guess I kind of widened my view of mathematics. It's a lot of theorems and definitions. On top of that, you have problems to solve. I guess I widened my view of things. [pause] Instead of using formulas and algorithms to solve a problem, I'm given tools and definitions to solve another problem or to optimize a way to solve a problem.

Tony broadened his view of mathematics as a result of taking Real Analysis. He specifically referred to it as hitting a wall. In other words, he realized that math encompassed much more than numbers and formulas, which is a common conception of what the discipline entails. His challenge boiled down to understanding what essentially constitutes mathematics and how to solve a problem with this newfound command of the subject. As mentioned in the previous section, this caused him to work with peers, which strengthened their resolve to persist.

In another example, Jared commented about his challenges while taking Real Analysis.

> When I took Reals 1, it was just strictly proofs, you're proving everything that you're doing in Calc 1 and Calc 2, you know, so it was just in the beginning, it was all over my head, like, what was going on. But eventually, one day, it just kind of clicked, like that's what they're saying, like if you have a ball of radius x and it's centered at this point, you know that this set is going to be open if you can continuously have a ball at each point in that set and, you know, things just all started to come together.

Jared revealed that Real Analysis requires a robust understanding of Calculus but that concepts started to make sense to him. Like Jared, many of the majors were stumped in Real Analysis and realized they would need the assistance of other majors to learn the material. To illustrate, Asa shared: "When I got to Real Analysis, we started study groups. We still have those study groups even if we're not in the same class." Marcus shared: "In Real Analysis, you really need a group of people, at least one other person with you to bounce ideas off of." The students said that Real Analysis requires collaborative efforts to fully understand and master the content for the Black men in this mathematics learning community.

The participants' trials and tribulations extended beyond Real Analysis. Max's experience relayed this.

> I've just been clueless through the whole thing. I haven't really
> understood anything at all. I've been working with the tutor, and
> some things have kind of come to light, where I've been able to see a
> question, read the question, understand what it's asking, deliver, and
> deliver correctly. I've been able to do that with some questions, and I
> get an exam and those questions don't appear on the exam, and I go
> back to being clueless and just gasping for air.

Max had some challenges with making concepts click. To rectify the issue, he attended tutoring and experienced some short-term successes. However, when he encountered unfamiliar problems on exams, he resorted back to a state of "cluelessness." His narrative is common among some students who successfully complete math exercises but might not have a conceptual understanding of the big ideas, often positioned as procedural versus conceptual understanding (National Council of Teachers of Mathematics [NCTM], 2014).

In another instance, Max shared his difficulties with successfully completing Calculus 2. Strangely enough, he had to take the course four times. He explained:

> I'll start with Calc 2. The first time I took it, it was just ill advisement.
> I was taking a bunch of other difficult classes, and I wasn't able to put
> the time in. The second time it was in summer school; I was working a
> full-time job that summer. I just didn't do well enough. The third time
> I took it with Dr. Fractal here and that was a bust, and then I guess I
> took it four times because the fourth time went well.

Max's outside commitments and circumstantial issues prevented him from performing well in Calculus 2. During his first couple of tries, he had too much on his plate to properly focus on the content. During his third attempt, he referenced taking the course from Dr. Fractal. He, along with a few other majors, mentioned the abysmal pedagogical practices employed by Dr. Fractal, and this absence of culturally responsive practices can be detrimental to students' math education and identities (Gay, 2018; Jett, 2013a). On his fourth attempt, he was able to focus and pass the course.

Max shared even more about his situation to paint a portrait of his mathematical challenges:

> There's too many outside variables that inhibit me from basically
> meshing with upper-level math courses. And basically those outside
> variables would be, like, outside commitments, commitments to work,
> commitments to my fraternity, lack of foundation. I think those things
> all keep me from being successful in upper-level math courses.

Max conceded that outside influences hindered his ability to devote sufficient time to studying. He worked regularly and was an active member of a BGLO. In his interview, he said that he loves his fraternity and his chapter. He acknowledged that there were just not enough hours to be a star student. He also acknowledged his shortcomings, which reared their head in his upper-division coursework. Taken together, Max's many commitments prevented him from participating in some of the study groups.

Jared encountered an issue with an upper-level course. He elaborated:

> Advanced Linear Algebra. Nothing basically, I don't know, I'm just not getting it, it's just not clicking for me; it's coming towards the end of the semester, so I'm not so sure how it's going to work out. I know if I don't pass this course, it's one of the electives I need to get out. I'm just going to be one course away from a math major, but I can't afford to stay in Morehouse any longer so if I don't, I'll just graduate with a computer science major. I already have a math minor; it'll just be a really, really strong math minor. I'm not sure how that would affect my future, but I know if anything I would do, is to go back and still learn that Linear; even if I don't come out as a math major, I would at least know it; so when I go for a job or whatever or for grad school, I can say, "I'm only one course away; I didn't understand it then, but I understand it now." You know, if they say, "Well, prove this or explain this," I want to be able to do that and say, "I've learned it; I just didn't know it then."

Jared's narrative about his challenges in Advanced Linear Algebra substantiates math educators' assertion that students sometimes put forth the time and effort and the concepts still do not register for them at that specific time, which can be a daunting challenge (Dahlke, 2011; Schumacher & Siegel, 2015). Even if Jared is one course short of a major in math, he plans to go back and learn the material from the course. He understands how important it will be during his next steps as he attends graduate school in computer science and pursues a career in cybersecurity (see Chapter 7 for the brothers' career aspirations). Some students are mad at themselves for unsuccessful efforts, and some even throw in the towel if they do not understand advanced concepts. Jared is determined to master the Advanced Linear Algebra material now or in his future (independent) studies.

Other participants employed different strategies to overcome their dilemmas. For Michael, this meant going to office hours and expending additional study hours. He vocalized:

> My first difficult course was the Set Theory course they offered here, and I really struggled with that when I started. And I stayed up long hours, at least 4 to 5 hours a day to try to understand these Set Theory

concepts and went to office hours and stuff, and my first test I got a C. And every other test, just for going to office hours, I got As and I got an A+ in the course, and it was probably the hardest math course I took in sophomore year. And just getting that A really motivated me to take more math classes and do the same thing as that class.

As Michael shared, Set Theory was his first major challenge. Like others, his difficulty prompted him to be persistent by going to office hours and studying many hours. Because of his persistence, he was able to raise his overall grade in the course. After improving his grade throughout the semester, his faith was restored in his mathematical abilities, and he was able to overcome this hardship.

In an example that extends beyond coursework, Daniel affirmed:

I have mixed emotions [about mathematics]. I love it at times and sometimes it'll be real, real frustrating; it'll take a lot of time and a lot of studying to do it. But at the end of the day, you love it more because once you complete a task, it just seems so worth it because a lot of people can look at you and can see that you are a hard worker just from seeing you're studying mathematics. Because a lot of people just feel that mathematics is a tough subject and a lot of people don't want to fool with it, so when people say they're majoring in mathematics, you get that respect in a sense from people. So I really like that about it, and I've always loved it, again, because I've been good at it, and I like solving problems, and I like fixing things.

Daniel acknowledged that his mixed emotions intensify his love for the subject because it requires persistence to complete challenging tasks. Additionally, he realized that there is a certain level of respect ascribed to math majors. Alluding to the broader perception of math as a demanding or tough subject, he indicated that some students "don't want to fool with it" or attempt to avoid it at all costs, even in collegiate settings. Conversely, those who accept the challenge and overcome any trials and tribulations are generally perceived as smart.

DIVISION AMONG THE BROTHERS

Generally speaking, the majors were exceptional math students. However, data analysis revealed that there was some *division* between those who were deemed "stellar" and "mediocre" students, as mathematics has consistently established hierarchies between students. Martin (2009, 2019) exposed the dangers of racialized hierarchies in mathematics. This study uncovered that these mathematical hierarchies can manifest intraracially. This is plausible given that HBCUs are embedded within this Westernized society and Black male students encounter ability grouping in math classrooms, so efforts must be exerted to deconstruct such partitioning. The participants acknowledged that there were clear distinctions among the majors, and their interviews shed light on which majors were associated with each camp. In fraternal organizations, there might be *division* among members in a chapter. As such, many of them were forthright concerning the evident *division* among some of the majors.

> *division*: divisive behavior between brothers within a chapter

Jeremiah was positioned as one of the "good" math majors. He spoke about this *division*.

> I've actually been, increasingly, been less and less invested in students who I feel don't put forth effort in classes, as far as tutoring, stuff like that. Like one person, they keep telling me, "This is going to be the semester," "I'ma try harder," and stuff, and they have my phone number, they can call me on weekends, and I'll be at the library and you know I study a good portion of the weekend every weekend, and routinely what happens, they hit me up right before an exam and you know, they do decently, they do poorly, and it's a cycle that happens again, so stuff like that. . . . So that's why I lean towards those at the top.

Jeremiah distinguished the majors as those who put in little versus extra effort. Jeremiah had a consistent study schedule, and he made no qualms about gravitating toward what he deemed the stellar students in the cohort. Conversely, he mentioned becoming increasingly frustrated with students who do not put forth their best effort. On one hand, he noticed these students' utterances at the beginning of each semester such as: "This is the semester that I'm going to make a 4.0"; "I'm going to stay current with my homework and problem sets this semester"; and "I'm not going to wait until the last minute to prepare for my exams." On the other hand, he observed that many of these students continued to slack off with their studies in spite of these proclamations. Central to his narrative is a desire to lend a helping hand to his struggling peers, which demonstrates an empathetic aspect of Black masculinity and is an integral component of brotherhood (Pelzer, 2016).

Max self-identified as one who was not a part of the higher echelon of those within the mathematical brotherhood but attributed it to not knowing how to study.

> I'm not the best math student, but I'm not the worst. At the end of the day, I've never spent hours upon hours studying or preparing for a test or for a class, not that I'm that brilliant I don't have to, but it's just that I don't know how.

Earlier, Max pointed to his many commitments, but here he acknowledged that he does not know how to study math. Thus, one implication from his comment is that ongoing efforts must be in place to teach students, even declared majors, how to study math effectively. Therefore, teaching study skills, couched in culturally responsive practices, can foster community for Black men, which can in turn help facilitate mathematical brotherhood (Dahlke, 2011; Gay, 2018).

Epsilon referenced the *division* among the classes of majors, which was a different conceptualization of this concept.

> *Epsilon:* This department has set a clear line between the top students in math and the not-so-top students in math.
>
> *Chris:* You said the department classifies top students and not-so-top students. Can you elaborate?
>
> *Epsilon:* That's fine, so I think it's this class of students that's coming out, my class right now. I think we kind of turned this department into a fraternity kind of thing.

Epsilon admitted that the department contributed to this hierarchy, but he explained it as this particular cohort being set apart from other cohorts. The previous offering of *division* mentioned the intergroup issues between the "stellar" and "mediocre" majors. However, when elaborating, Epsilon expressed that this cohort turned the department into a fraternity because of their mathematical prowess and togetherness. Recall that a portion of Epsilon's quote was used at the beginning of this text to demonstrate the fraternal aspects of the mathematical brotherhood, and this exchange rounds out his thought process in this domain.

Whether the *division* exists within this cohort or between different graduating classes of majors, the participants sought to form an authentic mathematical brotherhood. Even though there were some mathematical hierarchies present, all the participants engaged in doing math. In the end, all 16 Black men persisted and succeeded together in attaining an undergraduate mathematics degree.

CONCLUSION

This chapter explored the participants' successes and challenges in the major. They had some victories in the major, and the Real Analysis course was repeatedly identified as their most challenging course. They hinted at some *division* between the majors. These collective successes and challenges channeled the persistence they demonstrated throughout their studies. In a nutshell, they were very serious about math and active participants in their overall mathematical development. As a result, they were able to persist in the major.

By and large, the mathematical brotherhood represents a dynamic group of 16 academically talented African American male students. During their time at Morehouse, they were motivated to achieve their goal of earning a mathematics degree. Many of their narratives touched upon the influence of their math professors. The next chapter depicts the brothers' views about the people who were primarily responsible for leading them to higher heights—the faculty.

CHAPTER 4

The Faculty

The Department is very engaging. A lot of the professors you go and talk to about things more than just math. I think they've done a good job here where everyone is friendly.

—Darius

This passage is extracted from Darius's description of Morehouse's mathematics faculty. He mentions that they are engaging because they show interest in the classroom and beyond. Also, his reference to conversing with them about other things demonstrates their overall support of the whole student, which is in sync with culturally responsive pedagogy's comprehensive characteristic that asks educators to teach the whole student (Gay, 2018). He believes the faculty has created a friendly environment, and the other participants overwhelmingly shared similar ideas about the faculty at this traditionally single-gender HBCU.

This chapter paints a picture of and analyzes the brothers' narratives about the people on the ground doing the work to ensure their success—Morehouse's faculty. I first discuss the mathematics faculty and then share student-generated descriptions of them. After that, I share information about the less highly regarded mathematics faculty, followed by the majors' recommended faculty improvements. Next, discussions about the non-mathematics faculty members ensue. I close the chapter by summarizing the students' ideas about the faculty at Morehouse.

THE MATHEMATICS FACULTY

Morehouse's mathematics faculty represent an eclectic group of professionals. At the time of this study, the full-time faculty consisted of three full professors, five associate professors, eight assistant professors (two tenure track and six non-tenure track), and two instructors (Crosby, 2013). Their research interests included bioinformatics, dynamical systems, noncommutative ring theory, and symplectic geometry, to name a few. They teach and advise the majors, but their role transcends picking courses and mapping out semester or yearly plans. They get to know each and every single solitary major by providing personalized attention throughout degree completion. In this way, they live by Delpit's (2012) assertion that "knowing students is a prerequisite for teaching them well" (p. 87).

While teaching and advising the majors, the faculty build a positive rapport with students, recognize their disciplinary leanings, and shepherd students into the field. In doing so, they expose and orient majors to graduate programs and career fields in unique ways. The faculty have achieved many accolades, and the 2016 AMS Mathematics Programs that Make a Difference Award mentioned in Chapter 1 was earned largely because of the faculty's efforts (Jackson, 2016).

The 18 faculty are a diverse group. Nine are Black, four are White, two are Asian, two are from other minoritized groups, and one is multiracial. Fifteen of the 18 are men, and three are women, which suggests the faculty could benefit from more women and that mathematics is a gendered field (Hottinger, 2016). Intersecting race and gender, six of the 18 are Black men, which is one-third of the faculty. All three women faculty are Black, so half the faculty are Black.

While non-Black faculty can be effective pedagogues of Black students (and this is true at Morehouse), the racial composition of the faculty is important because Black male students' relationships with Black faculty promotes a sense of belonging (Strayhorn, 2019). The considerable amount of Black mathematics faculty is pertinent given that much of the important guidance Black undergraduate and graduate students receive comes from Black faculty (Cooper, 2004). Also, findings from prior STEM higher education research suggest that Black professors have higher expectations for Black male students (Fries-Britt et al., 2012; Jett, 2013b). Therefore, the participants were able to learn from these Black experts who were equipped with both racialized and disciplinary knowledge about thriving in mathematics.

Michael's narrative indicates how much students value the fact that many of the professors with earned doctorates in mathematics are Black.

> This is a HBCU so a lot of faculty here are Black, so they can kind of relate to each student more. There are other HBCUs with not nearly as many African American mathematicians in the department, and I guess we value that a lot. There's quite a few Morehouse alumni who work in our department, a couple of Spelman alumni who work in our department, so they know how Morehouse works, and they were once like Morehouse students, and they know what we go through every day, and they can pretty much relate to what we're doing, so they can give us advice about how to go about in our future career and stuff like that.

Michael emphasized that the majors were enrolled at an HBCU and being taught by some HBCU graduates. Because some of the faculty earned undergraduate mathematics degrees from Morehouse and Spelman specifically, Michael recognized that they were able to relate to his plight. One advantage of being taught by these HBCU alumni is that they have institutional capital that can be drawn upon to support Black students. In addition, these faculty understand the nuances of Black culture, know the intricacies of the AUC, and offer valuable wisdom regarding what it takes to be successful beyond the undergraduate degree as emerging Black math professionals. This representation is important as it allows alumni to pass the baton to current students; this is commonplace among Black mathematicians who attended HBCUs (Walker, 2014).

Jeremiah also viewed his professors in high regard and positioned them as role models. He shared: "A lot of the professors that I've had here . . . In some sense, they're what I want to be; I wanna teach math while doing research while having an impact on students, teaching math in college." With aspirations to assume a faculty position, Jeremiah gets a glimpse of what faculty life might look like. Again, I must reiterate the immeasurable impact associated with studying math with Black faculty members at an HBCU, and the HBCU-related mathematics scholarship has emphasized the motivational roles these faculty play in the production of Black mathematicians, professionals, and college faculty (Borum et al., 2016; Walker, 2014).

Epsilon discussed benefits from having welcoming and accessible faculty.

> I've never been to an office and have the door closed on me where they don't have time. Everyone has an open-door policy. You kind of feel like this is your family, and they want the best from you. I love this place. I love them, each and every last one of them. I've received everything that I've needed from my math professors, from a kick in the behind when I wasn't doing right to a pat on the back when I did something good.

In his narrative, Epsilon spoke passionately about the faculty being truly committed to seeing students succeed. He acknowledged that he has received everything that he has needed from his professors. He also mentioned his love for and the family-like feel of this institutional space. His narrative depicts the nurturing and inspiring environment that HBCUs provide to Black math students, which has been captured in prior work (Inniss, 2015; Jett, 2013b; Walker, 2014).

Daniel reiterated how much students value their relationships with the faculty. He said:

> One thing I love about our faculty in our math department is that they're always available for office hours to sit down and converse about things you have questions about and that has been real, real

helpful, and they always look out for you, sending you emails on talks that somebody is coming to campus to give, emails on career fairs, things of that nature. Emails on math ceremonies, opportunities and internships, it's really valuable because I know you can't say that about every math department in every college.

In his statement, Daniel echoed the sentiments of other members of the mathematical brotherhood that the faculty support them mightily. The faculty ensured that these Black men were aware of math-related opportunities that would advance their outlooks and trajectories. Employing a critical perspective, Daniel conjectured that this dissemination of information may not happen in every math department in higher education, yet Morehouse's faculty cheerfully distributed information to these brothers.

Because there was so much praise for the professors, I share even more data. Marcus voiced:

The professors care about the students, and they really want us to pass. I don't recall any professor who won't make time to help a student. You don't even have to be in their class. My professor wasn't on campus that day, so I talked to another professor, and we sat down for like 10–15 minutes, and I got the answer. So it was like all the professors are open to answer your questions. It's just almost like a family up here on the third floor, you need help, you just go ask them and they help you.

Marcus indicated that the professors are a caring group of pedagogues. This caring persona aligns with conventional secondary education research suggesting that caring teachers are concerned with Black male students' academic achievement and their overall development as human beings (McKinney de Royston et al., 2017). Marcus likens the care and kinship on the third floor, which houses the math department, to that of a family, representative of HBCU culture.

Marcus continued about his professors:

You can fail a test, but your professors won't give up hope in you. They'll be like, "You can do this, but you'll just have to put forth that effort. My office is always open," they'd say, and it's true.

Marcus spoke about how his professors continually believe in their students. Even when students have slip-ups, their professors do not allow those mishaps to define their intelligence. Instead, they encourage them to put forth extra effort and seek out assistance. And although students can get tutoring or use other resources at their disposal, the main point is that the faculty here are willing and available to help.

While several students had a strong, positive relationship with the faculty, Jared yearned for a closer relationship with them. He shared:

> I feel like I'm maybe at a little bit of a disadvantage. Some of the professors you can see the relationship between the students and the professors, and I feel like mine is just not necessarily as strong. Not as strong as it could have been, but I guess that's just simply because I wasn't in the department the whole time.

Jared recognized that his relationship with the faculty was not operating at full capacity, especially in comparison to the other majors. He believes this is the case because he switched from the DDEP. Undergirding his narrative was an increasing desire to be intimately affiliated with the established camaraderie in this community. Jared's narrative speaks to the need to better welcome and embrace newcomers in the major.

As noted, the majors shared quite a bit about the faculty's strengths. Allen said: "I'd probably say the network or the togetherness of all the professors and how they use that network to benefit the students." Michael added: "They really want to see you learn the material; I really value that here." Jeremiah offered another strength.

> That's another thing I like about the department, Abs 3 [Abstract Algebra 3] was never a course, and I think they created that course just for us. And like, we could ask for a course, and they'd do it for us.

The mathematics faculty offered Advanced Abstract Algebra as a special topics course to this cohort. Abstract Algebra 2 is listed as the department's terminal Abstract Algebra course, but Advanced Abstract Algebra was offered to better prepare the majors for graduate school or a math-related position. In this department, the faculty meet African American male students' needs by any means necessary and provide invaluable support in doing so. This finding contributes to previous work that shows that HBCUs support and cultivate Black math majors (Borum et al., 2016; Jett, 2013b; Walker, 2014).

STUDENT-GENERATED DESCRIPTIONS
OF THE MATHEMATICS FACULTY

Because of the small nature of the department, it was easy for participants to frequently interact with the faculty. These constant interactions led to the closeness between the students and faculty. Similar to what might occur among Black families and lines within BGLOs, the brothers generated nicknames for the faculty—*superhero*, *math geniuses*, and *night shift*. Some faculty were placed into multiple categories; I discuss each moniker in turn.

Superhero

The participants positioned the department chair as a *superhero*.[1] Data analysis revealed that he was pegged as a *superhero* because of his leadership and amazingly effective method of recruiting students into the major. The chair's purpose is to oversee a top-of-the-line program for Black male math majors (Morehouse College, n.d.). Keeping undergraduate math education as the central aim, the chair worked to recruit, retain, and cultivate the majors. In this study, he served as a professor, mentor, leader, and advocate. Dr. Coefficient is a proud alumnus of Morehouse's mathematics program and member of a BGLO, so that adds an additional layer of nuance concerning his commitment to this role. Simply put, he serves as a model of Black manhood in conjunction with mathematics. In Black fraternal campus organizations, the *chapter advisor* is the authorial point person. In this case, Dr. Coefficient serves as the *chapter advisor*.

> *chapter advisor*: faculty member or staff professional who serves as the campus advisor for a fraternal organization

Max described the chair's leadership and referred to him as a *superhero*.

> I feel like Dr. Coefficient is probably the protagonist or the leader or the superhero in this story. I love smart people. That's why I think I like Dr. Coefficient so much. He's smart, and he has a personality, so you know, those two things are rare to come by.

This description indicated that the chair served as the front-line leader responsible for running a vibrant department conducive to supporting African American male students. Max went on to describe him as smart and having an engaging personality. These relational skills, echoed in the Black masculinity literature (Dancy, 2012; Pelzer, 2016), served him well in establishing and sustaining relationships with these Black men. Max pointed out that those characteristics were rare, so these attributes elevated the chair among his colleagues.

Michael expressed his thoughts about the department chair. He related:

> I had Dr. Coefficient who like, he'd stay here as long as the students need it, so sometimes 8 or 9 o'clock, sometimes 10 o'clock, just hoping he's in his office. . . . If a student has a question, he'll guide him to the right path.

Michael praised the chair's efforts to go above and beyond, which is indicative of a *superhero* who surpasses students' expectations. This example included staying in the office after business hours to steer students in the right direction. Therefore, it can be deduced that the chair is consistently around the department, spends an inordinate amount of time with students, and interacts with these African American male math majors on an individual basis to provide support, guidance, and mentorship, which is substantiated in the research with effective African American STEM mentors to African American undergraduate students (Mondisa & Main, 2021).

Before changing his major, Epsilon was a computer science major. He shared an exchange that spoke to the chair's skillful ability to win students over to the major.

> After I got out of class [Set Theory], he was like, "Did you like this stuff?" And I was like, it's alright, it's cool, so he's like, "Why don't you try Real Analysis then?" He's like, "It's kind of similar to this class, and it gives you the same types of proofs." I was like, all right, I'll try it, and at this point I was still a computer science major, and he was like, "The Real Analysis isn't for computer science majors, but it's a good way to think about stuff." So I tried it, so I took Dr. Coefficient that semester, and he failed me, but that was like the best class I've ever had in my life. I love Real Analysis, I really do, it was such a great class, and so I came back in the fall, and he wasn't teaching it in the fall, but I could have taken someone else for Real Analysis, but I didn't; I waited for him. Around here, he's the hardest teacher. I'm not scared of him, so that's what I did, and that's where I just loved it.

It is important to note Epsilon's love for the content and the professor even though he failed the course. Dr. Coefficient's nudge for Epsilon to enroll in Real Analysis piqued his interest about the proof-based subject matter, and this was another example of recruiting a math major "by induction" (Schumacher & Siegel, 2015). In Figuero Charles's (2017) study with six African American male actuaries (actuarial science is one of the most competitive areas in applied mathematics), she found that they used failure as motivation to succeed. Moreover, Epsilon still felt motivated and empowered in this learning community after failing a course. The chair was skillful in fostering belonging and recruiting students into the major despite their difficulties. As mentioned in Chapter 3, Real Analysis served as the course that initiated the majors into the brotherhood.

In summary, each and every major spoke highly of Dr. Coefficient. Even though he used language such as "real man" (see Chapter 3), which has been critiqued for promoting male-centered dominion and power, to heighten Black male students' math identities, the majors who were in relationship with him expressed that, at the core, he wanted them to succeed (Jett, 2022b). The participants repeated similarly positive sentiments about his accessibility, approachability, and supportiveness. They applauded his content expertise and dedication to their studies, and this challenged them to produce high-quality mathematics deliverables. The chair's example adds to the scholarship suggesting that Black faculty serve as highly effective educators, leaders, and mentors to Black students in mathematics contexts (Cooper, 2000; Inniss et al., 2022; Walker, 2014).

Math Geniuses

The students referenced the *math geniuses*—Drs. Coefficient, Histogram, Simulation, and Unbounded, who all happened to be Black women and men faculty—when discussing the faculty who exhibited exemplary mathematical competence. The language of *math geniuses* was used during my observations of the majors and documented in my field notes. Data analysis revealed that the majors had profound respect and admiration for these professors. While discussing the faculty, Marcus said:

> I'd say the professors here, they know their stuff. Of all the professors I've taken, it's like, I don't think it's easy to become a professor at Morehouse to tell you the truth, because everyone is like so real in their subject, and I was, like, Dr. Histogram, and I just asked him a question, and he like off the top of his head, he just started writing stuff out, and it was correct. And he knows it was correct, and I got a better understanding of it, and I've done it to all my professors. So I'd say the level here is pretty high, they know their stuff. I think 15 are PhDs, so the math department is pretty strong.

Marcus suggested that it must be competitive to join the Morehouse Mathematics faculty given how knowledgeable the professors are. In addition, he referenced the approximate number of professors with doctorates. Crosby (2013) indicated that there were 16 faculty members with doctorates in the mathematical sciences, as a new faculty arrived the spring of data collection. The point is that there are a large number of PhDs on the faculty, which underlines the breadth and depth of their mathematics knowledge.

In Asa's interview, he mentioned two Black male math professors explicitly who were categorized as *math geniuses*.

> I would say that all of them are inspired with what they teach. They never look like they're bored. Dr. Coefficient is always energetic. Dr. Histogram, his class lasts longer because he always wants to talk about stuff at the end of class and stuff like that. So it's cool to have professors like that so that you don't lose that fire to keep on going.

Asa mentioned that his professors are inspired by the content that they teach, so it stands to reason that they are energized. He praised Dr. Coefficient's enthusiasm and Dr. Histogram's passion for delivering the content, evidenced by his desire to talk about mathematical ideas even after the class session had ended. As Asa shared, these two Black male professors motivated him to persist with his studies because of their superb pedagogical skills, and these men furnished impeccable representations of Black manhood in this mathematics learning community (Jett, 2022b).

The majors sought out the *math geniuses* more earnestly when enrolling in courses, searching for adequate resources, and seeking general advice. Andre used different criteria to choose a broad group of instructors. He said:

> I've chosen what may or may not be considered the top professors here. I wanted to get the full experience. I didn't want to sell myself short for lack of better words. Those were people I felt comfortable with; people that have been here the longest. Not necessarily where they got their degrees from. I asked some of the top students that were here, and they suggested those professors, so I took those professors.

Andre spoke to the high-achieving students to solicit their recommendations for professors who would offer him a "full experience." Andre's narrative encapsulates the dedication of these faculty based on their time on the Morehouse faculty (although new or early career faculty can also be dedicated and top professors), but it extends beyond that as well. It encompasses their ability to deliver a high-quality math course; being able to do so was not necessarily tied to institutional prestige.

Malik discussed these faculty and suggested that their teaching style was learning-centered.

> They don't teach to the test. They just teach, they actually—I know some professors don't make the test until test day, so they really are just learning-based, and I remember specifically, I asked one professor what's on the test, what should I study for the test, and he said, "If I taught it, you should know it." I was offended, but I'm thankful now.

In this case, Malik commended one professor for being learning-based as opposed to test-based. His initial offense was that he expected a test review, list of learning objectives, etc. to prepare. His professor's reply implied that his teaching would result in command of the concepts, and this learning-based approach caused Malik to become a more independent math learner. Demonstrating independence by knowing what and how to study has been linked to success in collegiate mathematics (Dahlke, 2011; Schumacher & Siegel, 2015). Reflecting on this exchange, Malik admits that he is now appreciative of this pedagogical approach.

Night Shift

The participants referred to a small group of faculty as the *night shift*[2] (which was also documented in my field notes based off the participants' natural conversations during my observations of them) given that they remain in the office until dark to assist students. This sacrifice is commendable given the familial responsibilities and other commitments that faculty have. Staying in the office for long hours demonstrates the professors' deep commitment to students and students' earnest desires to learn more. Working at night also shows their strong dedication to the mathematics enterprise. The chair was included in this group as evidenced by Michael's previous admission that the chair went beyond the call of duty timewise to help students. In a different instance, Marcus shared an encounter in which he spent many hours working on Real Analysis proofs.

> My professors really want you to learn; they aren't just going to give you an A, but they really want you to learn. They are not just gonna say: "Oh, you don't get it? Well, I don't care. I don't have office hours today." Like I have been in this room until 9:30 at night doing Analysis on the board; I mean like the professors here really care about us.

Marcus praised the faculty for going the extra mile. He recounted staying in the department's conference room (which was also this study's designated interview room) after hours completing Real Analysis work. As his narrative attests, a few of the faculty are known for staying in their offices after business hours to help students learn material, and he equated that to really caring about them as Black male math learners. These observations extend to the undergraduate level, prior work showing that access to caring secondary educators improves academic engagement for Black male students (Jett et al., 2015; McKinney de Royston et al., 2017). Morehouse's professors were deeply invested in their students' academic performance.

Extending this *night shift* discourse, Jeremiah provided another example:

> I've always been going to office hours a lot; I've been kicked out of office hours before like the professor needed to leave, so I actually got one of my professors to get pizza once because we stayed that late.

Jeremiah goes to later office hours often, and he has even been "kicked out" of office hours. In other words, his professor was not rude or dismissive; rather, he meant it was time to go home because of the exhaustion associated with how much time and energy had been spent on math that day. In another instance, he remained there so late that his professor ordered pizza to serve as their dinner. The act of breaking bread while doing math is a powerful example of how students affiliate with faculty at Morehouse. This professor's act of ordering food represents a unique outward expression of dedication to Jeremiah's mathematical studies, and it corroborates Gay's (2018) finding that culturally responsive pedagogues, at HBCUs especially, attend to the whole student.

To recap, the participants generated nicknames for the faculty and praised them for being dedicated to their studies. The majors' expressed sentiments paint a vivid picture of the faculty's commitment and validate the family-like traits exemplified by the faculty. Narratives in this section reify the notion that Morehouse motivates Black men in mathematics and that faculty foster mathematical brotherhood. Narratives simultaneously confirm that HBCUs provide a family-like environment for Black students (Borum et al., 2016; Jett, 2013b; Walker, 2014).

LESS HIGHLY REGARDED MATHEMATICS FACULTY

Even though the participants applauded the efforts of the faculty, they also critiqued some of them. I must reiterate that this study was conducted with the majors only; I did not interview the faculty to uncover their thoughts, rationales, or responses for any of their decision-making processes. Also, similar to many other higher education institutions, the Department of Mathematics has its full spectrum of professors. In practical terms, there are faculty who exert extra efforts to support students, there are those who exert less effort, and there are those somewhere in the middle.

The participants mentioned Drs. Factorial and Fractal when discussing the less highly regarded professors. John critiqued Dr. Factorial's teaching style in particular.

> It's not that he can't teach, because he knows the material, but he doesn't know how to get that information across to the students well. He doesn't write notes, so it's kind of like we still have to piece the pieces together, and he's so stern about classroom attendance, but he gives us the homework that's in the book, and you just have to do whatever the section is assigned, you just have to do all the problems. So literally, it's like, okay, you wanna learn, here's the book, but come in here and listen to me talk about you. So I ended up withdrawing out of that class.

In this case, John critiqued Dr. Factorial, who taught an advanced math course. From John's standpoint, there was a mismatch between his professor's teaching style and the majors' way of learning. Instead of effectively teaching the content, his professor merely talked about them. As a result of his professor's incompatible pedagogical style, John decided to withdraw from the course. In prior work, I argued how some math pedagogues at the collegiate level serve as "identity thieves" regarding African American students' racial and mathematical identities (Jett, 2013a). Thieves come to steal, kill, and destroy (John 10:10, King James Version), and professors who diminish Black students' racial and mathematical identities are emblematic of identity thieves. These professors rarely embody culturally responsive practices, and John's example shows how students are taught in culturally unresponsive ways.

John also referenced Dr. Fractal in his interview.

> You have some that are great, some that are mediocre, and you have
> some that are horrible, but for the most part, the horrible teachers
> are gone . . . and that potentially could be why I'm not up to par
> as I should be in the mathematics department because like I said,
> Dr. Fractal, I had him and he literally didn't teach us, you know, so it
> was kind of he recycled tests and everything.

John mentioned that Drs. Factorial and Fractal are no longer on the faculty at Morehouse. Dr. Fractal was labeled as a terrible professor by a few participants who took him for foundational coursework. John indicated that he even recycled tests. To him, recycling tests was not a mathematical challenge as students were aware of this practice and obtained copies of old exams to pass the course. These professors do not embody the culturally responsive practices found among HBCU math faculty (Ellington et al., 2021; Jett, 2013a).

Malik's narrative about the less highly regarded mathematics professors shows that their ineffective pedagogy could have severe implications for students' subsequent coursework. He shared:

> People navigated the weak professors in Calculus 1, Calculus 2, and
> Set Theory. In Probability and Statistics, we ended up doing College
> Algebra because we couldn't learn any of the real material, because
> they didn't know how to do Calculus; they couldn't do any of the
> theories because they didn't know how to write a proof, and it was
> just, obnoxiously dumb it down. And people who know the material
> suffer from it.

Malik argued that this simplification of content did not adequately prepare students for the more advanced courses, and it did not challenge those who were prepared for the course to the fullest extent possible. Therefore, he suggested that these students had neither a strong Calculus knowledge base nor a solid foundation on the logic of how to construct proofs, which are essential for succeeding and thriving in upper-level courses. Malik's narrative is in tune with previous work showing that not knowing math concepts well from earlier coursework comes back to haunt students in later coursework (Dahlke, 2011; Schumacher & Siegel, 2015).

In another example, Max admitted:

> Some are very much masters of what they do. They are very good, they can explain things to you clearly. And some are horrible, they make things too difficult, they can't explain what they're doing, they are stubborn, they're stuck in their ways, they're mean, they're rude.

Max acknowledged there are some skilled professors because they know their content well and can explain mathematical ideas clearly. Max also alluded to the less highly regarded professors. From his vantage point, they cannot explain concepts comprehensibly. On top of that, he has found them to be insolent. Max continued his critique of said professors.

> I split them up in like two tiers or whatever—professors that I enjoy taking their classes and actually learn or professors that I dread seeing them. I have a distaste for them. I have a lot of bad feelings towards them. I think the math faculty here, if you look at the people that I enjoy, I think their biggest thing is that they're very smart, very masterful of the concepts that they teach. If you look at the people that I don't enjoy, they have zero strong points. They don't do anything right in my eyes.

Max placed professors into two distinct categories, which coincides with Black masculinity theory's relational tenet (Pelzer, 2016). The first category represented professors he deemed excellent scholars, and the second category represented professors who were unsatisfactory mathematics teachers. Based on these categories, he had either a pleasant or unpleasant relationship with the faculty member. Max did not appear to have any in-between feelings about his professors, so none were in the middle of the spectrum for him.

In his interview, Epsilon also acknowledged that there were some differences among the professors.

> It just depends on who you get; there's a set of professors here that will prepare you for any graduate school that you go to, any job that you go to, there's a set who won't. There's a clear distinction with that, too. I hope that changes one day.

Epsilon spoke passionately about the professors. In so doing, he cautioned that there is a demarcation between faculty who adequately prepare students for next steps and those who do not. He is optimistic and hopes that this phenomenon changes in the future. Stated differently, it appears that he wants a 100% committed faculty who will fully prepare Morehouse's students for the next steps in their professional careers.

FACULTY IMPROVEMENTS

Among any group of mathematics professors, there is always room for improvement. The same is true for the faculty at Morehouse. Study participants noted some improvements that could be made. Jared shared:

> I'd say maybe more problems that would help me visualize the problem, more so than all things based on the theory side. Maybe if I get a problem that actually exemplifies what I'm doing. I mean you have some professors that do that and some that don't. I'm not the best at finding problems. Maybe something simple like eigenvalues or eigenvectors of a matrix, you can find something like that easily, but if you need to find a problem that deals with the Weierstrass Theorem or something, it's just kind of hard to find problems.

Jared suggested that faculty incorporate more application exercises. While he can find application problems for straightforward concepts, he struggles to find them for more advanced topics. His narrative hits on a popular myth that advanced math is not applicable to real-world situations; however, it serves as the disciplinary underpinning for the majority of our modern-day capabilities including medical imaging, digital structures, and Internet-based innovations (National Research Council, 2013). Jared's point is that application problems bring rich imagery to high-level topics, and this reinforces previous recommendations to link application and theory, especially with Black male mathematics learners (Jett, 2021; Schumacher & Siegel, 2015).

Jeremiah's recommendation also had pedagogical implications. He said:

> Because some professors will give out test corrections, there are situations where points should be given back on a test, and that'd be good, but some professors do it for every test, so that means if I got like a 50% on every exam but did test corrections on every exam, then I'd get up to a 75%, which is a passing grade, which I don't think you should get, if you're getting 50% on your exams.

Jeremiah believes some professors abuse the test correction process. Again, because interviews were not conducted with faculty, it cannot be determined what factors led to them enacting a test correction system, and it is beyond the scope of this chapter to discuss the pros and cons of test corrections. From his vantage point, test corrections were not warranted for every single test. In essence, he thought that this practice allowed students to obtain passing grades who would have otherwise failed. Essentially, he wanted a more equitable grading system and noted this as an area of improvement.

It was clear that Jeremiah had some passionate thoughts about improving things. He continued:

> Some professors, they go a bit slow, because of the class, but I think sometimes, the problem with that line of thinking is that you slow it down for the class, and you slow it down to where the students currently are, then of course your top students know they're not being challenged the way they should. Even though a lot of times, the students that you're slowing down for, they are not being challenged the way they should, so they're actually bringing it down too far, because I understand bringing it down to some happy medium, so yeah, I mean it's hard. . . . So that kind of happens in a range of classes.

Jeremiah recommended that professors find suitable middle ground with the content. If students need some prerequisite skills, then professors might devote some instructional time to that background knowledge. The problem with this ideological paradigm, Jeremiah argued, is that students might not get everything that could have been potentially offered in a course. Also, delivering the content at a much slower pace does not adequately account for students who pick up on mathematical ideas rather quickly. Jeremiah emphatically wants a full mathematical experience for him and his brothers, which maps onto the relational aspects of Black masculinity (Pelzer, 2016).

Max saw things in a different light and offered a contrasting recommendation.

> The one thing they can do better is focus more on the students and focus more on struggling students instead of devoting all your time to this kid who already knows what he's doing and you just want to make him better.

Max suggests there are tighter relationships between faculty and stronger students than with mediocre math students, which supports the argument in Chapter 3 that there is some *division* among the brothers. This example touches upon the hierarchy of students that often happens within math communities and suggests that faculty contribute to establishing these hierarchies. In order to improve things, he recommended that faculty focus more on the students who are having some challenges instead of allocating the majority of their energy to students who appear to be mathematically astute. In short, Max believes that a concerted effort should be made to include both camps of students.

In this final suggested improvement, Daniel brought up a separate issue, course scheduling.

> I think, what should be improved is—so there are certain math courses that are only available during the spring or fall semester, I feel like it'd be better if the math department were able to allow every course that we have to be taken each year, like give it a possibility to be taken each semester. For example, somebody who, okay, maybe messed up in Abstract Algebra 2 and has to retake it. For the next semester, it may not be available. They'd have to wait for a whole year to retake it.

Daniel's recommendation was for the advanced courses to be offered each fall and spring semester. He used Abstract Algebra 2 as an example, indicating that the course is offered once a year, which is a notable lapse in time. In the upper-level courses, students are further along in their program of study, so waiting a full year to take a course could potentially prolong graduation. Logistically, there are administrative concerns associated with enrollment numbers and such, but Daniel's point is well taken regarding this course scheduling issue.

NON-MATHEMATICS FACULTY

In order to capture the majors' full Morehouse experience, I asked about their relationships with other professors (i.e., non-mathematics faculty). This question caused them to pause. Data analysis revealed that this was because they took most of their courses with, and ultimately became more acquainted with, the math faculty. However, there were some discussions about other professors, voiced primarily from the majors who switched out of a different major. Max was previously enrolled in the DDEP. He shared:

> The last physics class I took was like E&M [Electricity and Magnetism], so we started classes on Wednesday here at Morehouse and you have until the following Friday to drop, so by that following Wednesday, he said in class, "If you don't understand the things before this and you don't understand this, you might as well not take this course." I didn't understand anything prior to that, you know, so he's talking to me; this isn't the first time I've been in this situation with this kind of warning sign, and I ignored it, so I got out of there, never looked back.

As Max shared, his physics professor advised students not to take the course if they were already having difficulties. Arguably, the professor could have used more inviting language or admonished the students to pick up the pace with their studying. STEM education researchers have found that it can be extremely discouraging when students are presented with unfamiliar material that other students seem to have knowledge of (Seymour & Hunter, 2019). In Max's case, he had been in this predicament before, so that prior knowledge caused him to think and react differently. Given that he did not understand the first week's material, he dropped the course. In fact, he dropped the physics major and the DDEP. In doing so, he switched his major to math.

In his interview, Max's time as a physics major struck a nerve with him as he wished to share more.

> Another guy was a physics professor who kind of like disrespected me and hurt me. I had to go to a funeral. My uncle actually passed away. My mother called me, told me her brother passed away. I could tell she was upset. I immediately got myself ready to catch the next flight out, so we had a test, and I wrote him a note, you know, "Family member passed, I have to leave right away, I'll miss the test." Slipped the note underneath his door. I come back maybe a week later and he goes, "You're not my girlfriend, don't be sliding me notes, that's one of your dropped tests, I gave you a zero." This is the second test, and I already did poorly on the first test, and it just felt like my best interest wasn't at hand, and you make this lewd comment about me not being your girlfriend. That's another example of me wanting to revert back to old ways and really having to have some kind of self-control.

Instead of Max's professor being understanding about the uncontrollable situation, he made the coarse comment about Max not being his girlfriend. Max mentioned that he had to maintain self-control and not resort to his old ways, which suggests that this situation could have turned ugly. This exchange strengthened his desire to leave the physics major. Both of Max's shared encounters corroborate a key finding from the American Institute of Physics' (AIP) team regarding African American persistence in physics and astronomy; that is, "Faculty interactions have a powerful effect on student retention in, or departure from, the major" (AIP, 2020, p. 64).

On a more positive note, Jeremiah verbalized: "I know particularly one of my [redacted] professors, very strong relationship, he even asked me to tutor his daughters in math so that's umm, yeah, think he owes me a dinner actually." Jeremiah had a close relationship with this professor because he started out as a history major and took a few courses in the humanities. Moreover, this relationship grew stronger because he tutored his professor's daughters. Reflecting on that experience, he recalled that his professor might have still owed him dinner for his tutoring services, which highlights the ways extended family connections are associated with HBCUs' familial aspects (Albritton, 2012).

Regarding other professors, Darius replied:

I spend the most of my time up here, but I do have a good relationship
with some of my professors. Just with an HBCU, especially with a
small HBCU, you're gonna have more professors that are inclined
to engage the students and want everybody to do well. I have good
relationships with some of my other professors but not as close as with
the math department.

Darius spent most of his time in the math department. He specified that
Morehouse is a smaller HBCU and indicated that professors are more inclined to want students to succeed, which is in line with prior work about
the crucial role of HBCU faculty regarding the development of Black math
students (Borum et al., 2016; Jett, 2013b). With that, his narrative suggests
there are dedicated faculty in other disciplines at Morehouse, but he is not
able to witness, experience, or get to know these faculty well because of the
significant amount of time spent in the Department of Mathematics.

Most of the participants' thoughts about other professors were like
Darius's. Allen shared: "I wouldn't say I have a strong relationship with
them, just because I'd only have one class with them or only see them for
one semester and not have to take their classes anymore." On one hand,
Allen shared how close he was with his math professors because he had to
take multiple courses with them. On the other hand, he acknowledged that
he did not have a strong relationship with professors with whom he only
had one class. Similarly, Andre shared: "Honestly, what other professors?
I take all math classes." Again, these comments solidify that the majority
of their time was spent with math professors and underscore the need for
math professors to be inviting and inclusive if the goal is to have Black male
students enroll in multiple courses and persist in the major.

CONCLUSION

From these African American male students' viewpoints, the math professors
at Morehouse are effective, supportive, and available to induce meaningful
learning. This cohort talked at length about establishing stronger bonds and
spending more time with their math professors than their other professors,
which is not a surprising finding because they took several courses with
them. It can be deduced that they benefited greatly in instances where they
had to take a highly effective professor for multiple courses. There were a
couple less highly regarded math professors, but these bad apples did not
spoil the bunch.

Overall, the participants' narratives commended the Black faculty, as
they praised the support and guidance received from them. Even though

there were some hiccups, the brothers still generally reported positive relationships with them. By creating classifications of faculty—*superhero, math geniuses,* and *night shift*—the students enacted their respect and admiration for these scholars, which suggests that these scholars positively influence the students' attraction to and retention in the major. These stellar faculty members served as mathematical role models and mentors for these Black men. The following chapter goes a step further to bring Morehouse's mathematics learning community to life.

CHAPTER 5

Morehouse's Mathematics Learning Community

It's something they call third floor respect. In order to be on the third floor in the Math Lab, we need to respect your mathematics.

—Asa

Asa's narrative alludes to a key concept in Morehouse's mathematics learning community, that is, the nuanced concept of *third floor respect*, which will be explored in this chapter. He mentioned the Math Lab, where third floor respect was often manifested. The majors took great pleasure in this phenomenon—third floor respect was used to signify respect for math skills among members of the Morehouse Mathematics learning community.

This chapter paints a portrait of Morehouse's mathematics learning community. It draws heavily from fraternal language to establish the links between this community and the Black fraternal tradition. First, I discuss the Math Lab. Then the brothers' ideas of third floor respect are unpacked, followed by the inverse—*third floor disrespect*. Next, I share information about the activities and events that occur among the majors and the alumni, respectively. After that, I summarize the activities that build community for these Black men and portray them in a concept map. I conclude the chapter by summarizing the uniqueness of this collegiate community.

MATH LAB

Dansby Hall houses the Physics Department on the first floor, the Psychology Department on the second floor, and the Mathematics Department on the third floor. Because of math's ascribed intellectual prestige, the third floor arguably represents the pinnacle of majors for students.

In the midst of the third floor is the Math Lab. It is a larger space that can accommodate about two traditional classrooms. There is a chalkboard where students complete exercises, and tables for students to sit in circles and work together. There are 8.5×11-inch placards including short biographies of Morehouse's math graduates. There are also math journals, professional newsletters, and published papers on display; most of these publications were authored by Morehouse faculty and (former) students. In addition, there is a wall displaying posters from some of the majors' current and previous research projects. In short, the Math Lab provides these African American male students with mathematically accomplished images from those who look like them, sends a strong message that Black men are exemplars in mathematics research, and sets the expectation that they, too, will make significant contributions to the field.

The Math Lab brings the majors together to study and allows students in all majors to partake in walk-in tutoring sessions. In it, math is presented as an interesting and intriguing discipline among peers, and students watch, listen, conjecture, and learn how others solve problems. The space is used to validate, motivate, affirm, and support students and simultaneously promote a healthy campus ethos in support of Black men in math. The participants utilized this space to problem-solve, complete problem sets, and delve deeper into mathematical structures. The Math Lab also served as a space for the majors to get to know one another, build community, and strengthen their brotherhood while solidifying their bourgeoning content expertise. Allen referenced the Math Lab as a space that strengthened the majors' relationship.

> I think we're all really close since it's a small department, and there's a Math Lab; we call it our hall, so in between classes, most of us are usually right there in the Math Lab, and we're either tutoring people or asking each other about homework or generally just socializing, and I think that allowed us to be pretty close.

As he shared, these brothers made the Math Lab their home when they had breaks between classes, when they were tutoring or studying, or when they simply needed to socialize and fellowship among the brethren. Allen also pointed out that they referred to the Math Lab as "their hall." In other words, it served as a space for the majors to congregate, which is similar in nature to the *yard*. With BGLOs, the *yard* is where members of a fraternity congregate on campus. At Morehouse, the Math Lab represents the *yard* for the mathematical brotherhood.

yard: physical space where members of a fraternity congregate on campus

The participants took ownership of their learning in the Math Lab. They researched ideas, explained abstract concepts to their peers, and resolved mathematical conflicts. Instead of waiting on professors to validate their arguments, the students themselves evaluated their mathematical argumentation. Fundamentally, they were engaged in the practice of presenting mathematical ideas, and presenting math is comparable to *stepping* in the Black fraternal tradition. *Stepping* has a rich history steeped in African origins (Branch, 2005), and the behind-the-scenes preparation fosters group cohesion, which promotes a brotherly bond.

> *stepping*: a BGLO tradition characterized by completing hand and foot movements, chanting songs, and performing dance routines

Darius illustrated the comradery and group dynamics that occur while doing math within this institutional space.

> I think our relationship is really good. The math department in particular, I haven't seen it in other departments like how close the students really are. Like I said in physics, we all kind of went our separate ways. Talking to people in other departments, it seems similar where everybody's doing their own thing. We're all friends. You know, we have 12, 13, or 14 of us all hanging out together in the Math Lab doing math.

As a former physics major, Darius noted that they were not as close as the math majors. He also referenced the group dynamic in which a critical mass of African American male majors was working in the Math Lab, and this group effort presented a captivating portrait of a Black manhood into which mathematics is woven (Jett, 2022b).

Having so many Black men posted up in the Math Lab generated *math talk* (i.e., disciplinary discussions, debates, critiques, and rationalizations) (Hufferd-Ackles et al., 2004) to get the attention of the other majors. *Math talk* is analogous to the *call* in fraternal organizations, which is an utterance to gain the attention of fraternity members. *Calls* also have African origins; they serve as a form of affirmation and foster fraternal pride (McCoy, 2005). When several majors were studying in the Math Lab, *math talk* or their *call* produced a siren song, so to speak, motivating other Black men to join in the free-flowing mathematical discussions.

> *call*: an utterance to gain the attention of the other fraternity members

Marcus shared how being in the Math Lab boosted his mathematical self-confidence and self-efficacy.

> Every time I go to the Math Lab, where all the math majors study and, you know, doing something on the board and your fellow math majors

> behind you goes, "Yeah that's pretty good, you're doing alright." And
> I was like, yeah, I know what I'm doing. So it feels pretty good when
> like you do something right and the rest of the math majors' feedback
> says you know what you're doing; it gives you some confidence to go
> pass the next test.

When Marcus presented the correct mathematical justifications, his brothers applauded those efforts. This encouragement motivated them to succeed on subsequent work. Marcus's example reinforces Noble's (2011) findings with six Black male HBCU students who excelled in math: that supportive peer relationships heavily influence math self-efficacy among African American male college students. And again, it must be pointed out that Morehouse's Math Lab is uniquely occupied with an abundance of Black men engaged in doing math.

Overall, the atmosphere of the Math Lab is convivial and exhilarating. Moreover, this gathering of Black men focused on math debunks deficit narratives that suggests a group of Black men are likely up to no good. Malik shared: "In the Math Lab, you don't have to tell anyone to watch your stuff. No one steals in the Math Lab." Malik's narrative counters stereotypes about stealing, especially among Black men, and underscores how trusting the majors are with respect to their belongings and other personal items, which extends beyond mathematics. In a similar vein, Marcus explained:

> I like the atmosphere of the Math Department, it's like my home
> away from home, and I could be in my room, and I would think I'd
> rather be at the Math Lab right now, and you can ask anyone in the
> department, and you don't have to just ask a professor. You can ask
> anyone.

As Marcus's quote attests, this atmosphere is welcoming. Instead of passing time in the dormitory, he felt compelled to spend that time learning, doing, or practicing problems in the Math Lab. He stressed that students could ask anyone for assistance, indicating that tutors and peers were knowledgeable and could help others arrive at a solution to their problem. The majors had profound math knowledge and were positioned as such. Therefore, the majors learned from each other as well as from their professors at Morehouse, and the Math Lab was the bedrock for this learning community that helped promote the idea of third floor respect.

THIRD FLOOR RESPECT

As mentioned in the opening of this chapter, the majors ascribed to and relished the phenomenon of third floor respect. This was bestowed upon the majors who demonstrated deep math knowledge and contributed meaning-fully to Morehouse's mathematics learning community (Jett, 2022b). Also, the third floor served as a place of fictive kinship whereby Black male vali-dation, support, and liberation ran free within the context of mathematics (Chatters et al., 1994; Martin et al., 2019). Accordingly, third floor respect was constructed and legitimized among these Black men, uniquely linking mathematics and Black manhood.

During his interview, Asa added more to bring this nuanced concept to life.

> I work very hard. Usually, I kind of like compare myself to Epsilon and Jeremiah. I'm like, am I on their level yet? Because I know I'm not there, but I know I need to get there, and I work hard to get there, like understanding proofs like they do. Like ever since I've started taking classes with them, and seeing how they work hard at it, and how they understand it, and how I should be working as hard as they are.

As Asa's narrative suggests, Epsilon and Jeremiah were positioned as top-notch students in their cohort. Asa aspired to be on their level mathemat-ically, as he saw firsthand how deeply committed they were to it. Asa's narrative revealed that he respected his peers' profound work ethic and pro-found understanding of mathematical ideas. In addition, his narrative con-firmed Noble's (2011) findings with Black men who excelled in math at two HBCUs that seeing others similar to them acquire success improved self-efficacy. Similarly, seeing these Black men succeed prompted Asa to strive for mathematical self-improvement.

As one of the majors whom third floor respect was thrust upon, Epsilon stated:

> I tutor pretty much every class that's offered here besides like two [of them]. Everyone knows that; everyone acts accordingly, so I noticed, it's going to sound crazy, but someone was like, "You're the Jesus of math." I didn't like it; I didn't like it at all. It made me feel so uncomfortable, so umm, but it was a joke, but he was looking at me like you're like a titan. I'm scared because everyone gases me up like so great, but I know that graduate school is going to humble me, prob-ably the first week.

Because of Epsilon's ability to tutor students in many of the upper-level math courses, his peers placed him on a pedestal. On one hand, this admi-ration resulted in a deity-like reference to his mathematical prowess. On the other hand, earlier in the interview, Epsilon shared that he recently re-ceived his second acceptance letter into a prestigious graduate program, so he expressed being nervous about going to graduate school, hence the latter portion of his comment. As a result, he believed that his graduate experience would humble him since he would be surrounded by other exemplary students from their respective undergraduate programs. Epsilon's narrative also suggests he is aware of the harsh realities of graduate mathematics programs; efforts should be exerted to produce more racially affirming graduate programs, especially for Black men who are underrepresented in these programs (Jett, 2019a).

Like Epsilon's, Jeremiah's name was offered swiftly when discussing third floor respect. He genuinely wanted to help his peers with their studies, but he lamented:

> Sometimes it's tutoring, and helping people really understand the concept. Why is that? When someone is trying to do something, umm, and they need help at it, I naturally want to help people when they're trying. What bothers me is when people don't really want to try, and they do something last minute or something like that.

It bothered Jeremiah when some students did not put forth their best efforts or when they would come in the Math Lab to complete various tasks right before an assignment's due date. The Math Lab is a walk-in establishment, so students can come in at any time for assistance. Jeremiah was critical of students who would come to the Math Lab at the last minute, not for a quick clarification but for time-intensive interventions.

THIRD FLOOR DISRESPECT

Third floor respect was the desired goal for the participants, but the inverse also existed—third floor disrespect. *Third floor disrespect* entailed being disrespected mathematically or otherwise. Participants did not call it third floor disrespect, but they described some incidents they deemed disrespectful. Marcus offered a poignant example.

> The math majors, we really value like, knowledge, and we found out someone was cheating on a test in Abstract Algebra 2, and it was like, man, you ain't even real; nobody's cheating on a test. We don't like cheaters, Morehouse Mathematics, we want to stay strong and if we got cheaters—it's like we kind of frown upon cheaters here. Like you go and put some bad math on the board, and it's like hey man, you might need to go back to College Algebra bruh.

On the third floor, the majors did not tolerate cheating. A couple of the majors mentioned the Abstract Algebra 2 cheating scandal, as dishonorable behavior did not warrant third floor respect. Marcus's use of the word *strong* indexes the notion of what constitutes Black manhood (Neal, 2013). That is, the mathematical brotherhood upheld a moral code, making the department strong. Responding to follow-up questions, he shared even more about this ordeal.

> They had like a bet going on, like "Who's going to get the highest grade in the class?" I honestly don't know why he cheated, but they saw him cheating on the test, so he walked into the Math Lab and he [the cheater] was like, "You all think you got the highest grade" and he [a fellow major] was like, "I saw you cheating bruh." And he [the cheater] just packed his bags and walked out. I mean it was like he was shamed. You were caught cheating, like not by a teacher but by your fellow students, so it was you know, he felt bad, and we don't respect your mathematics no more.

In this case, a brother confronted the cheating student. In some departmental spaces, cheating might be ignored. In other spaces, cheating might be reported to the respective professors or administrative authorities. With this scandal, the majors handled the situation themselves. On another note, this scandal unearthed a shortcoming of competing for the highest score; that is, it can potentially lead to problematic practices such as cheating. The student never surfaced in the Math Lab again, and the majors saw less of him on campus. This example is reminiscent of a *drop* within BGLOs. A *drop* is usually a person who has decided not to continue the pledge process (although the reason might not be linked to a dishonorable act). A mathematics *drop* represents someone who has decided to leave the major for whatever reason.

> *drop*: a person who has dropped line when pledging a fraternal organization

Disrespect also manifested itself in the form of dissing. "Dissin" or "dis" is to speak to someone in a disrespectful manner (Smitherman, 2000). The exchange with Malik captured this:

Malik: There's a lot of sneak dissing, like making fun of them on the low. I don't really know. They don't study, so I don't study with them, so I don't spend much time with them.
Chris: You said sneak dissing, like dissing them on the low. Can you give me an example?
Malik: So they'll be in a 400-level math course, and say okay, consider 3 divided by 0, like it's College Algebra, that's one of the big no-noes, and you're like, "Oh you dividing by zero, bruh? Aw naw, you got it, you a genius!" Stuff like that.

Malik's narrative provided additional evidence about some *division* between the majors, as alluded to in Chapter 3. His recap of dissing represented the underhanded comments directed to those either not putting sufficient time into their studies or not displaying mathematical intelligence. Division by zero is undefined; he expected a student in an upper-level course to possess that foundational knowledge. The point is that Malik's response of describing the act of dividing by zero as genius was a sarcastic dis.

Max was on the receiving end of some of the disrespect. As mentioned previously, Max had a very demanding schedule, and he admitted that he could not devote as much time to his studies as many of his peers. He noted:

> This semester is the first semester I can say I've enjoyed everyone else's company. I feel like there's a huge divide. Previously, I mentioned they cultivate a few, and that few that they cultivate previously, there's been a huge divide between them and us, and like they almost like look down on us, disrespect us, say little catty things that I don't particularly care for, like I come from a place that you're not going to disrespect me, and that goes back to high school.

Max recently came to enjoy the company of his fellow majors, but he expressed that some majors were being cultivated while others were viewed in a less favorable light. In some cases, disrespectful comments were made, and Max acknowledged that he did not appreciate the disrespect. He held strong to this philosophy even during his secondary schooling days at his rather tough, urban high school. The interview continued:

> *Chris:* When you say disrespect, can you give me an example of something that happened?
>
> *Max:* Well, something happened this semester, and I really had to catch myself. It was after class, and I asked someone who had already finished the course for help in the course, and he was like, "You need to sign in." You're my age; you don't need to tell me what I need to do. You will never speak to me like that, ever.
>
> *Chris:* Like sign in, in the Math Lab?
>
> *Max:* Yeah, and the second thing, I came to you humbly and that's already, you know, that's something you have to work for, like you're lowering yourself to your peer, and then you like step on me. Like that's just, we can easily take that outside, but that's another story.

Max cited when a peer flippantly requested him to sign in at the Math Lab. Max had to humble himself to ask for tutoring, so he believed that requesting him to sign in was an affront to his ego. Arguably, this comment revealed aspects of Max's masculinity. Taking something outside suggested that he was thinking about throwing some hands (or fighting), and a contentious debate is centered on whether physicality or physical prowess is synonymous with Black masculinity (Neal, 2013; Richardson, 2007). In Max's case, there was some evidence of physicality being linked to Black manhood as he grappled with this disrespectful situation.

This idea of disrespect also extended and manifested itself uniquely on Spelman's campus. Malik's example showcased this:

> When I first got here, they talked about the blacklist at Spelman. Once you're on that list, it's the list all the girls talk about: "Don't talk to him, he's a player" or whatever, "womanizer," or whichever word. I thought it was a joke, but I came into Morehouse knowing Calculus 1 fairly well already, and so I was in a position where I could tutor a lot of Spelmanites, and I had fun doing that. I had so much fun; I ended up on the blacklist. I wasn't even doing anything with them; it was just we were behind closed doors; nobody knew what was going on, just always at the dorms, in somebody else's room, you know, tutoring.

Malik referenced Spelman's blacklist, which he described as an underground list of men to avoid when seeking dates and romantic partners. The fact that Spelman women composed a blacklist indicates that there are some deeply troubling issues regarding the sexual objectification of Black women. Because Malik frequented Spelman's residence halls to tutor women in Calculus, he was placed on the list. His narrative sheds additional light on his quote in Chapter 2: "Came for the women; stayed for the math." In addition, his narrative rejects hypersexual constructions of Black masculinity and challenges discourses that seek to position Black men as players or womanizers (Pelzer, 2016). Notwithstanding, his altruistic mathematical gestures resulted in women at the sister institution not trusting him.

COLLEGIATE ACTIVITIES AND EVENTS

In Morehouse's mathematics learning community, there are several activities and events that bolster students' learning outcomes and earn them respect. These include undergraduate research, the Mathematics Colloquium Series, the Math Club, and the Putnam Team. There is also a Mathematics Awards Day Ceremony as well as a Morehouse Mathematics Breakfast at the end of the spring semester. In addition, students get the opportunity to expand their mathematical thinking via study abroad opportunities, conferences, and other opportunities. I briefly discuss each of these, in turn, to provide some flavor to these activities and events.

Undergraduate Research

Previous work with college students shows that engaging them in undergraduate research enhances their intellectual development, leads to increased persistence in the major, enhances collaborative skills, and ushers in the next generation of professional mathematicians (Adams et al., 2013; Sturner et al., 2017). Morehouse stakeholders champion undergraduate research, so students are expected to take part in it (Morehouse College, n.d.). The participants learned about research opportunities through the faculty and their fellow majors. They engaged in research projects at Morehouse, Research Experiences for Undergraduates (REUs) programs such as the Mathematical Sciences Research Institute Undergraduate Program (MSRI-UP) summer institute, and internships. Regardless of where students conduct research, they can present their research at Morehouse's Harriet J. Walton Symposium on Undergraduate Mathematics Research. Table 5.1 provides a list of research topics this cohort worked on.

This smorgasbord of research topics can be used to solve practical problems that evolve. These specialty areas are listed as course options in graduate programs and research areas for practicing mathematicians (AMS, n.d.; MAA, n.d.; NAM, n.d.). One benefit is that projects provide the majors with an opportunity to make connections between their undergraduate coursework and mathematics research. These topics also reveal the potential research streams participants could pursue and ultimately make contributions to. Therefore, their research experiences exposed them to concepts they were likely to encounter later in the field.

Table 5.1. Brothers' Research Topics

Combinatorics	K-theory
Commutative rings	Lie groups
Complex variables	Manifolds
Field theory and polynomials	Matrix theory
Fourier analysis	Numerical analysis
Global analysis	Operator theory
Graph theory	Optimization
Group theory	Partial differential equations
Integral equations	Stochastic procedures
Integral transforms	Topological groups

Mathematics Colloquium Series

The Mathematics Colloquium Series is a seminar series where professionals share results from previous or current work. Because Morehouse is an undergraduate institution, the seminar series is designed to be accessible for an undergraduate mathematics audience. Through this series, students get to learn from others' firsthand math experiences. This series includes a vast array of topics to expose, entice, and steer students in different mathematical directions. During the year of this study, topics presented ranged from the Cauchy-Schwarz inequality to elliptic curves to the quadratic assignment problem, to name a few.

What is unique to this study is that most of the speakers for this series included Black male math-oriented professionals. Coupling the Black male math faculty members with the Black men who were invited to speak in this series, Black men at Morehouse get to regularly witness and interact with Black male math scholars. Therefore, the brothers in this mathematics learning community were able to engage in rich dialogue with these same-race and same-gender speakers to expand their thinking and expose them to various math-intensive research pathways. Collectively, these Black men contributed to the climate of the department, helped to facilitate the students' socialization into the discipline, and served as tangible models of mathematical excellence combined with Black manhood.

Math Club

The Math Club is a student-led organization that brings together students who have an interest in math. The club primarily consists of math majors, but students from other majors can also join. The Math Club holds events each year, such as social and Pi Day events; the primary goal is to bring awareness and generate excitement about math. Michael, who served as the president of the Math Club, revealed:

> I have different events on campus to show like different sides
> of mathematics, so the first event was a social with Spelman's Math
> Club. We have a Ms. Math Club, they're pretty much responsible
> for one event per year related to math, like women in mathematics
> or they highlight women in mathematics.

As president, Michael was responsible for spearheading math events on campus such as the social in conjunction with Spelman's Math Club. He mentioned the title of Ms. Math Club, which he shared was open to any woman in the AUC. During the year of this study, Ms. Math Club was a math major at Spelman. This disciplinary ambassador promotes women in math, which is beneficial within this male-centric HBCU space (see Jones, 2019, and Shetterly, 2016, for inspiring depictions of African American women in mathematics). In all, the Math Club stimulated discipline-specific thinking, allowed Black men to hold a disciplinary leadership role, and exposed them to other Black mathematical intellects.

Putnam Team

The Putnam Team consists of a group of students who prepare to participate in the collegiate William Lowell Putnam Mathematical Competition (Kedlaya et al., 2002). Administered annually by the MAA on the first Saturday of December, the Putnam Competition is an intercollegiate competition where college students extrapolate popular theories in undergraduate coursework. Putnam problems have been the inspiration of new mathematical theories, modern research directions, and unique problem-solving techniques. As a member of Morehouse's Putnam Team, Darius described it in the following manner:

> There will be like seven to 10 people. We'll meet down in the Math Lab. Dr. Coefficient would just put Putnam problems up on the board, and we work on them for like an hour, and he'd help us if we needed help. We'd meet once a week.

As Darius corroborated, the Putnam Team meets weekly to tackle difficult problems used in previous Putnam Competitions. Some Spelman scholars practiced with them, including Ms. Math Club. Morehouse's department chair served as the faculty leader with this team and provided mathematical assistance as needed. Jeremiah expressed: "There's a Putnam Practice Team at Morehouse, so yes, in some sense, it's practice for the exam, but I mean, also, it's a way to like learn some cool math." In this way, he substantiated the fascinating and deeply educative experience associated with being on the Putnam Team.

Five majors participated in the annual competition. Also, some members of the Putnam Team, along with others from interested majors, worked with students in local K–12 schools to expose and prepare them for math competitions. In this way, the brotherhood functions to build the next generation of mathematicians. Returning to the BGLO language, a mathematics research, Math Club, or Putnam Team meeting constituted a *chapter meeting* given that these three activities occurred with some regularity.

> *chapter meeting*: a meeting to discuss the business of the chapter

Awards Day Ceremony

In addition to the ongoing activities, there are annual events held in Morehouse's mathematics learning community. One example is the Mathematics Awards Day ceremony. This ceremony is designed to give each math professor the opportunity to recognize an outstanding student(s) in each course. The award is given to the student(s) who has exemplified all-around outstanding math performance. Both majors and non-majors are considered for an award.

The speaker for the Mathematics Awards Day Ceremony is usually a graduating senior who shares a research presentation. As an up-and-coming mathematician, this student presenter receives feedback from professors and attendees. Importantly, this presentation signals to underclassmen that they could aspire to be the selected featured speaker. After the event, refreshments are served in the Math Lab to facilitate student and faculty mingling and socializing.

Daniel talked about getting an award for his achievements in a Pre-Calculus course during his first year at Morehouse.

> My first mathematics award was when I was a freshman. I got an award in my first semester, and I told my mom and everything and everyone about it. I was so excited, and I was just so proud of myself and proud of my knowledge in math and everything. I felt real good. That was just Pre-Calculus but later on I received two more math awards: Calculus and—it was so long ago I can't remember [the other one].

Daniel was so proud of his Pre-Calculus award that he called his mother to inform her of the accolade. His call back home provides additional evidence of the supportive role Black families play during Black male students' collegiate journeys, especially Black mothers, and confirms findings from Hrabowski et al.'s (1998) foundational research regarding Black parents' support and encouragement to academically successful African American male students. Such encouragement fosters a belief in self. Daniel's achievement also reinforces Noble's (2011) findings that previous success elevates self-efficacy among African American male math learners. This victory heightened Daniel's mathematical self-efficacy and encouraged him to continue in that path (i.e., earning two additional awards). For Daniel and others, the Awards Day ceremony served as a public affirmation of these Black men as mathematical scholars in this collegiate community.

At the Awards Day Ceremony, a Morehouse Mathematics sweater vest is bestowed upon majors who have demonstrated unwavering commitment to their studies. It reflects the signature style of Dr. Robert E. Bozeman mentioned in Chapter 1 as displayed in a frame in the center of the Math Lab.

In fraternal life, *paraphernalia* represents the clothing items with the fraternity's name and/or Greek letters. In the Black fraternal tradition, it is worn with the utmost pride to represent the organization. The Morehouse Mathematics sweater vest is the *paraphernalia* that the majors seek to earn at the culmination of their degree program.

> *paraphernalia*: clothing items and gadgets that bear the fraternity's name

Morehouse Mathematics Breakfast

The year of this study marked the first Morehouse Mathematics Breakfast, a home-grown event that occurs on Saturday morning during commencement weekend (see Appendix B for observational notes about the breakfast). The celebration honors the graduates and their families. It also allows them to have direct interactions with their fellow majors, institutional stakeholders, and other supporters. Memorable stories are shared about their experiences in the major while eating breakfast, creating a synergy among those in attendance. This event represents something more than simply having breakfast, as this culminating event provides this cohort one final intimate moment of collective fellowship before the Sunday morning commencement ceremony.

Other Activities and Events

The participants were able to take advantage of other math-based opportunities during their time at Morehouse. For example, Michael spoke about his study abroad experience, which touches upon the notion that Morehouse Men are well traveled, as mentioned in Chapter 1.

> Last year, at Morehouse, it was called Germany–U.S. STEM exchange. We went to Berlin and Munich, and we explored a couple of schools in Berlin and Munich, so we explored BMW [Bayerische Motoren Werke] and the German version of NASA and the Berlin Mathematics School, and it was pretty much like *the* math school in Germany. And we just pretty much explored a different company and a different industry because they wanted to expose STEM students to the idea of working outside the country for the most part. It was two and a half weeks of exploring the company, studying the company, and looking at different options, at international jobs and careers.

In his narrative, Michael shared that studying abroad broadened his view of the domestic and international opportunities available to mathematically talented students. Covington (2017) advocates for HBCUs to be positioned to increase the number of Black students who take advantage of study abroad opportunities, and this cross-cultural STEM exchange program exposed Michael to what working outside the country might entail. By visiting the best companies and the top math school in Germany, he was able to witness and explore career opportunities through an international perspective, which is critically important in today's global economy (National Research Council, 2013).

Another opportunity in which some of the majors took part was the post–Dansby Lecture dinner. As mentioned in Chapter 1, the Dansby Lecture serves as the premier research presentation within the Morehouse Mathematics domain. This year, the college Provost's home discipline was mathematics. He gave the annual lecture. At the end-of-year breakfast, the students were still talking about their brother who spent the dinner doing Linear Algebra in a corner instead of taking advantage of the dining and conversational opportunities. They mocked him, but they also admired his dedication to his studies.

There are also community events for these brothers. Max participated in a mentoring program that was developed by one of his Morehouse fraternity brothers. He shared the goal of this initiative serving school-aged children:

> To see somebody in Jordans who didn't have to sell drugs to get them, to see somebody in college who doesn't talk like a square or isn't White. Just talk to them about things we've experienced and just basically hand them the answer key to life.

Max's counternarrative debunks the idea that Black men have to engage in criminal activities to acquire material goods. While mentoring, he wants local students to see someone who is relatable with a shared racial identity, and the sound advice can motivate students, especially Black boys, to succeed in life (see Kafele, 2009). In another example, Daniel became involved in a community-centered activity that he learned about through his fellow major, confirming that peers are a great resource for information:

> Actually, another math major asked me if I would like to be a part of it, and so I did just give it a shot and just teach and everything to see how it goes. And a lot of people said I did well, and I enjoyed it . . . to just encourage the students.

Daniel volunteered a couple of hours each week tutoring metro Atlanta students through an organization whose mission is to provide a positive culture and expose students to educational and career opportunities. This is not surprising given Daniel's comment in Chapter 2 about not being stingy with his math gift. Like Max, Daniel's involvement within this local organization as an HBCU student is congruent to Albritton's (2012) assertion that "HBCUs have long been important cultural centers that contribute to the life and the vitality of the Black community" (p. 323). These examples, along with the Putnam Team's *community service* efforts and college-wide service initiatives, emphasize the service that Morehouse students perform with, for, and in service to the Black community.

> *community service*: an activity in which fraternity members provide service to the Black community

Furthermore, there were other activities and events in this mathematics learning community. Chapter 3 mentioned the Real Analysis parties that occurred throughout the year. In December, there was the singing of Calculus carols during the holiday party. To promote summer research, there was a meeting where students shared presentations and posters from previous experiences. This meeting occurred during the early part of spring semester—an opportune time for submitting summer research applications, thereby promoting a culture of Black men applying for programs en masse. Drawing from language used within BGLOs, this meeting served as an *informational*.

> *informational*: a meeting where prospective pledgees can learn additional information about a fraternity

ALUMNI-RELATED ACTIVITIES AND EVENTS

Morehouse's alumni are a loyal group who have access to wider networks in the field. Members of the mathematical brotherhood were able to interact with the institution's alumni through homecoming activities.

Morehouse Mathematics Homecoming Activities

Morehouse and Spelman have a joint homecoming, referred to as Spel-House. HBCU homecomings represent a family reunion of sorts that includes alumni, students, faculty and staff professionals, community representatives, family members, and friends.

One special feature is the Morehouse Mathematics Tent, which is displayed during Saturday's homecoming tailgate. The tent serves as a home base, allowing current majors to have fun with math and connect with alumni.

Within fraternal organizations, a *prophyte* refers to an older brother. In this case, a Morehouse math alumnus represents a *prophyte*.

> *prophyte*: an older member of a BGLO

At the Morehouse Mathematics Homecoming Tent, the majors, alumni, and any attending faculty receive free food and drinks. Others have to participate in the classic game—"proof or pay"—whereby they have to either produce a proof or pay for their lunch under the tent. This impromptu request to prove a theorem was done in a joking manner to determine if others were on their toes, so to speak, mathematically. On a more serious note, it is also a testament to these brothers' dedication to the mathematical enterprise. And what a powerful message for Black children to see, witness, and receive during this homecoming excursion!

Regarding the homecoming tent, Michael said:

> We have a homecoming tent every year to showcase different mathematicians, people who major in math and different math games, just different homecoming stuff, I know they definitely have barbecue, poker, or something like that, some card games, something related to math. [We highlight] people who went to Morehouse, so generally people in the math department who graduated from Morehouse and just came back, so old math majors come back, and guest-speak about what they're doing, so we can get a sense of where they are.

Robert's narrative echoed this description of the homecoming tent.

> Each club, Greek organization, everything basically at Morehouse has a tent where people from that organization or major can go to the tent, and we would have food, cups of water, drink, and juices and chips and kind of spread the word about their organization. It's kind of a tent where we want to expose people to math but also have fun during homecoming.

As Michael and Robert indicated, this tent allowed students to interact with alumni who work in math-intensive fields. The interesting thing about the homecoming tent was that events revolved around math—showcasing (Morehouse) mathematicians, playing poker, playing card games, etc. During homecoming week (as well as other random times throughout the year), alumni visited the department, Math Lab, and classes, all on the third floor. In doing so, they reminisced about their undergraduate experiences and shared details about their contemporaneous careers. Many majors referenced how the testimonials from alumni served as motivational offerings of what they could accomplish in the future.

Morehouse Mathematics Alumni Conference

Another mechanism for the majors to engage with alumni was through a Morehouse Mathematics Alumni Conference (see Appendix B for observational data about the conference), which included several African American men. The conference functioned as a mentoring meeting in that stakeholders across the educational spectrum were in attendance—undergraduate students, graduate students, alumni (many with advanced degrees), and (Morehouse) math faculty. Presentations, panels, and outreach activities ensued that offered these Black men discipline-specific support, knowledge, and guidance about succeeding in post-undergraduate mathematics contexts. In this way, the alumni served as living examples of Black men who were thriving in graduate school and employment. Through the conference's professional development efforts, the participants were granted access to Black male math capital in unique ways.

Alumni Connections

This study unearthed other ways participants were able to capitalize on the connections from alumni. An example was embedded within Jeremiah's narrative:

> Turns out one of the math alumni at Morehouse is going to be a graduate associate with the program. He's actually a graduate student at Tetrahedron University, but I heard about it from another undergraduate student and in some sense it's great because we hear things from one another, and in some sense, we help each other out.

As Jeremiah mentioned, he learned of this summer program from a fellow student. A math alumnus was slated to be a graduate associate (i.e., math mentor) with the program. This example demonstrated the power of networking with, between, and among these Morehouse Mathematics Men. This example also provides disciplinary evidence of how Morehouse Men benefit from the larger institutional brotherhood (Eaves, 2006).

In another example, Robert was connected with a Morehouse alumnus in his hometown while participating in an internship. He recounted:

> It was a large insurance company, and there was a program that I was involved in that was available to all interns where we were given various projects, and we put together a presentation, and the director of the program, I became really close to her and she knew

that I was interested in math, and she saw that I was good at it, so
she actually worked on the same floor as the other guy, and she
knew him really well. So she sent me to talk to him one day, and I
went over and emailed him a couple times, and we set up a meeting
to talk, and we talked about math and school and just various things,
so ever since then, every summer, at least 3 or 4 times a summer,
I sit down and talk to him, email him throughout the summer
and kind of see him as a mentor and kind of what I would have
eventually done.

Robert's program director introduced him to a Morehouse alumnus working at the company. As a result, Robert was able to leverage his Morehouse
affiliation. Even though he plans to pursue a different career pathway, he
views the Morehouse alumnus as a mentor. Robert has been strategic about
taking advantage of this connection, especially during the summer months
when he is home, to propel his goals and aspirations. In this way, he has
made a meaningful connection in the broader mathematical community, as
other majors have also benefited from connections with alumni.

Professional Conferences

In addition, eight majors attended the Joint Mathematics Meeting (JMM),
which at the time was the largest national, professional mathematics meeting, and were able to attend a Morehouse Mentoring dinner with faculty
and alumni during the JMM. Further, NAM's Undergraduate MATHFest,
which was initially geared toward HBCU students (encouraging them to
pursue graduate degrees in mathematics and mathematics education), inspired MAA's undergraduate-focused MathFest (NAM, n.d.). These events
are not reported in detail here because in-depth information about them
was not part of this study. It is highly probable that there were other aspects
of these opportunities that may be significant. However, the overarching
finding is that, taken together, this wide assortment of activities and events
fosters a robust math identity for the African American men at Morehouse,
which ultimately influences their persistence in the discipline.

SUMMARY OF ACTIVITIES AND EVENTS
TO PROMOTE COMMUNITY

Figure 5.1 provides a concept map of the activities and events that tran-
spire at Morehouse; these institutionalized practices assisted in developing,
promoting, and sustaining community for the Black men in this study. In
the figure, mathematics community is centered as the overarching phenomenon, followed by the supporting attributes—math coursework, Math

Figure 5.1. Mathematics Community Concept Map

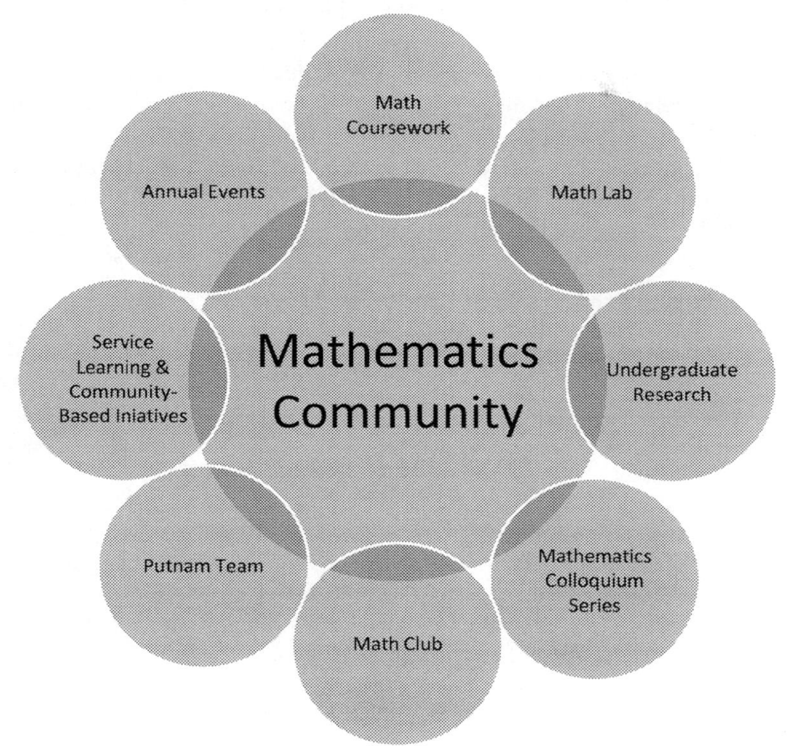

Lab, undergraduate research, Mathematics Colloquium Series, Math Club, Putnam Team, service learning/community-based initiatives, and annual events (i.e., Homecoming activities, Awards Day Ceremony, Breakfast, and Alumni Conference). These activities and events are used as touchpoints to establish a vibrant connection between mathematics and Black manhood, and they comprise the infrastructure that produces Morehouse's thriving mathematics learning community.

CONCLUSION

Morehouse's mathematics learning community is a sacred one that Black men can call their own. The Math Lab allows majors to congregate, hold discussions outside of class, and earn third floor respect. In addition to the Math Lab, the activities and events mentioned in this chapter jigsaw to produce a humanizing space for the students. Crucially, these efforts provided the 16 participants access to Black men in mathematics career fields. As such, they have family, alumni, faculty, and peers who provide wider academic, mathematical, and social networks to connect them to math-related internships, study abroad opportunities, research programs, graduate programs, and career opportunities. Further, mathematical attributes are wedded to fraternal language in this chapter, which uniquely extends the Black masculinist frame.

At Morehouse, these brothers were empowered via the aforementioned activities and events. What is abundantly clear is that these Black men got personal meaning and satisfaction out of these endeavors—being in the Math Club, participating on the Putnam Team, engaging in community service, and partaking in homecoming festivities. While being a Black man is celebrated at this traditionally single-gender HBCU, this is not the case in many contexts outside of this one. The next chapter explores some of these encounters by examining the brothers' racialized experiences.

CHAPTER 6

The Brothers' Racialized Experiences

I think the negative stereotype about Black males is that there are no positive stereotypes.

—Michael

Michael's statement presents a troubling reality regarding stereotypes about Black boys and men. This country has a troubled racial history; therefore, society's racial problems run deep. Segregation, educational inequality, unequal funding, and discriminatory practices and policies are some of the drugs that give racism its consistent high. Unfortunately, Black men deal with essentialist notions that attempt to thwart Black manhood. The good news is that Black-affirming spaces like Morehouse counteract these deficit notions about Black men.

In this chapter, I paint a picture of the brothers' racialized and gendered experiences drawing on CRT and Black masculinity theory. I use [n-word][1] instead of the derogatory term, as it surfaced during data collection. First, I report on the participants' racialized K–12 experiences, followed by their racialized experiences in other math-related contexts. Then, descriptions of their racialized experiences in everyday life are shared. After that, I highlight how the participants positioned Morehouse as a racially affirming space. I conclude by summarizing this chapter's race-related main ideas.

RACIALIZED K–12 EXPERIENCES

In educational settings, deficit-oriented narratives attempt to position Black male students as academic catastrophes. As a result of these racial biases, Black boys and men are overwhelmingly stigmatized within academic settings. In view of the gendered racism in schools, African American male students have been at the forefront of race-based analyses (Howard, 2014; Wright & Counsell, 2018). These works have used CRT because it recognizes the normalcy of racism (Delgado & Stefancic, 2000). Dumas and ross (2016) nuance this theory via BlackCrit and demonstrate that anti-Black racism reproduces Black suffering and oppression. Consequently, Black boys deal with the anti-Black racism that is commonplace in K–12 settings.

Racialized Early Childhood Years

The brothers in this study were from racially diverse neighborhoods across the country, so the racial composition of their schools varied. Although many early childhood educators think children do not notice racial differences, the participants were aware of the racial undercurrents surrounding being Black and male. As a matter of fact, the vast majority of the study's participants were confronted with racial issues as early as kindergarten. While racial differences extend beyond Black and White binaries, the participants overwhelmingly operationalized race in this way. In one example, Tony shared how he experienced racism during his elementary school years.

> I lived in a predominately White town, so I would get picked on a lot because I was the only Black kid, so I used to fight a lot. I used to be upset. I remember my best friend; we were playing around, and I was chasing him. I grabbed him or something like that; I can't remember what we were doing. But he pushed me off of him, and he said, "My dad said I can't play with [n-words] anymore." That's the last time I talked to him, and I was like 7 or 8 at that time.

Tony recalled playing with his former best friend and the racial slur later directed toward him. This exchange dissolved their friendship, but it left an indomitable mark on him. More specifically, the boy said that his father commanded him not to play with [n-words] anymore, further demonstrating the intergenerational aspects often affiliated with nefarious racist ideologies. Tony's example shows how racism is taught and passed down from generation to generation, indicating that Whites love Whiteness to death and pass this White dominance complex down to their children (Matias, 2016).

Malik also recounted a scenario of navigating and grappling with racism at school.

> When I went to the White school, they were racist, ridiculously racist. One time, a few White dudes came up to me and asked me if I would prefer being called a [n-word] or a boy. I beat that dude, and I beat him something crazy, and his friends just watched. I thought they were going to help him. So it was just really racist.

As reported elsewhere, this incident stood out to Malik because it resulted in a fistfight with a White male (Jett, 2016b). Malik was involved in other racialized altercations at school. These incidents lead to out-of-school suspensions and expulsions for Black boys at a heightened level, disrupting their learning, and school discipline data often do not account for the ways in which race-related acts provoke these incidents (Dancy, 2014). Moreover, Malik's case illuminates the racism that is normal in society and entrenched in students' psyches, as revealed in the CRT literature (Delgado & Stefancic, 2000).

John, who identified as multiracial, lamented about grappling with racism.

> Oh yeah, I was bullied a lot, I was called "sand [n-word]" all throughout elementary school. I was talked about because I couldn't hang out with the Black people because I was too light to hang out with them, and I couldn't hang out with the White people because I was too dark to hang out with them, so it's like
> it was just me by myself.

John was bullied, treated as an outsider, and called "sand [n-word]" because of his skin tone. "Sand [n-word]" is a demeaning phrase referring to a person of Middle Eastern or North African descent (de Brito, 2013). The usage of the disparaging phrase toward him exposes the racial challenges that John had to endure as a Black mixed-race boy (see Howard, 2019), providing additional evidence that his elementary-aged classmates were exposed to and used racist language. One difference is that John felt excluded from both Black and White peer groups because of his multiracial background. This suggests that systems and approaches should be in place to provide better (historical) education for students across racial groups regarding engaging with persons of mixed-race, especially in light of the increasing multiracial population (Rousseau Anderson, 2020).

On another note, Robert elucidated how he came to grips with and about race as a young Black male student.

> I would say 4th grade when I switched schools. It was 1st through 3rd [grades] was 98% Black and the other percent was Latino, so it wasn't really different, but when I switched schools, and it became 90% White, it was a little different because I was outside the norm, outside of my comfort zone, and only my dad had moved out to where the school was, and my mom was still in Abacus, so at that time, I noticed it [race]. Because at first I was kind of oblivious to it, but that's when my parents sat down and talked to me about the Civil Rights Movement; they kind of went in-depth to make sure I understood certain things about being in a predominantly White neighborhood. So I'd say, the first week or so of being at the other school was when I noticed it, because it was kind of brought to my attention to make sure I understood.

Robert spent his first few years of school living with his mother because of his parents' divorce. While doing so, he attended a predominantly African American school in an urban city. He expressed that the decision was made for him in Grade 4 to move with his father to a suburban neighborhood with a high-performing school district. His narrative reveals that this co-parenting situation was constructed to provide him with access to more educational opportunities. In this new neighborhood, there were different racial demographics, which resulted in his attending a predominately White elementary school. It was during this transition that Robert recognized racial differences.

Whitaker and Snell (2016) noted that Black parents have "the talk," or the race talk, with their children, especially their sons, to increase their chances of survival in a racially hostile situation. Lesane-Brown (2006) reviewed the body of research examining racial socialization within Black families. Her analysis revealed that Black families utilized different, deliberate modes of discussing race-related topics with Black children, such as during dinner conversations, via Black art, and through books with race-related themes. She found that Black families did so to establish racial pride and foster a positive racial identity among their Black children. Black families must have a pointed talk with Black children about race relations at an early age. For Black boys in particular, discussions surrounding race relations are more salient because they could be a matter of life or death. As a result, race-based discussions commonly occur before Black boys reach the adolescent stage, and that was the case for Robert and many of the other participants.

Racialized Secondary School Years

Like the early childhood years, the secondary school years presented racial challenges for some of the participants. Michael interpreted his racialized experiences in the form of not having access to the same academic preparation as his White peers, which also points to the ways systemic racism impacts the quality of education students receive.

> After elementary, I was supposed to go to a really, really bad middle school, but my mom kind of found a way for me to go to a better middle school. And when I got to middle school that was the first time that I had [inaudible] concept of White people. I honestly felt that they were more prepared than I was in middle school, and I didn't go to one of the better elementary schools, and I felt like they were more prepared for the courses, and I had to really work hard to get on their level in terms of their knowledge and that kind of thing, so I had a really steep learning curve.

As Michael mentions, his mother advocated for him to attend a predominantly White middle school. There, he began to understand the concept of Whiteness and grapple with racial issues (see Matias, 2016). Reflecting on this experience, Michael believed that his White peers were more prepared academically than he was. Despite this belief, however, Michel became and remained an honor student, served as the president of MATHCOUNTS, and received several math awards. In addition to his K–12 accomplishments, he received math awards at Morehouse and even served as the president of the Math Club, as highlighted in Chapter 5. He persevered and persisted with his math studies in his middle school space in spite of the racial disparities.

Jeremiah shared a racialized experience. He was the only Black student in an AP Biology course:

> I noticed I was the only Black person in class, and that was part of it, and every once in a while, during class a race situation will come up and people will, you kind of notice everybody will look at you. And I mean in some sense, it's understandable, and I don't think anybody actually meant it in a negative way, so those situations, you just kind of know.

Jeremiah believed that racial issues were at play and reasoned that it might be understandable for his secondary classmates to look at him when racial issues surfaced because he was the only Black student in the class. The disproportionately low numbers of Black students in gifted and AP courses leads to experiences where Black students are made to feel as if they have to be the spokesperson for the entire Black race (Ford, 2013). There is, however, an unspoken burden associated with always having to educate classmates or peers about race. On another note, Jeremiah's experience of being the only one is consistent with Black male mathematicians who have spoken out and received public attention about being the only one in educational and professional settings (see Doan, 2019; Harmon, 2019). The next section examines the racism succeeding the participants' K–12 years in math-related contexts.

RACIALIZED EXPERIENCES IN MATH-RELATED CONTEXTS

Because mathematics is entangled within a racialized system, racial profiling and stereotypes infiltrate Black male students' math experiences (Jett, 2019a). Some participants experienced bouts of racial stereotyping in math-related contexts. Given that this study took place at Morehouse, none of the brothers offered any experiences of dealing with racism at college. As with BGLOs and other HBCUs, Morehouse's high concentration of Black people served as a buffer to anti-Blackness. This finding supports previous literature indicating that HBCUs have elevated concentrations of Black students, faculty, staff, and administrators who racially empower African American mathematics students (Jett, 2019a; Walker, 2014). However, the participants grappled with racial stereotypes, microaggressions, and the like in non-HBCU mathematics research apprenticeship settings. One example included being stereotyped as mathematically incapable, and Epsilon's experience was illustrative of this.

> I was in this algebra group in my research [internship], and it was me and three White girls. And a lot of times, before I started to put my foot down and said I'm not going to do this, some of the project assignments, they kind of just like handed me the easy ones, like "Here, you can do these, and we'll do these"; it's like, no, this is trivial, you can give me some of those, and we can split this stuff and that'll be fine.

Epsilon reflected on his participation in a summer program at a historically White institution (HWI). His group members, who happened to be three White women, were making all the executive decisions for the research group without his input. More importantly, he witnessed the young ladies assigning him the trivial math tasks. His narrative suggested that these White women held some racially misguided beliefs about his mathematical intelligence, and there is a troubling history of White women upholding stereotypes about Black boys and men.

He revealed more about the racial slights he experienced at the same institute.

> I had this one heated argument with one of my graduate assistants because she didn't believe that my proof was right. And the way she came at me about it, you can tell it was like, "Hey boy, don't do it like that." And I was like, really? If I was at any other place right now, I'd call you some names right now, but I can't so let's just relax a little bit. It was just crazy that no one came to me like, you're Black, but it was just a presence that was there.

In this account, Epsilon described an encounter where one of the graduate students approached him in a disrespectful manner about a proof. He acknowledged that there was a sense of rudeness and condescension in her tone, which he equated to racial tensions being present. Also, "boy," which surfaces as thug in today's vernacular, has racial undertones and has been weaponized by Whites to racially undermine Black men (Adamson, 2016). In any other context, Epsilon disclosed that he would have given her a few choice words. Despite his displeasure, he decided to subdue his natural response, keep calm, and defuse the situation in order to remain and be perceived as professional in this research environment.

Epsilon's math experience at the HWI is in stark contrast to his HBCU experience. At Morehouse, he was positioned as a competent and developing math professional, while the people in his research group at the HWI viewed him as someone lacking math acumen, which is consistent with prior work contributing to the HBCU versus HWI debate in mathematics contexts (Jett, 2019a). Racism was couched in skepticism and criticism about his mathematical arguments, justifications, and proofs. Also, Epsilon was outnumbered in this research group. In other words, there were more of them (i.e., three White women) in comparison to him (i.e., one Black man), so issues of power and privilege were also at play.

Like Epsilon, Jeremiah is another student who was viewed as an astute math student at Morehouse, and he faced racial challenges in a summer REU. The following exchange unearthed details about his experience at an HWI:

> *Jeremiah:* At Protractor University, I noticed there was a lot of racism there, and I remember going to a party at a frat house and whew, I could just feel it in the air.
>
> *Chris:* How so?
>
> *Jeremiah:* So we showed up to the party, it was three Black guys, including myself, one Black woman and one White woman. So we showed up to this party, so you know, so I saw some people I knew up on the driveway, but they said you had to come through the front of the party; as soon as they said that I knew it was going to be kind of interesting. They said, "Do you know someone here?" and the White woman said she knew someone; she said, "I know such and such," so then we have to wait on the porch until such and such can verify that he knows her, and he does, so we walk in. It's not even a party, people are just standing around and drinking and like, I don't even think there's music being played, I don't even see anyone dancing so like, it's not even really what I came for, let's go ahead and leave. And then they said, "Oh, actually, he doesn't know you, so you guys all have to leave."

In this case, Jeremiah mentioned going to a house set, a gathering where folks were hanging out, socializing, and drinking. Within his group, the White woman had to vouch for knowing someone to let them all in the party. The White woman speaking on behalf of the group further represented the power and authority that was manifested in this space. Shortly thereafter, Jeremiah and his friends were informed that the guy did not know them after all. As a result, they were instructed to leave, confirming Jeremiah's hunches that racism was "in the air." This example is similar to Garcia et al.'s (2011) work regarding when parties become racialized. Using CRT, the authors found that White people dress up representing racial stereotypes or mock racial groups at their parties. As a result, White people's parties tend to turn away Black people. Therefore, parties, house sets, etc. like the one Jeremiah attended are pegged as being inherently racist.

Jeremiah provided another example at the HWI that was different in comparison to most of the race-related narratives that were shared during the brothers' interviews.

> I had a very opposite experience at Slide Rule University last summer. I was coming back from a math meeting at like midnight or 1 a.m. with one of the White guys, and the police stopped us like on the way back. So I think, I'm the only Black male in the family who hasn't had a gun pulled on me by the police, so there's a reason for my trepidation, so it turns out I was pretty worried, and he said, "Where are you guys headed?," and I was like, I know how this happens: "The dorm," and you know I was already feeling like, okay, this is going to probably go to the third degree, and he said, "Have you seen a White guy running around campus?" and gave some description, and I thought it was the most hilarious thing because I had all this stuff filled out in my mind. And I was like "No!" but in my mind, I was like, I hope you catch him.

Because of the racism endemic in society (Delgado & Stefancic, 2001), Jeremiah expected this situation to lead to interrogation at the least. His expectations were not far-fetched, given Black men's racial experiences with campus police at HWIs coupled with the unstable relationship between Black men and police officers writ large (Baldwin, 2018; Jenkins et al., 2021). As Jeremiah mentioned, all the Black men in his family have had guns pulled on them by police officers, which is a tragic and unfortunate state of affairs.

As with other Black men in this cohort, to recount all of his racial incidents could have led to a lengthier and exhausting interview with Jeremiah. To keep the study grounded in their personal experiences, I focused on the students' own experiences with racism and not that of their friends, families, and community members, even though I recognize that others' experiences influenced their racial understanding. Jeremiah reflected the impact those incidents had on him. He mentioned, however, that it was refreshing, so to speak, and rather ironic to have the police officers look for a White man as he was departing his math meeting.

On another note, there were some critical comments shared about race, and Robert's racial criticisms had some explicit connections to math.

> I feel like math is a great major to go into; it can be broad and be used in basically everything, but there needs to be more people

exposed to more than just what they dislike about it, especially in the Black community.

As Robert explains, there are innumerable applications of math concepts for many fields, and this point hits on the interdisciplinarity of mathematics knowledge (National Research Council, 2013). However, Robert recognized the necessity of more exposure to the broad array of applications associated with math. His plea that this exposure needs to especially happen within the Black community reveals the disdain typically associated with the discipline. As already noted, African Americans are racially mischaracterized with respect to their mathematical perspicacity because of structural and institutional racism; therefore, exposure to the benefits and practical uses of math in service to the Black community is a crucial way to legitimize Black students' interests and desires to go into the field.

RACIALIZED EXPERIENCES IN EVERYDAY LIFE

For centuries, Black people have had to contend with racism as a fact of life. The Black Lives Matter Movement has brought racial injustices to the forefront (Baldwin, 2018). The movement has spurred action on many fronts to value Black life. In spite of these public awareness efforts, Black lives are still undervalued. The 2020 murders of unarmed Breonna Taylor, Ahmaud Arbery, and George Floyd illuminated the deadly force that police use as an ongoing threat to Black life. Thus, the permanence of racial contestation has material consequences for Black people.

The sum total of being Black and male equates to a way of life where one must routinely deal with racial disgust, hostility, and malice. Early on, Black boys are bombarded with messages, visually, symbolically, or otherwise, that they are violent and criminal, among other negative portrayals. It is indeed a sad reality that "when a Black boy walks down the street, plays in a sandlot, or drives a car, his presence immediately conjures up associations of fear, threat, aggression, and danger" (Brown, 2018, p. 12). Because of these pervasive and pernicious stereotypes, Black boys must prepare for the racism that ensues throughout their entire lives.

The participants encountered racist acts in everyday life. Max commented on how he came to understand how racialized stereotypes manifest themselves.

> I remember one time, I was really young, maybe 12 or 13, I played
> a lot of basketball and one time my mom was at the bank, at
> the grocery store bank teller thing, but I came in playing, and I had
> on like basketball shorts, socks, flip flops, and undershirt. And I was
> like looking for the key or trying to get a dollar to get a drink. I wasn't

> dressed appropriately . . . so I like snuck up on my mom and grabbed her purse and this White woman got so startled and dropped her purse and got the attention of like over half the room, and I looked at her and went like, "Why are you scared? What did you think I was going to do? She's my mom."

Max had an eye-opening racial experience during his adolescence. As he communicated, his attire was not up to par in light of his contemporary thinking of what constituted appropriate attire. (It can be argued that street wear or athletic attire is a form of acceptable dress for an adolescent child or even an adult, for that matter.) The point here was that Max playfully snuck up on his mother and grabbed her purse, which also was typical, playful behavior for an adolescent child. Despite his innocuous intentions, he was shocked at the response from a White woman. Because of this White woman's misreading of Black boys' culture, her reaction caused others to follow suit and believe that he was committing an act of larceny—theft.

In this case, Max was playing with his mother, and there is nothing wrong with joking with *his* mother. However, to do this as a Black boy has severe broader racial implications when some onlookers perceive Black boys as violent and destructive. His example corroborates Bryan's (2021b) assertion that Black boys are harshly stereotyped and severely punished for and during childhood play. Recall that Tamir Rice was a 12-year-old Black boy who was killed while playing with a toy gun in the park because a White man called 911 and mentioned that there was a Black man in the public park with a gun (Baldwin, 2018; Bryan, 2021a). As a result, Black boys' routine play experiences could result in their death, as Max's adolescent experience in the presence of this White woman could have turned out differently.

Jared recounted being racially profiled in a store.

> It's got to be you know, it's some things you notice sometimes, when you walk into the store with a group of your friends, and you notice the clerk is really going far out of their way to check on you and your friends, to really keep an eye on you, instead of paying attention to the other group there, whose skin isn't necessarily dark.

Jared's statement indicated how some store clerks went out of their way to keep a tab on Black youth versus non-Black youth. His example was another instance of anti-Black racism where some store clerks acted as if Black youth would commit criminal acts (see Pittman, 2020). In another example, Marcus shared: "I'm pretty sure I have been racially profiled, like this lady followed me from the store one time, and I was like, why is this lady following me." This example conjures up the reprehensible killing of Trayvon Martin (de Casanova & Webb, 2017; Love, 2014). Again, these examples demonstrate the racist profiling that occurs with Black boys, and it is well-documented that Black male youth are regularly racially profiled (Adamson, 2016; Baldwin, 2018; Bryan, 2021a).

Jared also realized that there was some racial tension when he changed his hair as a young Black man.

> When I first got my hair twisted into locs, that first month I might
> have gotten pulled over three times, and it was just like pretty much
> for no reason. One time, I was in my mom's car, and the cop walks up
> to the car and he's like, "Let me see your license and all that," and he's
> like, "There's a robbery nearby and your car fits the description," and
> it was like, the car fits the description? I feel like it was more I fit the
> description: Black male, dreadlocks.

Jared grew up in predominantly Black contexts, so he acknowledged that being surrounded by Blackness in some ways shielded him from racism. However, he began to realize how race operates when he was pulled over a few times after he had dreadlocks. The incident he referenced stood out because it seemed fishy that the police officer would say that his car fit a description for a robbery. He believed it was a cop-out; in other words, he believed that he fit the description as a Black man with dreadlocks. Jared's narrative is consistent with the research of Smith et al. (2007) who argue in the article with the fitting title, "Assume the Position . . . You Fit the Description," that college-going Black men, too, are under increased surveillance via policing tactics.

Regarding racialized experiences, Epsilon's interview was one that stood out as intense and filled with emotion. He vocalized one life-altering experience with the Special Weapons and Tactics (SWAT) team.

> One time I was at my mother's house, they were actually looking for
> [redacted], the police came to the house, well the SWAT team came to
> the house. . . . I was coming out of the door, trying to get to my car
> because I didn't even know they were out there, and like, they rushed;
> and when I tell you, I've done some crazy things in my life, but it is
> a very humbling and very scary thing for 20 people to be standing
> around you with guns like this and I'm like, Please, whatever you do.
> I won't repeat everything that they said to me but like, basically, "Hey
> man, if you move, I'm going to fry you."

According to Epsilon, the SWAT team was looking for someone at his mother's residence. That person was not there when the legal authorities arrived, but Epsilon was. While seeking to go to his car, he was rushed by this team. He described begging and pleading for his life—begging the SWAT team not to kill him. He chose not to repeat the degrading things shouted at him during this awful ordeal, but he said that it succinctly boiled down to the possibility of having his life ended right there on the spot. Relatedly, Epsilon's experience touches upon Black men's ongoing challenges with law enforcement and the racial trauma that ensues as a result of it. Participants shared that several men in their family had negative experiences with police officers. This included Black men with and without advanced degrees, thereby countering the false reality that education makes Black men immune to the venoms of racism (Harcourt, 2009; Joseph, 2011).

Black men also contend with racism through digital media.[2] In these technologically savvy times, videos, blogs, and think pieces often circulate depicting the harsh treatment Black people receive from police officers, among other entities. Marcus brought attention to this and personalized it.

> I've seen some videos online about how police officers would treat Black people as opposed to White people, and there's a huge difference, like they always assume we're going to be hostile. And that's why I'm thankful I've never had a racial encounter with a police officer, knock on wood, but like, I don't know. I've learned that you don't wanna scare police officers because they're already scared as it is, and then on top of that, I'm a Black male, and I'm not a small Black male either, so I'm very wary around White people, more so because I feel they're gonna claim that I was gonna do something to them and do me more harm.

Although Marcus did not have any run-ins with police or law enforcement, his inclusion of the phrase "knock on wood" indicated that he knew he was not exempt from having one. His narrative unearthed the stereotypical messages in the mainstream about folks being afraid of Black men. Moreover, he mentioned how White people are more likely to claim that he, as a Black man, was going to do something to harm them. In his case, an argument could be made against him based on his body size alone. Marcus is a relatively stout Black man and could be falsely accused of inciting fear among those who ascribe to racist tropes about Black men. Thus, physical body size adds an additional layer to the complexities associated with Black manhood, and the gruesome killing of unarmed Michael Brown in Ferguson, Missouri, is a clear-cut example of using body size as a bogus excuse to claim being threatened by the Black male body (Bonilla & Rosa, 2015).

Without question, negative stereotypes pervade the discourse regarding Black people. The participants were cognizant and critical of these racial interpretations. Ray's narrative confirmed this.

> Someone was talking about, Blacks composed 12% of the
> population but commit 90% of the crimes. I'm like, I'm pretty
> sure those numbers are skewed. They say like we don't aspire to be
> anything, I will say that is completely untrue. Even amongst those
> of us that don't go here, I've hardly seen anyone that just wants to
> remain on the streets.

Ray believed the reports on the numbers of crimes committed were skewed in order to paint a negative picture of Black people. Essentially, he claimed these statistics are ludicrous. His critique is parallel to Toldson's (2019) argument that several of the stereotypes used to shine a negative light on Black people are bad statistics (BS). Even in areas that have been designated as "high-crime areas," Baldwin (2018) points out:

> We must be clear that there is not always a direct correlation between a
> "high-crime area" and actual high rates of crime. . . . These high-crime areas
> are heavily policed, the citizens in these communities are stopped and detained
> at enormous rates, and the residents are disproportionately represented in our
> prisons and jails. In short, because of their racial and sometimes economic
> make-up, these neighborhoods are disproportionately subject to greater levels
> of interaction and management at the hands of police agents and through the
> medium of the criminal justice system. These communities have become over-
> criminalized. (p. 442)

In all, these fallacies "support a false premise that African Americans are more dangerous and prone to criminal behavior" (Baldwin, 2018, p. 433).

Robert's narrative also illustrates how deficit societal perceptions can influence the public's views about Black people.

> Society perceives Black men as threats in the sense that they probably
> perceive Black men as violent or dangerous or committing a crime
> or ignorant or not as smart as they are, or not as smart as the rest of
> society; basically, as a threat, not in a good way, but something bad
> was gonna happen when Black men are around.

Again, Robert's narrative highlights the many ways that people in society are misinformed about Black men. As he indicated and as is echoed loud and clear in societal discourse, Black men are often viewed as menacing, treacherous, and unintelligent. As a result, masculinized racism thrust upon Black men suggests that something bad will occur while interacting with us.

As an extension of these misguided notions, there are also standards associated with what constitutes an exceptional Black person. Malik critiqued this line of thinking:

> One person told me, I had to be the exceptional [n-word], because
> when you go to interviews and you're Black, and the stuff they
> write down—he talks well, and stuff like that, not really credentials.
> I think it's all stupid. Even Black people do it too, they're like "Take
> your hat off, pull your pants up, talk better," so you can be more
> White, because they think if you're more White, you can be more
> successful.

Malik indicated that racist ideologies shape perceptions concerning who can and cannot be successful. These deficit philosophies equate Whiteness with success and erroneously equate Blackness with failure. Malik spoke passionately about challenging these racist ideas, and he pointed out that some Black people are beholden to these race-based viewpoints as well. Conversely, scores of examples substantiate that being dressed in a suit, speaking with proper grammar, and acting in a professional manner does not protect a Black man from racial discrimination (Harcourt, 2009; Joseph, 2011).

MOREHOUSE AS A RACIALLY AFFIRMING SPACE

As noted earlier, HBCUs have been heralded as spaces that racially empower, inspire, and motivate Black students, and this has been true since their inception (Albritton, 2012; Favors, 2019). In the face of the ever-present racism in society, HBCUs provide a safe haven for Black students to thrive. Thus, HBCUs are antiracist educational spaces for African American students. Morehouse is the only HBCU whose mission is squarely centered on racially empowering Black men. Distinct from studies that report on Black men's racial discrimination at HWIs (e.g., Harper, 2015; Smith et al., 2016), this traditionally single-gender Black institutional space is a disruption from the racism that is pervasive in other higher educational spaces and in society in general.

Asa explained how this institutional space was an affirming one for him during college.

> Just the experience, and not just the math department, just the
> experience of being around more African American males who want
> to achieve and who want to make a difference in the world has been
> an amazing experience for me. Because like I said in high school, I
> didn't see any of that. There weren't a lot of African American males.
> I was always the only Black male in my AP classes and stuff, so I
> wouldn't see that. And so, coming here, I'm able to see that, and it's
> really just been a great experience for me.

As he indicated, the experience of being around so many Black male academics was astonishing. These Black men aspired to achieve their goals and make a difference in the world. Juxtaposing his educational experiences, he expressed that his Morehouse experience was in direct opposition to his high school experience where he was the only Black male student in an AP class, for example. To reiterate, Morehouse's critical mass of Black male scholars affirmed these Black men as academics, (peer) role models, and leaders.

These brothers also spoke about race generally when talking about Morehouse. As they did, they talked relentlessly about the negative stereotypes surrounding Black people. Darius shared:

> Stereotypes come from somewhere, so a lot of the stereotypes that go on about Black people, there aren't truths to them. Clearly, you can't make absolute statements about people. People are different. At the same time, by me coming here, I have seen a lot of progress that we've made. It's good to see people try to break those stereotypes.

Darius emphatically stated that there is no truth to many of the stereotypes about Black people (see Toldson, 2019). He emphasized that absolute statements cannot be generalized to represent an entire racial group of people. Attending Morehouse, he has seen and witnessed the progress being made by Black people, and he reported that these Black people break those deficit stereotypes. In other words, being in this institutional space has not only countered these stereotypes but also provided him with even more hopeful outlooks about Black people.

Michael noted his positive collegiate experience and mentioned how prospective employers and other professionals come to Morehouse to seek out Black men.

> I mean my experience at Morehouse has been pretty good. Opportunities that I never thought or dreamed of happened here at Morehouse, just opportunities, awards, me meeting different people, networking with different people just because I went to Morehouse, so people come to Morehouse to look for Black males for like jobs. That's one of the reasons why I came here. It was clear that people come to Morehouse to look for Black males for something. And coming to Morehouse has definitely given me the idea that I can do anything that I put my mind to.

In the excerpt, Michael notes that he received opportunities because of his institutional affiliation. These things, he argued, led him to attend college at Morehouse, bolstered his self-efficacy, and left a favorable impression of his college experience. Like Michael, the other participants shared that they had a positive experience at Morehouse. The participants' contemporary narratives during their time as college students mirror the inspirational stories of 30 alumni spanning the 1948 to 2001 graduating classes profiled in *Speakers of the House: Morehouse Men Reflect on their Journeys to Manhood* about the positive developmental impact that Morehouse had on them as Black men and leaders (Eaves, 2006).

In Chapter 5, I provided some examples of the majors' interactions with math alumni, but their interactions with alumni extended beyond their disciplinary connections. For example, Marcus was welcomed to lunch with more mature alumni in Chapter 3. In another instance, Allen drew attention to this phenomenon.

> Even random alumni you see on the street, if they see you wearing a [Morehouse] hat or the keychain, they'd stop to just have a conversation with you and just be extremely supportive and just tell you to keep on going.

Allen also benefited from Morehouse's network of Black men. He spoke about how random alumni would stop current students who were wearing institutional *paraphernalia* to denote their enrollment at the college. These alumni would engage in small talk with the students and offer encouraging words to these young Black men to support them along their collegiate journey. Thus, this large quantity of Black men—administrators, faculty, staff, alumni, and students—cultivated the racially affirming space at Morehouse and strengthened the institutional brotherhood.

CONCLUSION

This chapter reported on the brothers' racialized experiences. They experienced subtle forms of racism such as being negatively stereotyped, being followed, and grappling with bogus statistics regarding the criminal acts committed by Black men. They also experienced overt forms of racism such as dealing with law enforcement, being assaulted with racially loaded talk, and having their intelligence questioned in academic spaces. The 16 participants hailed from and completed internships in different geographical areas, so these racial incidents happened with frequency all over the country, debunking the myth that overt racism only happens in the deep South. Therefore, Black boys and men writ large must deal with the deeper racial problems in society that also manifest in math-related contexts.

Overall, racial issues remained salient in the lives of these Black men. However, the participants did not allow racist attributions, attitudes, beliefs, and stereotypes to diminish their confidence concerning their mathematical abilities or stifle their mathematical achievements. In addition, racist discourses did not alter their desires to persist in the field. The final chapter explores their career aspirations and outlines the implications that emanated from this ethnographic study.

CHAPTER 7

Moving Forward

That's the thing I like most about Morehouse in general—the family feel of it. That's how I feel about the math department; it's like my family.

—Jeremiah

Jeremiah's excerpt confirms the family-like feel of the department. As the previous chapters have shown, the brothers' times together have been fun, comical, serious, demanding, and sometimes confrontational, all of which are reminiscent of the dynamics associated with biological family members. In this study, the family unit consisted of peers, faculty, staff, and alumni. This family dynamic provided the majors with what they needed to move forward with their goals.

This final chapter concludes the reporting of the entire study while participants' voices continue to be amplified. I begin with a portrait of their future goals and aspirations and then discuss the implications for undergraduate math education. Implications for families, K–12 math educators, and stakeholders concerned with broadening the participation of Black men in the mathematical sciences are presented. Additionally, recommendations for policymakers and researchers are offered. I close the book by reiterating the familial and fraternal bond in this study.

FUTURE GOALS AND ASPIRATIONS

Morehouse's undergraduate mathematics program uniquely encourages, supports, and challenges students, so it stands to reason that it also has a consistent track record of launching Black men into math-intensive graduate programs and career pathways. As highlighted in Chapter 1, Morehouse is the top producer of Black male math majors in the nation (U.S. Department of Education, 2019). Morehouse is also the number one baccalaureate-origin of African American male doctoral degree holders. Table 7.1 depicts the participants' career aspirations. Their time at Morehouse has strengthened their resolve to achieve these goals.

Table 7.1. Brothers' Career Aspirations

Brother	Grad School	Anticipated Area of Study	Career Aspiration
Allen	Yes	Engineering	Engineer
Andre	Yes	Mathematics	High School Mathematics Teacher
Asa	Yes	Computational Finance & Risk Management	Undecided
Daniel	No	N/A	Minister
Darius	Yes	Applied Mathematics	Mathematics Professor
Epsilon	Yes	Mathematics	Mathematics Professional or Professor
Jared	Yes	Computer Science	Cybersecurity Professional
Jeremiah	Yes	Mathematics	Mathematics Teacher & Mentor
John	Yes	(Secondary) Mathematics Education	Financial Analyst or Mathematics Teacher
Malik	Yes	Statistics	Public Health Professional
Marcus	Yes	Mathematics	Mathematics Professor
Max	Yes	Public Policy	Diplomat
Michael	Yes	Economics	Academic
Ray	Yes	Mathematics	Cryptographer
Robert	Yes	Applied Mathematics, Computer Science, Actuarial Science, or Law	Business Owner
Tony	No	N/A	Engineer & Serial Entrepreneur

The brothers' graduate school aspirations hold a lot of promise for the mathematical sciences. As highlighted earlier, Black men account for approximately 2.37% of undergraduate mathematics degrees annually, and those small numbers are even more miniscule at the graduate level. Thus, Black men's enrollment and persistence in graduate mathematics programs is also of significant national concern (Jett, 2019a). Figure 7.1 indicates that 14 out of 16, or 87.5%, of these Black men plan to attend graduate school. Further, 10 out of 16, or 62.5%, plan to attend graduate school in the mathematical sciences. This percentage is much larger in comparison to the 17% of all graduating senior math majors from bachelor's degree granting institutions (with 15% from doctoral-level institutions and 12% from master's level institutions) headed to graduate school in the mathematical

Figure 7.1. Brothers' Graduate School Aspirations

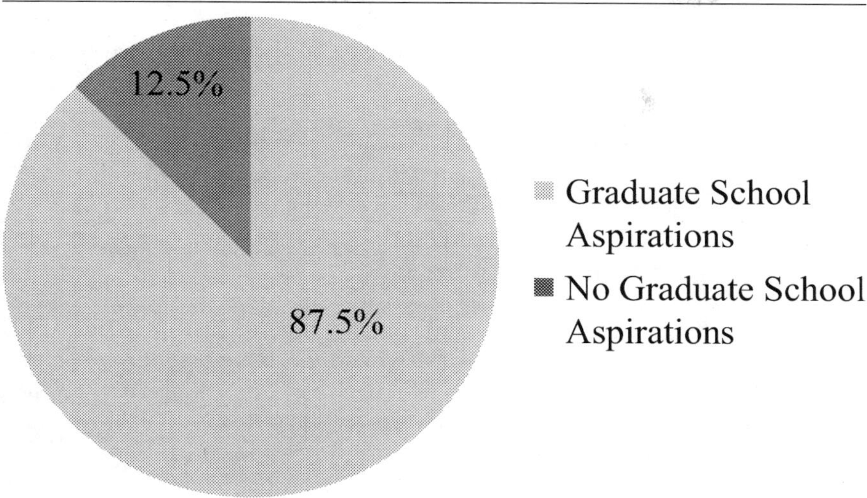

sciences (Blair et al., 2013). This large percentage of African American male participants with graduate school aspirations as they approach their undergraduate degree completion is encouraging, especially given that they are earnestly desirous of a career in the mathematical sciences.

The majors' professional aspirations provide a similarly encouraging glimpse of their potential contributions to the field. Their career goals include occupations within and beyond the traditional mathematics ecosystem. Interestingly, quite a few of the majors, 7 out of 16 to be exact, are interested in pursuing careers in math education[1] (i.e., teacher, professor, or academic). This striking realization suggests that an empowering undergraduate mathematics space can be an incubator for propelling African American men into teaching-oriented positions. The majors can see themselves as math faculty because of their day-to-day interactions with the Black math scholars at Morehouse.

Darius, who plans to enroll in a graduate mathematics program, pointed out:

> The support I've gotten here. Like I said, my growing interest in it [mathematics] has made me feel like there's nothing else I'd want to do more. Like I said, the professors here, my parents and people just telling me I can do it and move forward.

Again, Darius applauds the support that he has received at Morehouse. Additionally, his interest in the field has grown during his matriculation in this math community. As a result, there is nothing he wants to do more than fulfill his mathematics career goals, and he acknowledged his village with providing him the motivation to move forward.

Epsilon is another brother who plans to enroll in a graduate mathematics program. He boasted:

> I feel like I'm smart enough to do it [mathematics], I feel like I can do it, and I feel like I can succeed. So I feel like my brain in math is good enough so that I should be talked about amongst elite mathematicians, so that's the reason I want to do it. You guys are going to give me my props because my props are due.

Without question, Epsilon loves math and feels compelled to earn a PhD in the discipline. He believes that he should be talked about like other elite mathematicians (see Graham et al., 2018, and the associated website, *Mathematically Gifted and Black* [mathematicallygiftedandblack.com], for profiles of distinguished Black mathematics professionals). In other words, he believes that folks should put some respect on his name, as commonly touted in hip-hop discourse.

In many ways, Morehouse is a launching pad for this cohort to build their math identities and leap forward with their career aspirations. The institution has provided them with access to admirable Black men, and they are building on and extending Morehouse's rich history of Black male math excellence mentioned in Chapter 1. The ending of their undergraduate mathematics degree program is the beginning of their life as professionals, and their experiences provide substantive implications that are instructive for the field.

IMPLICATIONS FOR UNDERGRADUATE MATH EDUCATION

This study unearthed the concept of mathematical brotherhood with this cohort of majors in this collegiate community. The salient themes encapsulate the distinguishing characteristics of mathematical brotherhood found within it. With that, the following implications, although not exhaustive, complement and extend these big ideas and are especially pertinent for undergraduate math education:

- Cultivate a racially affirming institution.
- Develop a robust peer network.
- Establish a culture of respect.
- Build a dedicated and committed faculty.
- Promote collective persistence across the college years.
- Give back and empower others.

First, this study suggests that Black men matriculate in racially affirming institutions to foster mathematical brotherhood and build community. This finding is consistent with prior work using Black masculinity theory and CRT with Black male college students to emphasize the relationship between racial-affirmation and collegiate success (Brooms, 2017a; Dancy, 2012). Because Morehouse is a traditionally single-gender institution, its mission is devoted to empowering Black men. As mentioned, HBCUs and BGLOs also provide racially affirming environments for Black men. Regarding undergraduate mathematics programs, this study suggests that systems be in place to buttress brothers' racialized and gendered identities.

Another implication is centered on establishing a robust peer network. Given that students must frequently work collegially to solve math problems, this study suggests that peers are integral to building brotherhood and community. The Black male participants indicated that they spent an inordinate amount of time in the Math Lab, and they reported spending time in peer groups in math apprenticeships outside the institution. Thus, peer intervention at the student level is critically important so that Black men can thrive in a safe, trusting, and empowering mathematics learning community.

The next implication builds on the finding of third floor respect. That is, the mathematics community must respect Black men in practice to establish a culture that welcomes and validates them. This study suggests that collegiate educators should position Black male math majors as peer leaders and invite Black male professionals to courses, seminars, and other campus events so that Black male math majors can see themselves following a similar, albeit personalized, math pathway (Jett, 2019a, 2022b). The chief takeaway is that Black men represent a large untapped talent pool of individuals who can enter the field if they are provided with educational opportunities that respect and affirm their humanity in mathematics contexts.

As noted in Chapter 4, this study showed that this cohort spent a significant amount of time with the department chair and other dedicated and committed math faculty. This engagement over the years fostered stronger longitudinal relationships with the faculty, and the participants overwhelmingly expressed positive interactions with them. It bears repeating that they gravitated toward the Black math faculty. This suggests that Black students positively relate and interact with Black faculty and underscores the need to hire and support more Black faculty in undergraduate mathematics spaces, recognizing that Black faculty should not be burdened with an excessive amount of mentoring to minoritized students. Also, the participants expressed that the math faculty believed in and anticipated their success. In mathematics, if and only if, commonly abbreviated iff, indicates that "two sentences are necessary and sufficient conditions for one another's truth" (Borowski & Borwein, 1991, p. 280). With that, this study asserts that math faculty should be allowed access to African American male math students iff they honestly believe in their natural brilliance and they work to manifest it within college settings.

Connected to that, a faculty implication is centered on the messages sent to Black male students. In this study, affirming messages were conveyed to students by publicly acknowledging their mathematical accomplishments, encouraging them to enroll in subsequent math courses, offering special topics courses for them, and helping them to secure research internships. Also, professors' supportive comments on students' papers and exams made a huge difference for the participants. Therefore, faculty should not underestimate the power of an encouraging word or act to affirm African American male students' mathematical intelligence.

The IPEDS national data regarding Black men in undergraduate mathematics programs shared in Chapter 1 indicate that programmatic structures must improve if persistence rates are to do the same. This study, in highlighting the participants' successes and belonging early on at Morehouse, points to the need for undergraduate mathematics educators to pay particular attention to the first academic year. While students' declaration of the math major is a significant first step, research shows that students who persist through the first year often succeed in attaining mathematics degrees (Bressoud et al., 2015; Seymour & Hunter, 2019). The first year often includes Calculus 1 and 2, which are key courses linked to mathematical persistence (Ellis et al., 2014). Thus, the first year serves as the base year for math majors, and the pedagogy in these courses is crucial for supporting and retaining Black men in the major.

Even though the first year is critical, subsequent years are equally important for supporting and increasing persistence in the major for African American male students. The following years include math courses that require students to function at a higher cognitive level. To support students in later years, one recommendation comes from Michael, who remarked:

> Every tutor in this department can tutor a Calc 1 student. But only one person in this department, that's like hired to tutor like a Differential Geometry course or an Abstract Algebra 2 course or something like that, so somehow find helpful outside resources for students who are taking Abstract Algebra 2 . . . or Real Analysis.

Michael revealed that one way to offer support in upper-level courses is to locate resources or hire tutors for advanced math content. His assertion that everybody can tutor students in Calculus 1 implies that the majors would either know Calculus 1 exceptionally well or not struggle with it in the same manner associated with upper-level courses. Recall that Epsilon mentioned tutoring students in several advanced math courses. This study's data suggests that the majors served as each other's peer tutors in these courses, and they took advantage of faculty office hours. However, Michael's recommendation extends beyond having a single tutor for upper-level courses. His point yields an exploratory opportunity to address this issue, especially for those in (primarily) undergraduate institutions without the luxury of graduate mathematics assistants.

Linking persistence to the mathematics curriculum and coursework, Table 3.1 showed that the vast majority of the majors identified Real Analysis as their most challenging course. In this way, Real Analysis was a high-stakes course. An in-between course could have eased this burden, and John's statement gets at the heart of this: "Set Theory, of course that's the basis of theory, but I think there should be another class that connects from Calculus to Analysis. A transition course . . . with a transition course, it'll probably be a lot easier." To facilitate a more seamless transition to Real Analysis, John suggested adding a transition course[2] to bridge the gap between the Calculus sequence and Real Analysis. As such, a practical recommendation would be to include a transition-style, introduction to proof-writing, or seminar in advanced math course to improve students' mathematical persistence.

In tandem with John's recommendation, Andre's statement addresses this issue on a broader scale.

> If everything were more interconnected where we could walk from one class and say, oh yeah, we were just talking about this; if it were clearer to more students, it would probably bring more students into the major. Maybe it would bring more credibility to the department.

Andre's recommendation is for faculty to better link concepts in a conceptually coherent manner. Because of the AUC's cross registration process, Morehouse students can take math courses at consortium institutions. While these diverse course offerings are commendable, this recommendation specifies that efforts should be shored up to systematically interweave mathematical ideas across courses.

Taken a step further, departmental representatives could partner with Business, Industry, and Government (BIG) professionals to stay current with ongoing needs and developments in the field (Levy et al., 2018). Levy and colleagues recommend that math faculty "invite BIG scientists to provide curriculum review and advice" (p. 115). Pragmatic feedback provides real and fresh insights from working professionals in the mathematical sciences, satisfies the participants' desire to link theory and practice as mentioned in Chapter 4, and gets at Andre's recommendation to "bring more credibility to the department." Similarly, Allen shared:

> I'd say having a more uniform expectation of what students should learn because I could take one class and there's a second level to

that class, and you may be in that second level of the class. They might expect you to learn something that you should have learned in the beginning of . . . well, something you should have learned in the previous class that may or may not have been taught or reviewed.

Allen voiced his concerns about having more uniformity across courses. Many courses in the math major are sequential wherein disciplinary skills are built incrementally; hence, success in the subsequent course requires profound knowledge of the ideas learned in the prerequisite course (Dahlke, 2011). Thus, Allen's recommendation is for faculty to adequately cover important topics, especially those that will resurface in future coursework, for these brothers to stay the course across the undergraduate years.

In addition, these brothers expressed wanting to reach out, work with, and mentor younger math learners. This desire by HBCU students to give back to the broader Black community finds support in the research literature (Albritton, 2012). As suggested by this study, this desire is prominent among Black men and satisfies a need to present more positive images surrounding Black manhood. Many of the study participants were tutoring local students to complete the required service hours for scholarships, and some were volunteering through community organizations. With the benefits and growth of service-learning courses,[3] opportunities and incentives exist for college students to receive course credit for assisting math learners in local schools, community programs, and other outreach initiatives. Along with a desire to give back outside the institution, it is important to reiterate that these brothers also rendered their talents to and empowered each other in this collegiate community.

IMPLICATIONS FOR FAMILIES

This section unpacks the implications for families (the term *families* is used expansively to include parents, grandparents, family members, guardians, and caregivers). Education begins at home, and families play a crucial, continual role as educational guides, agents, and champions. Implications for families include:

- Incorporate math in daily activities.
- Facilitate participation in math-related events.
- Seek educational settings that build robust math identities.
- Use resources to scaffold math learning.
- Engage in ongoing conversations about race and racism.

One recommendation is to involve Black boys in math activities early. Chapter 2 described how the participants' families used out-of-school, everyday activities such as shopping, dining out, and playing games to build the participants' number sense and fluency. Other activities such as cooking, traveling, and attending athletic events provide unique math enrichment opportunities. To the fullest extent possible, families should engage in these activities with their Black boys to ensure they regularly practice their math skills, which ultimately helps them gain some mathematical footing. Considering the majors' home-based experiences, families should build Black boys' mathematical confidence in the home early so they develop robust math identities that will later serve them well.

Deeper analysis of the 16 participants' experiences reveals that Black boys are mathematically inquisitive, astute, and ambitious. As substantiated by this cohort's experiences, families should make certain that their children participate in math clubs, friendly competitions, and related events. Also, families should explore different methods of approaching problems at home when helping their Black sons. In addition to school-based programs, families should utilize local programs, community initiatives, and online resources to further develop their Black boys' math skills. In sum, families should be in Black boys' mathematical corners and provide opportunities for them to nurture their mathematical abilities.

Contrary to deficit-based mindsets about Black families, research shows that African American parents are deeply concerned about their children's education (Cooper, 2009; Hrabowski et al., 1998; Thompson, 2008). Even more telling was Thompson's (2003) study with 129 African American parents, which created a list of their 10 most frequently cited school-related problems. The top item on the parents' list was the school district's racial climate, and the second was centered on their children's struggles with mathematics. This suggests, as this study's findings attest, that Black parents should especially be on guard and advocate for their Black boys in these two critical areas.

As it pertains to race, the 16 participants showed that racism is so entrenched within the American fabric that for students to thrive and fulfill their potential, they must learn to confront racist ideologies. Racist epithets were spewed at them as early as kindergarten. Boutte and Bryan (2021) say that "White children are 'apprentices' who learn [racism] through observation" (p. 241), and many White children observe racist practices from parents in their homes. One piece of evidence that supports this finding was found within Tony's example in Chapter 6 when his former best friend, a White child, informed him that he was instructed by his father not to play with Tony because of his race. Such racist tropes plant the seeds that sustain White supremacy and ensure that racism continues to flourish and thrive in American society. Therefore, a recommendation for White families is to have ongoing race-related conversations with their children to awaken their racial consciousness, especially with respect to anti-Blackness, and obliterate racist ideologies, remarks, practices, and tactics.

IMPLICATIONS FOR K–12 MATH EDUCATION

This study lends itself to implications for K–12 math education that are centered on making the classroom space more amenable to Black male mathematical brilliance. For practitioners, the implications include the following:

- Awaken and nurture Black boys' math identities.
- Create transformative learning environments.
- Legitimize Black males' innovative thinking.
- Don't negatively stereotype Black boys.
- Recommend Black boys to gifted programs.
- Connect with and learn from Black families and community stakeholders.

Table 2.1 showed that almost all of the participants pinpointed a schooling experience whereby they solidified their interest in math. This finding clearly demonstrates that math teachers across the K–12 grade levels play a crucial role in awakening, nurturing, and cultivating African American male students' math identities. Evidence-based recommendations for doing so include assessing Black male students' funds of knowledge, infusing cultural math referents, and setting high expectations for math success (Berry et al., 2011; Jett et al., 2015; Stinson et al., 2013). Alongside this, the Benjamin Banneker Association advocates infusing justice-oriented concepts into the curriculum to augment Black students' math learning (BBA, 2017).

What is clear in the study described in this book is that members of the mathematical brotherhood at this HBCU reported, with excitement, valuable school-based learning experiences where they could be innovative regarding mathematical ideas. They persevered with mathematical problem solving, reasoned, and modeled as well as represented mathematical ideas in multiple forms. These characteristics constitute the hallmarks of mathematically proficient students (NCTM, 2014). With that, there is an urgent need for K–12 teachers to transform learning environments so that African American male students become excited about math. This study's findings also point to a critical need for educators to appreciate and legitimize Black male students' multiple ways and methods of expressing and representing mathematical ideas.

As discussed, these 16 Black male students' exposure to math in their home lives influenced their schooling experiences. Ellington and Frederick's

(2010) study with eight Black math majors found that all were from two-parent households; the participants in this study differ because they were reared in two-parent households, households with a stepparent, and single-parent households, and raised by grandparents. They also hailed from households with a diverse range of social strata. The point is that all of these home environments represented spaces where mathematical brilliance resided. Therefore, one recommendation for K–12 practitioners is not to stereotype Black male students based on home dynamics or resources but to recognize their inner mathematical prowess.

Adding to the body of knowledge regarding Black children's mathematical brilliance (Leonard & Martin, 2013), many of the participants were enrolled in TAG programs and AP Calculus. K–12 educators should ensure that Black boys have access to these rich learning opportunities to build their disciplinary knowledge (Davis et al., 2019). The participants also overwhelmingly used discourse that elevated their mathematical self-efficacy. These phrases, informed by a strengths-based paradigm, included: "I've always liked math;" "I've always been good at math;" and "Math is my favorite subject." These internal musings were supported with actionable behaviors and consequently manifested outwardly to bolster their math identity.

Compare the participants' sayings to the comments of students impaired by negative mathematical self-talk, such as: "I've never been able to understand math;" "I'm not good at math;" or "I'm going to fail this math class." The issue with the latter is that these counterproductive phrases are a misrepresentation of mathematical virtuosity and can become a self-fulfilling prophecy. As a result, K–12 teachers should include validatory pledges, inspiring songs, and positive affirmations that allow Black male students to embrace robust math identities so that they ultimately affirm their mathematical brilliance.

Moreover, K–12 math teachers should continue to connect, partner, and leverage Black families and community organizers' expertise to support African American male students. A community-based disciplinary example is the M^3 program (Bellamy & Berry, 2017). The aim of the "Math, Men, and Mission" (M^3 or M-Cubed) program is "to increase Black boys' participation in upper-level mathematics and to provide Black boys with mentors to support their social and academic development" (p. 28). Another example is Eagle Academy of New York City that was founded when parents, community leaders, corporate partners, and members of the 100 Black Men of New York, Inc. joined forces to improve the academic achievement outcomes for African American male students (Quigley & Mitchell, 2018). Malik's narrative enriches this recommendation.

> You [Black boys] gotta see people like me, I talk to girls, I still
> go to parties, I still have fun, I still dress like I have swag, I still

wear Jordans, I don't wear Clarks like that, I still own a chain; but really, send someone back like me who they can relate to, and then also, guide them: you know, just because you sag your pants and wear a chain doesn't necessarily mean you will be successful either. Let them know they can be themselves and guide them when they get there, and don't tell them to change themselves. Don't tell them they're not good enough as themselves.

When entering these programmatic spaces, Malik draws upon Black masculine style and recommends that Black male students see Black men with whom they can relate. He challenges traditional thinking about the apparel and behaviors that are characteristically associated with professionals, and his critique links to scholarship on *respectability politics* with respect to Black boys (Oeur, 2017). He cautions that young Black boys should understand that sagging pants and chains will not necessarily lead to success either. In essence, he advocates for a (math) space that allows Black boys to be their authentic selves. Interventions that conjoin school district and community organization personnel should leverage the individual strengths of Black male youth to remedy race-related and gender-specific challenges in math.

IMPLICATIONS FOR BROADENING THE PARTICIPATION OF BLACK MEN IN THE MATHEMATICAL SCIENCES

Within the last decade, national reports and professional organizations have called for the full participation of *all* individuals in the mathematical sciences, and we have much work to do regarding the full participation of Black men in the mathematical sciences (AMS, n.d.; NAM, n.d.; NSF, National Center for Science and Engineering Statistics, 2017). Implications for broadening the participation of Black men in the field include:

- Facilitate success during the undergraduate years.
- Improve dual-degree programs.
- Welcome Black men into math spaces.
- Socialize Black men into the mathematical sciences.
- Provide Black mentors.

I agree with Saxe and Braddy (2015) that "The fact that our community has been unable to attract and retain a diverse student population in the mathematical sciences is a dreadful shortcoming that must be remedied" (p. 24). And without a pool of potential African American male mathematics graduate students, efforts for increasing Black men's representation in the mathematical sciences are dead ends at worst and fantasies at best. As such, success during the undergraduate years has significant implications for maximizing Black men's propensity for post-undergraduate mathematics study. Therefore, swift action must be taken, especially at the undergraduate level, to broaden the participation of Black men in the mathematical sciences.

At Morehouse, the DDEP is one mechanism to expand opportunities for Black men in the mathematical sciences. In this study, five out of the 16 participants began college enrolled in the DDEP but switched their majors to math. While this is a win for the mathematical sciences broadly, this study's findings suggest that a more nuanced course of action is needed to improve the DDEP's timeframe across institutions given that these majors estimated that successful completion of the DDEP would take more than the 5 proposed years. Overall, the takeaway gleaned from these participants is that they desire to enroll in institutions and programs that have a positive racial climate and steadfast track record of supporting African American male students.

Examples of the racial challenges that African American male students continuously endure in the mathematical sciences have been presented throughout this book. Chapter 6 referred to the racial undercurrents that were present in Epsilon and Jeremiah's summer programs. Thus, one implication is for Black men to be authentically welcomed into mathematics research groups, institutions, and graduate programs. Jeremiah planned to attend this HWI's graduate mathematics program; what messages might such an experience teach him about his sense of belonging in that space? Therefore, math professionals should be aware of how Black men's experiences in REUs, internships, and so on can either inspire or hinder their desires to study math or seek employment opportunities in these places.

One promising feature about this study is the finding of the efforts exerted to socialize these Black men into the discipline—both within this institutional context and on a national scale. As mentioned, the participants presented their research at the Harriet J. Walton Symposium and learned from African American speakers via the Mathematics Colloquium Series. Some participants were able to attend the post–Dansby Lecture dinner, go to the JMM, or participate in the Putnam Competition. Similar efforts with accessible role models could hold significant promise for fostering belonging and ultimately broadening the participation of Black men in the mathematical sciences.

As this study shows, participants sought out, spoke with, and were inspired by several Black math professors, so the increased presence of Black faculty holds promise for broadening the participation of Black men in the (undergraduate) mathematical sciences. If there are no Black math faculty at higher education institutions, then where can Black students turn for direction, mentorship, and guidance that is responsive to their racialized experiences? Also, what impact might the exiguous amount of Black math faculty have on national efforts to broaden participation in the mathematical sciences? The good news is that many of the participants plan to enroll in graduate programs in the mathematical sciences, and this is especially promising given that over half of those with doctorates in the mathematical sciences begin employment in an academic position (Levy et al., 2018). This cohort may itself contribute to the growth of the Black male math professoriate. On the opposite end of the spectrum, imagine being a Black man and pursuing a PhD in mathematics with a critical mass of Black male scholars in a racially affirming institutional space such as Morehouse!

IMPLICATIONS FOR POLICY

The framing of Black boys and men in policy requires a paradigm shift. Incorporating more asset-based perspectives and findings from strength-based research could bring about more pragmatic policy changes. The findings from this study yield the following implications for policymakers:

- Establish partnerships with a variety of stakeholders.
- Dismantle racial tensions in educational policies.
- Increase federal funding to HBCUs in the mathematical sciences.
- Increase investments in early childhood math programs.
- Implement policies that respect Black men.

Policymakers must earnestly partner with scholars and laypersons who have the research and practical expertise regarding Black male students' experiences to develop policies catered to them, especially given that the Black male *voice* is often missing in these deliberations. A pointed example is My Brother's Keeper (MBK—see https://www.obama.org/mbka/network/ for more info). This policy initiative brings together Black men to strategize and act, "building on what works, when it works, in those critical life-changing moments" with respect to Black and other minoritized boys, as President Obama noted in 2014; policymakers should capitalize on the strengths of this initiative (U.S. Office of the Press Secretary, 2014, p. 45). Policymakers must include African American men in the policymaking process to offer invaluable insights to shape policy recommendations. Systemic and institutionalized racism coupled with other forms of discrimination impact Black men's math experiences (Farley, 2012; Harmon, 2019; Jett, 2019a). Bearing this in mind, policymakers should devise relevant reform efforts and federal mandates to mitigate these racial tensions in their formation, application, and implementation.

This study points to a need for more government spending to be allocated to this area. Certainly, policy should ensure that governmental expenditures are adequately targeted to HBCUs (Williams & Davis, 2019). HBCUs' significant production of Black mathematics graduates suggests that government spending and policy should be dedicated to continuously support this longstanding tradition. Given this study's findings regarding the crucial impact of early math learning, government spending and policy should be also directed to develop and sustain more meaningful early childhood math interventions for Black boys. Furthermore, policy groups should advocate for summer research opportunities given their strong relations to graduate school aspirations. Policy conversations should shift from access to completion of the major; as Chapter 1 drives home, Black male mathematics program *enrollment* is very different from Black male mathematics degree *completion*. Such conversations should lead to a purposive course of policy-related action to improve the undergraduate mathematics landscape for Black men.

The Joint Policy Board for Mathematics (JPBM) is a collaborative effort among math organizations to ensure that policymakers are aware of disciplinary initiatives. The JPBM should advocate for policy initiatives to advance discipline-based education research and for funding agencies to provide more financial support for DBER studies. Further, policy-making bodies should establish standing committees to stay abreast of policy-relevant research to inform governmental investment decisions, especially those targeted to Black men.

As it pertains to institutional policy, administrators and other stakeholders should create or revise policies so that they respect Black men in their multifaceted ways of being. Given that Black men grapple with racial stereotypes, microaggressions, and assaults in academic spaces, institutional policies should include conduct codes that minimize the likelihood of Black men being disrespected. On that point, procedures should be in place to enforce severe consequences on those who do not follow the established policies. A departmental policy implication could be to design an action council or advisory team charged with directing and ensuring that departmental spending priorities, programs, invited speakers, and faculty exhibit respect for African American male students. As opposed to the deficit orientations that attempt to eradicate the relationship between mathematical intelligence and Black masculinity, the policy implications from this study present vibrant alternatives to promote positive change concerning Black men's mathematical persistence.

IMPLICATIONS FOR FUTURE RESEARCH

This study suggests several notable directions for future research regarding the support of Black boys and men in math. Implications for moving the field forward include:

- Investigate children's racial consciousness.
- Examine collegiate mathematics communities.
- Explore the intricacies of Real Analysis.
- Study the impact of same-race and same-gender faculty.

- Utilize race-based frameworks.
- Collect longitudinal data.

Considering that issues of race and racism were a prominent feature in the participants' elementary experiences, early childhood researchers should study "what and how children develop racial attitudes" (Husband, 2012, p. 365). This current study suggests that overt racist tropes largely originated with White parents, so researchers should include parents in these investigations. In doing so, researchers could utilize CRT as a theoretical frame to promote transformative change regarding children's critical race consciousness. Moreover, race-related work deserves significant attention across the (math) education spectrum if we are to achieve true racial equity in the field.

Future DBER should fruitfully examine mathematics learning communities.[4] Given the participants' varying reasons coupled with the large number of African American male college students nationally who initially declare math as a major, RUME scholars should investigate their reasons for declaring this major. RUME scholars should also inquire why some Black men do not complete the major. As Tables 1.3 and 1.4 show, it is a national trend for Black men to switch out of math at an alarming rate. Figure 3.1 shows that some brothers in this cohort changed majors as well. Recall that Max switched out of physics because of the accumulation of bad interactions with his professors. Similarly, future work should examine whether there are material and unintended consequences associated with Black men's interactions with math faculty. As a whole, future research should explore the intricacies of mathematics learning communities to impact students' persistence in the major.

Table 3.1 indicated that Real Analysis was a challenge for the majority of the African American men in this study, and Real Analysis parties were designed to address previously expressed concerns about the course. Based on this study's finding about Real Analysis, RUME scholars should consider what happens in this course. In previous work, Lew et al. (2016) found that six Real Analysis students did not understand the professor's expressed central ideas. Ironically, the Real Analysis professor's peers rated his lecture as a magnificent one, highlighting the bifurcated professor/student benefits of an advanced mathematics lecture. Future investigations that critically examine Real Analysis professors' pedagogical practices, textbook selections, and supplementary materials in concert with students' peer networks, support resources, and understanding of proofs could substantially alleviate students' challenges with Real Analysis and other heavily proof-based courses.

Future research should explore the variations associated with the influence and impact of same-race and same-gender dynamics on Black male students' math learning outcomes. Researchers have examined Black K–12 math teachers' agentic experiences with African American children (Clark et al., 2013; Frank, 2019; McGee, 2014); comparable studies should be conducted with Black math professors and mathematicians (see Walker, 2014, for a notable example), as there are many unanswered questions in the scholarly canon regarding Black men's math experiences. Also, this study occurred during the majors' final year. Including students from various classes in future work could yield nuanced findings across the undergraduate years. Further, researchers should collect data longitudinally to advance the knowledge base concerning Black men's mathematical participation.

Future studies should use a Black masculinist frame to explore Black men's experiences at HBCUs. Researchers should also investigate other minoritized groups' mathematics learning communities. Earlier, I mentioned Jones Williams's (2017) study examining the experiences of Black women who earned their mathematics degree from Spelman, in which she drew on Black feminist theory. Studying Black women at the undergraduate level offers insights to promote gendered-racial equity in the field and provides a more holistic picture of Black students' collective math experiences. Research grounded in Black feminist and masculinist frameworks could unearth aspects of collaboration versus competition, for example, and make sense of any gendered similarities and differences. An asset-based comparative study could crystallize how racialized and gendered identities, both individually and collectively, inform how Black students build mathematical camaraderie and community.

Additionally, researchers could use CRT to explore what happens once Black men leave their safe haven, such as an HBCU, and enter graduate programs at HWIs or the profession. On another note, future research should explore why some Black undergraduate mathematics degree completers choose not to pursue math-related graduate education, decide to later work outside the field, or do not enter the mathematics workforce at all. Drawing upon Frank et al.'s (2021) research design and national study exploring why Black math teachers consider leaving the teaching profession, researchers could adapt analogous methods to obtain a nationally representative sample of African American math majors to ascertain whether and why they consider leaving the mathematics workforce. Examining the experiences of African Americans who stay the course could also be a promising line of research and contribute much to DBER that will advance our understanding about the assets that African Americans bring to the field.

CODA

Black Male Success in Higher Education: How the Mathematical Brotherhood Empowers a Collegiate Community to Thrive highlights the stories of 16 awe-inspiring graduating senior math majors who shared information about themselves and their experiences in Morehouse's mathematics learning community, and thinks about those stories using Black masculinity theory and CRT. In a manner comparable with how fraternity brothers share the experience of pledging together, these brothers have the shared experience of majoring in math together. Of course, they did not get there alone; they had multiple sources of support, guidance, and encouragement paving the way for the possibility of this collegiate experience. This village that motivated them to persist with their undergraduate studies included their families, peers, teachers, professors, administrators, alumni, and community members. Often, individuals portray effortless achievement as the sign of true mathematical talent. However, this study demonstrates that, while these Black men had some mathematical curiosities, inclinations, and gifts—which earned them various mathematical accolades—they also worked hard to succeed in this space. Forthrightly, their narratives demonstrate that they were profoundly steadfast and deeply committed to their college studies.

As has been exhibited, Morehouse challenges, encourages, and supports African American men mathematically and offers much to the literature on Black manhood. Consequently, there is so much to learn from the Black men in this mathematics learning community as evidenced from the historical portrait presented in Chapter 1 to the contemporary study of this cohort of 16 majors. Morehouse's context asserts that Black men are: (1) scholars, experts, and leaders; and (2) burgeoning math specialists, brilliant mathematical thinkers, and venerable producers of math knowledge. An important takeaway here is the strengths-based framing of Black men in Morehouse's mathematics learning community. This positioning presents new possibilities, imaginations, and visions concerning what these brothers can achieve in the field.

In closing, the mathematical brotherhood represents a dynamic group who generally had an empowering, affirming, and liberating experience at this HBCU. Although everyone did not have the most glorious time in the Department of Mathematics, they cannot deny the influence of the mathematical brotherhood. That is, Morehouse Mathematics validates them by presenting constructive narratives about Black manhood and strengthening their mathematical acumen. In his treatise about the "Morehouse Mystique," Eaves (2009) argues that Morehouse makes a difference. This ethnographic study extends this assertion and demonstrates that the mathematical brotherhood made a significant difference to the 16 participants in this study. I hope this book provides a message of hope regarding the participants' experiences in this institutional space of Black male excellence and inspires many Black boys and men to thrive while achieving all of their math-related dreams, goals, and aspirations.

Afterword

How do we capture the essence of an institution—its most important work, its mission, its legacy? Christopher Jett has painted an incredible portrait of a slice of life at Morehouse College through its mathematics department, students, faculty, and alumni. Having spent quite a bit of time at Morehouse (which my late father attended) and the other AUC institutions, I can attest that there is indeed a palpable sense of alchemy in the air. History was and continues to be made there, as Jett writes so compellingly in *Black Male Success in Higher Education*. In addition to the feel of magic, there are very real structures and practices undergirding excellence that are deeply rooted in longstanding traditions. As I have written elsewhere, Morehouse, Spelman, and the other AUC institutions are much more than physical locations; they are incredibly important social and cultural spaces. We would do well to learn from them as such, and from Jett's powerful study.

In my study of U.S. Black mathematicians (Walker, 2014), I spoke with several mathematicians who attended and/or taught at Morehouse. As one can imagine, the professional Black mathematics community is an intricate and highly developed network; and while not all U.S. Black mathematicians attended HBCUs, as a participant observer (a role most generously afforded to me) in many meetings, conferences, programs, and classrooms, it is clear that the incredible connections that Black mathematicians' professional organizations, networks, and initiatives foster are reminiscent of the best of HBCUs. We often speak of genealogy in mathematics—in the common parlance, one's advisor is one's mathematical parent, and their advisor is one's mathematical grandparent. But as Jett's work and other works cited in this book about Black mathematics students and faculty note, this genealogy may be too limiting for the deep connections present in Black mathematics communities. Scholars have written compellingly about fictive kinships among Black Americans across a host of domains, but too rarely have these been used as a frame to understand the deep professional, personal, and communal ties of Black mathematicians.

It is beautiful and appropriate that Jett writes of a "mathematical brotherhood"; indeed, a number of Black mathematicians I interviewed referred to their mathematical "brothers" or "sisters" in the field. These authentic and meaningful relationships are incredibly important to the structures of success in a still too often hostile field. They form the backbone of both the nascent and enduring, informal and formal mathematics learning communities (Walker, 2012) that are often invisible to those outside Black mathematics networks. I'm reminded of the late David Blackwell sharing a story with me about how his fraternity brother in another discipline altogether gave him advice that was, in his words, "incredibly important" to his successfully completing his doctorate in mathematics. I'm also reminded of a group of Morehouse mathematics majors greeting me at the first mathematics conference they'd attended with their professor (a Morehouse graduate himself and the author of the foreword to this book). And I hear in the many stories told to me in *Beyond Banneker* the sense of family and connection shared across generations of mathematicians.

It is indeed "the family feel of it," as Jeremiah from Jett's study describes. Space does not allow me to name the many Black mathematicians—but we would be remiss not to highlight Stephens, Falconer, and Shabazz, as Jett emphasizes in this volume—who are responsible for the success of generations of Black mathematics students, faculty, and professionals. Stories that are passed down from "grandparents" to "parents" to "children" and "grandchildren" hold sage wisdom about succeeding in mathematics study, navigating graduate school, and making critical choices about careers and the profession. This book, with its careful attention to the lived experiences of students, faculty, and alumni of the Morehouse mathematics department, tells an important, yet often overlooked story, of both the magical synergies and serendipities and the practical aspects and norms that result in mathematics success. There is much to be learned, and hopefully, to be put in practice at institutions and departments who recognize the importance of care and real investment in students' potential.

For a moment I was thinking that the popular culture zeitgeist that propelled "hidden figures" Katherine Johnson, Mary Jackson, Dorothy Vaughn, and other Black women mathematicians and scientists working at NASA in the mid–20th century to recent recognition had left out Black men altogether. Then I remembered the first mathematical brother I can recall—Dwayne Wayne, a Black male mathematics and engineering major from the 1990s television show *A Different World*. There could and should be many more visible representations of Black mathematical excellence, but Dwayne Wayne is an important and enduring one. Attending college at an HBCU clearly inspired by the AUC, Dwayne Wayne's love for mathematics, his social evolution, and his enduring and simultaneous coolness and nerdiness is one of the first representations of a fully actualized Black mathematician. As a mathematician I interviewed recounted, she saw Dwayne Wayne on television doing math, so she knew it wasn't crazy to think that she could become a mathematics major.

The stories we tell about mathematics and mathematics doers—fictionalized or not—can have a lasting impact. And the young men that Jett has interviewed recognize this fully. It does not in any way surprise me that Jett's participants feel a deep responsibility to do community and student outreach, to show that Black men in all their rich diversity of interests, ways of being, and backgrounds are excellent mathematics doers. They know the importance of showing what is possible to young people so they can imagine more, and in turn, can imagine themselves doing anything they can dream. That is the rich legacy of Morehouse, and its many brotherhoods. We are fortunate to have heard the mathematical stories told by these wise and thoughtful students, brought to life by this talented scholar.

—Erica N. Walker
Teachers College, Columbia University
Clifford Brewster Upton Professor of Mathematical Education

Theoretical and Methodological Notes

THEORETICAL UNDERPINNINGS

Two theoretical frameworks guide this study: (1) Black masculinity theory and (2) Critical Race Theory. I briefly discuss each theory independently.

Black Masculinity Theory

Black masculinity theory is a theoretical frame that rigorously investigates the essence of Blackness and maleness/manhood. Scholars such as Elijah Anderson, James Baldwin, and Alfred Young have laid the groundwork for contemporary Black masculinist work. As it stands, Black masculinity theory draws from poststructuralism, cultural studies, queer studies, feminist studies, and Whiteness studies (Richardson, 2007). It also borrows from masculinist theorists to examine Black masculine practices and uncover how Black men form robust identities, among other things (Neal, 2013; Pelzer, 2016; Peretz, 2016). There are three core tenets that undergird Black masculinity theory: social construction of Black masculinity (hooks, 2004; Pelzer, 2016), relational aspect of Black masculinity (Dancy, 2012; Pelzer, 2016), and the deconstruction of hegemonic masculinity (White & Peretz, 2010).

By and large, this theoretical perspective correlates with previous work on Black men's collegiate experiences, as scholars ground and interpret their work through a Black masculinist theoretical lens (Dancy, 2012; Pelzer, 2016). This work presents asset-based framings and constructions of Black manhood. Thus, these publications substantiate that this theory has much to offer the field to better understand Black men's experiences and simultaneously advance research on and with Black men.

Critical Race Theory (CRT)

CRT is a theoretically and methodologically rich approach that centers issues of race and racism. The genesis of CRT is attributed to legal scholars such as Derrick Bell, the father of CRT, Richard Delgado, and Alan Freeman (Delgado & Stefancic, 2001). Through a racial lens, CRT offers tenets to engage and expose "the material, structural, and ideological mechanisms of White supremacy" (Ledesma & Calderón, 2015, p. 206). These include the normality and permanence of racism (Delgado & Stefancic, 2001), interest convergence (Delgado & Stefancic, 2001), social construction of race (Ladson-Billings, 2013), race intersected with other constructs such as sex, class, sexual orientation and so on (Crenshaw, 1991), and experiential knowledge through voice as counter-narrative (Solórzano & Yosso, 2002).

CRT has expanded to education (Ladson-Billings & Tate, 1995). Math education researchers have explicated how CRT-informed analyses can be applied in the field (Davis & Jett, 2019). Scholars have also conducted gender-based studies, grounded in CRT, to elucidate the experiences of African American undergraduate women and men (Harper et al., 2011; Patton & Ward, 2016). This work interrogates structures, policies, and practices with the goal of facilitating positive change regarding gender-based racial justice. Therefore, CRT is particularly useful for race-related examinations, and CRT proved useful in this ethnographic study of Black men's experiences.

METHODOLOGICAL NOTES

Ethnographies account for the behaviors and practices of people in a natural setting (Anderson-Levitt, 2006). Ethnographers embed themselves in a culture for an extended period of time to document and make sense of it. Preissle and Grant (2004) posit that "remaining in the field for at least one complete cycle of events is regarded as crucial for establishing the range and variation of activities in any group" (p. 178). I remained at the research site during the entire academic year—the complete cycle—to make sense of the activities within this collegiate community (Preissle & Grant, 2004). This immersion consisted of weekly data collection visits to learn about the participants' math experiences and lives.

As an ethnography, this study also employs portraiture (Lawrence-Lightfoot & Davis, 1997). Portraiture's aim is to explore, understand, and document what works well in great detail. "In the portraiture methodology, the researcher consciously seeks to identify the strengths of the site and the ways in which challenges are addressed" (Chapman, 2005, p. 32). Employing portraiture prompted me to look for the "goodness" in this community, examine student-generated concepts, and investigate the participants' challenges. The portraits shared in this text showed the multidimensionality of the majors' perspectives and experiences, especially within this learning community.

Graduating seniors were selected as participants because a characteristic of ethnography is that the group under study has been intact for an extended period of time, which suggests that there are some shared cultural values (Wolcott, 2008). All 16 graduating seniors agreed to participate in the ethnographic study. Data sources included historical documents and artifacts. Student-generated data included demographic surveys, semi-structured interviews, and observations. The demographic survey gathered information about the participants' upbringings (i.e., hometown, familial information, and childhood interests), K–12 experiences, and college information. The semi-structured interview allowed them to provide first-person accounts of their experiences in an open and unrestrictive manner.

In addition, observational data were collected to better understand Black men's interactions in Morehouse's mathematics learning community. Repeated observations provide deep engagement within a site and enable ethnographers to observe how participants perform culture (Preissle & Grant, 2004; Wolcott, 2008). Observations occurred via tutoring sessions and peer interactions, research talks, and other events. The yearlong observations served multiple purposes: to get to know the members of the mathematical brotherhood, understand routines and norms in the Math Lab, become acquainted with the institutional stakeholders, and document the math-related practices as the ethnographic researcher. In consonance with ethnographic methods, I fully immersed myself within this collegiate community via the three data streams to understand and paint a picture of its culture (Lawrence-Lightfoot & Davis, 1997; Wolcott, 2008).

Throughout the data collection process, my graduate research assistant and I transcribed the interview data. I read through each individual transcript line by line to make sense of each participant's math experiences and formally begin data analysis. While doing so, I created *episode profiles* for each participant to tell his math story (Maietta et al., 2021). I shared the written account with each participant to member-check the data and make certain their experiences and perceptions were reported accurately. Four participants provided minor changes via the feedback, and I incorporated those changes.

After that, I analyzed the 16 participants' stories multiple times to identify keywords, phrases, and ideas. Then, I employed analytic coding to develop code categories for the data (Saldaña, 2013). Example codes that emanated from data analysis included: family, math awards, DDEP, and teaching. During this analytic process, I continuously read and consulted the Black masculinity and CRT literature. My objectives were to deepen my understanding of the theoretical frameworks and note consistency (or not) of my findings with the theories' tenets and findings from prior literature. Finally, I compared and contrasted the (coded) data to make sense of and ultimately generate an ethnographic portrait of Morehouse's mathematics learning community.

Observational Data

Here, I provide a snapshot of the observational data. I share reflective field notes from the Morehouse Mathematics Alumni Conference held on September 3, 2013, a student-led study session conducted on February 27, 2014, and the Morehouse Mathematics Breakfast held on May 17, 2014. These data were selected because they occurred at three distinct times—at the beginning, during the middle, and at the end of the ethnographic study. I also share notes from an alumni panel at the Transforming Post-Secondary Education in Mathematics (TPSE Math) meeting held on June 10, 2019, at Morehouse. Although pseudonyms are used for professors' names in this text, professors' real names are used here.

Morehouse Mathematics Alumni Conference: It was the Tuesday after Labor Day. I had just returned from spending the long weekend in Nashville to attend the John Merritt Football Classic and visit with college friends. I was on my way to attend the Morehouse Mathematics Alumni Conference. As I walked into the Dansby Auditorium, I sat in the back to observe the setting and ensure that I could witness everything during the panel discussion. As the program began, the students listened intently. I noticed that there were no cell phones visibly displayed, which suggested to me that the two panelists, Drs. Johnny Houston and Benjamin Martin, had these young men's undivided attention. Below, I share the takeaways that I gathered from each panelist.

Dr. Houston provided a historical arc about Morehouse Mathematics. In doing so, he emphasized that Morehouse took in many first-generation students who were not prepared academically, but they felt extremely fortunate to be there. He mentioned that students had to live up to a certain image, have the proper decorum to enter the dining hall, and wear a shirt and tie on Sundays. During the presidency of Dr. Benjamin E. Mays, many high-profile Black male intellectuals were invited to chapel, and students were expected to model themselves on those intellectuals. Regarding math, he shared that they had problem sessions at 8 o'clock on Friday nights and that Professor Dansby told them that "if you really know math, then you should be able to pull out a napkin and explain it to someone." His final words were: "Don't just be a receiver. Ensure that the next generation is better off than your own."

Dr. Martin also had a memorable Morehouse experience. During his time as a Morehouse student, there were three math professors, and math majors formed one of the largest groups of majors on campus. He served as Professor Dansby's teaching assistant. Coincidentally, Professor Dansby was also the chapel attendance checker, which meant that he had to be there each and every time. Relatedly, there was a Religious Emphasis Week, offering spiritual nourishment to maximize students' academic outcomes. In his remarks, he shared how there was a profound respect for Morehouse and Dr. Mays. He told a story of two students who got into trouble with the law. At the station, they gave their home addresses rather than their Morehouse affiliation and claimed that they were just "passing through town," in order not to bring shame on Morehouse. His final words were: "The challenge of the future is to come back 50 years from now and share your accomplishments with current students." As a 1963 graduate, he earned his degree 50 years prior. (Dr. Houston earned his degree in 1964, so both of these men were Golden Tigers—those who received their degrees 50 years prior.)

Student-Led Study Session: I was sitting in the Math Lab on Thursday afternoon, my usual data collection day. The majors have grown accustomed to seeing me on the third floor. One of the majors asked another one, "Have you had your interview yet?" perhaps confirming that I was the "interview guy" or wondering whether I was scheduled to go to the main office with one of them, which would have disturbed their impending study session. A couple of other guys entered the room shortly thereafter. They all engaged in completing the assigned problem set, which involved proving theorems. Because of the natural, communal peer learning taking place, it was clear that their math education also came from their fellow majors.

The brothers earnestly put forth mathematically sophisticated explanations and avidly shared their discoveries to help others understand the proofs. One major referenced a previous lecture and tied in the Mean Value Theorem, a theorem from foundational Calculus, to drive home the point to the major who was having some challenges making connections across the mathematical ideas. They worked collaboratively (reminiscent of the student-centered learning, active learning, and cooperative learning strategies such as math circles that appear in the math education literature). They were still providing peer explanations and instruction upon my departure. This observation—the sight of Black men collaboratively presenting math—was astonishing and signified many similar encounters I would observe throughout the academic year in this learning community.

Morehouse Mathematics Breakfast: The academic year was coming to a close, which meant that this study was reaching its conclusion. It was early Saturday morning, and Sunday (i.e., May 18th) would be the brothers' big day—graduation. This breakfast, accompanied by the melodious sound of jazz, was the last—math exclusive—event where the majors enjoyed their time together as undergraduates in community and reflected on their time together at Morehouse. In attendance were the majors' families, friends, and faculty members. A few alumni attended, and they too referenced the small population of students at Morehouse. One of the graduates recalled an alumnus, who served on the admissions board of an Ivy League institution, knocking on his door during his freshman year and sharing stories of being an occupant of that same dorm room.

The majors agreed that you become a math major when you shake Dr. Duane Cooper's hand, explaining that the handshake welcomes you into the math community after you sign the major declaration form. There was also a Morehouse Mathematics wristband gifted to students. They laughed about a brother who earned his tenure, making light of the fact that he had been a student at Morehouse "forever" (i.e., beyond the traditional 4-years associated with obtaining a college degree). Photos were shared from events throughout their college years. All things considered, it was apparent that a metamorphosis had taken place and that Morehouse does an exceptional job of creating a community of, for, and with Black men in math.

TPSE Math Meeting: I was excited to attend my first TPSE Math Southeast Regional Meeting. It had special meaning because it was held in Morehouse's Shirley A. Massey Executive Conference Center, and I was definitely looking forward to eating some scrumptious Southern fried chicken for dinner later at the nearby Paschal's Soul Food Restaurant. The icing on the cake was that it included an alumni panel with a Spelman mathematics graduate and four Morehouse mathematics graduates. The Spelman graduate took an upper-division math course at Morehouse with Dr. Ulrica Wilson. She mentioned that she appreciated Dr. Wilson for telling her about the EDGE program and applauded her mentoring efforts, indicating that Dr. Wilson still serves as a mentor to her. (Dr. Wilson received a Presidential Award for Excellence in Science, Mathematics, and Engineering Mentoring for her extraordinary mentoring.) Two of the panel members—the Spelman alumna and the Morehouse alumnus—had defended their doctoral dissertations. In a field where Blacks are disproportionally underrepresented, it gave my heart great joy to see these young Black math professionals attain their PhDs, and it was especially refreshing to see that the Morehouse graduate was a participant in this study. The mathematics alumni panel provided confirming evidence to support the claims made in this book, and I focus here primarily on three takeaways concerning Morehouse Mathematics as extracted from the TPSE Math meeting.

First, it was clearly evident that exceptional mentoring takes place at Morehouse. The graduates emphasized that quite a few of the math faculty went above and beyond in their duties to ensure the success of the graduates. Dr. Cooper was included in that list of stellar faculty, and one panelist jokingly shared: "I should have paid him rent," referencing the huge amounts of time spent in Dr. Cooper's office. Second, it was abundantly clear that the majors were challenged. One referenced (and the others quickly agreed) that passing Cooper Reals—Dr. Cooper's Real Analysis course(s)—was a significant accomplishment because of the blood, sweat, and tears, so to speak, associated with successfully completing it. A similar reference was made to the late Dr. Rudy Horne's challenging theory he gave to students and expected them to build on it as the semester unfolded. Third, it was clear that these graduates developed close and lasting relationships with their math professors because of Morehouse's nurturing environment and the fact that the "professors are always there," as noted by one of the panelists. All in all, this panel at the TPSE Math Meeting reminded me that Morehouse's mathematics learning community is an affirming one for Black men.

Fraternal Vocabulary

The vocabulary in this book mirrors the language associated with BGLOs. Common terms are defined and operationalized to place the fraternity-style language in concert with mathematics.

Call: The call is an utterance to gain the attention of the other fraternity members. *Math talk* represents discipline-specific discussions, debates, critiques, and conversations that capture the attention of the other majors.

Chapter Advisor: The chapter advisor is the faculty or staff professional who serves as the campus advisor for a fraternal organization. The Department Chair serves as the chapter advisor for members of the mathematical brotherhood.

Chapter Meeting: A chapter meeting is used to discuss the business of the chapter, vote on various items, etc. Within the context of this study, a math club meeting, study session, or research seminar constitutes a chapter meeting.

Community Service: Community service represents community-based efforts in service to the Black community. For the participants, community service entails mentoring and assisting local K–12 students with their mathematics studies.

Crossing: A crossing is a process whereby a pledge goes from being on line to becoming a member of a BGLO. In this collegiate community, crossing is when majors earn third floor respect.

Division: Division is often used to denote any divisive behavior between brothers within a chapter. In this text, division exists between the "stellar" and "mediocre" students.

Drop: A drop is a person who has dropped line when pledging. A drop represents someone who has decided to leave or switch out of the math major.

Hazing: Hazing is the act of engaging in challenges or rituals that can be humiliating or embarrassing. Mathematical hazing consists of completing extremely difficult tasks to demonstrate disciplinary prowess.

Informational: An informational is a meeting where prospective pledgees receive additional information about a fraternity. A math informational is when students attend a session to learn about internships, research programs, and career opportunities.

Legacy: Legacy represents a pledgee whose family member is a member of a BGLO. The math legacy represents familial ties to the discipline.

Line: The line could represent the new members of a fraternal organization that develop lifelong friendships. In this study, the line typically represents students who successfully completed the Department Chair's Real Analysis course, but the line could consist of an entire cohort of majors—such as the 16 graduating senior math majors.

Line Number: The line number is the number a fraternity member is assigned based on his order in the line. Usually, fraternity brothers are lined up according to height. With this study, the chronological order of the interviews determined the line number.

Neophyte: A neophyte refers to a new member of a BGLO. In this study, a newly declared math major represents a neophyte.

Paraphernalia: Paraphernalia represents the clothing items and gadgets that bear the BGLO's name and/or Greek letters. The Morehouse Mathematics sweater vest is the paraphernalia that brothers seek to earn and wear with distinction.

Pledge Class: A pledge class represents a group of brothers who form a fraternal bond that could last a lifetime. The 16 members of the mathematical brotherhood represent the pledge class.

Prophyte: A prophyte refers to an older member of a BGLO. In this study, a math alumnus represents a prophyte.

Stepping: Stepping is characterized by completing hand and foot movements, chanting (historical) songs, and performing dance routines. Within this all-male group dynamic, presenting math is comparable to stepping.

Yard: The yard denotes where members of a fraternity congregate on campus. In this mathematics learning community, the Math Lab represents the yard for the majors.

Acronym Glossary

This glossary includes the acronyms used in this text.

AIP = American Institute of Physics

AMS = American Mathematical Society

AP = Advanced Placement

AUC = Atlanta University Center

BBA = Benjamin Banneker Association

BGLO = Black Greek-Letter Organization

BIG = Business, Industry, and Government

BMW = Bayerische Motoren Werke

BS = Bad Statistics

CAARMS = Conference for African-American Researchers in the Mathematical Sciences

CAU = Clark Atlanta University

CRT = Critical Race Theory

DBER = Discipline-Based Education Research

DDEP = Dual-Degree Engineering Program

DREAMS = Discovery Research Education for African American Men in STEM

EDGE = Enhancing Diversity in Graduate Education

E&M = Electricity & Magnetism

HBCU = Historically Black College/University

HWI = Historically White Institution

IPEDS = Integrated Postsecondary Educational Data System

ITC = Interdenominational Theological Center

JMM = Joint Mathematics Meeting

JPBM = Joint Policy Board for Mathematics

MAA = Mathematical Association of America

MBK = My Brother's Keeper

MSRI–UP = Mathematical Sciences Research Institute–Undergraduate Program

MWP = Mathematics Workshop Program

NAM = National Association of Mathematicians

NASA = National Aeronautics and Space Administration

NCES = National Center for Education Statistics

NCTM = National Council of Teachers of Mathematics

NFL = National Football League

NSF = National Science Foundation

PAESMEM = Presidential Award for Excellence in Science, Mathematics, and Engineering Mentoring

Q.E.D. = *quod erat demonstrandum*

REU = Research Experience for Undergraduates

RUME = Research in Undergraduate Mathematics Education

SAT = Scholastic Aptitude Test

SEMINAL = Student Engagement in Mathematics through an Institutional Network for Active Learning

STEM = Science, Technology, Engineering, and Mathematics

SWAT = Special Weapons and Tactics

TAG = Talented and Gifted

TFA = Teach for America

TPSE Math = Transforming Post-Secondary Education in Mathematics

TSU = Tennessee State University

Notes

Introduction

1. *African American* and *Black* are used interchangeably in this text.

2. *Participants, majors,* and *brothers* are used interchangeably and refer to the 16 graduating seniors who participated in this study.

3. See Bell (1995) for a discussion regarding attacks and critiques of CRT.

4. Bennett College, an all-women's HBCU in Greensboro, North Carolina, is also a sister institution to Morehouse.

5. Dr. Raymond Richardson was one of Atlanta University's 109 graduates under the tutelage of Dr. Shabazz. Dr. Richardson went on to earn his PhD in mathematics from Vanderbilt University and later joined the mathematics faculty at Tennessee State University (TSU). Dr. Richardson taught me Linear Algebra at TSU, so I am also indirectly connected to Dr. Shabazz's mathematical legacy.

6. Walker (2014) also notes Howard University's PhD program in mathematics for its production of Black doctoral recipients in the field.

Chapter 1

1. Some institutions are women's colleges, so they do not produce any male math majors. On the other hand, similar arguments can be made about Black women in undergraduate mathematics programs, especially Spelman given that it is the top producer of Black women in math (U.S. Department of Education, 2019).

Chapter 3

1. See Jett (2010) regarding the role of spirituality among African American male mathematics majors.

2. Coincidentally, it rained when the 16 participants received their undergraduate degrees, so many of them began and ended their collegiate journey in this memorable fashion.

3. See Thompson et al. (2016) for information about the Hopps (named after Morehouse's former Provost, Dr. John J. Hopps Jr.) Program's approach to preparing Black men for graduate programs in STEM.

4. This discussion is not meant to delve into the negative connotations associated with hazing or to critically examine the no-hazing policies associated with BGLOs (see Parks & Brown, 2005).

Chapter 4

1. The word *superhero* is often used to suggest that Black youth need *saving* without a critical interrogation of the structural inequities that fortify these inequalities (Baldridge, 2017). The use of *superhero* here is not intended to perpetuate this line of thinking.

2. This *night shift* language is not intended to suggest that faculty *must* remain in their office after hours to demonstrate their dedication to students' math education.

Chapter 6

1. See commentary concerning abolishing the [n-word] via the hashtag #abolishthenword across various social media platforms, websites, and clothing items.

2. Black people use digital counterpublics (e.g., Black Twitter) to expose racially biased encounters and events and argue that Black lives are worth protecting (Hill, 2018). As such, "Black Twitter operates as a digital counterpublic that enables new and transgressive forms of organizing, pedagogy and, ultimately, resistance" (p. 297).

Chapter 7

1. In related work, see Trawick et al. (2020) for results of Morehouse's Discovery Research Education for African American Men in STEM (DREAMS) to Teach program—a program that targets and supports African American male high school students to subsequently pursue K–12 STEM teaching positions.

2. For math programs that offer transition courses, efforts should be made to improve them.

3. Regarding service-learning courses, Butler (2013) reported on a fourth-credit option (i.e., adding an additional hour of service learning to an existing three-credit hour math course).

4. Future work should also examine Mathematics departments, as discipline-based scholars are calling for research on change within them (Reinholz et al., 2020).

References

Adams, J., Younge, S., Wilson, U., Pearson, W., & Leggon, C. B. (2013). The undergraduate STEM research experiences of African American males at a historically Black college. *Journal of Women and Minorities in Science and Engineering, 19*(2), 165–183. https://doi.org/10.1615/JWomenMinorScienEng.2013005706

Adamson, B. (2016). "Thugs," "crooks," and "rebellious Negroes": Racist and racialized media coverage of Michael Brown and the Ferguson demonstrations. *Harvard Journal of Ethnic and Racial Justice, 32*, 189–278.

Albritton, T. J. (2012). Educating our own: The historical legacy of HBCUs and their relevance for educating a new generation of leaders. *The Urban Review, 44*(3), 311–331. https://doi.org/10.1007/s11256-012-0202-9

Alcock, L., & Weber, K. (2005). Proof validation in real analysis: Inferring and checking warrants. *The Journal of Mathematical Behavior, 24*(2), 125–134. https://doi.org/10.1016/j.jmathb.2005.03.003

American Institute of Physics: National Task Force to Elevate African American Representation in Undergraduate Physics and Astronomy. (2020). *The time is now: Systematic changes to increase African Americans with bachelor's degrees in physics and astronomy.* Author.

American Mathematical Society. (n.d.). American Mathematical Society. www.ams .org/home/page

Anderson, J. D. (1998). *The education of Blacks in the South, 1860–1935.* The University of North Carolina Press.

Anderson-Levitt, K. (2006). Ethnography. In J. L. Green, G. Camilli, & P. B. Elmore (Eds.), *Handbook of contemporary methods in education research* (pp. 279–295). Lawrence Erlbaum Associates.

Atlanta University Center. (n.d.). *About our library.* https://www.auctr.edu/about /overview/about-our-library/

Baker, C. E. (2015). Does parent involvement and neighborhood quality matter for African American boys' kindergarten mathematics achievement? *Early Education and Development, 26*(3), 342–355. https://www.tandfonline.com/doi/full /10.1080/10409289.2015.968238

Baker-Bell, A. (2020). *Linguistic justice: Black language, literacy, identity, and pedagogy.* Routledge.

Baldridge, B. J. (2017). "It's like this myth of the Supernegro": Resisting narratives of damage and struggle in the neoliberal educational policy context. *Race Ethnicity and Education, 20*(6), 781–795. https://doi.org/10.1080/13613324.2016 .1248819

Baldwin, B. (2018). Black, White, and blue: Bias, profiling, and policing in the age of Black Lives Matter. *Western New England Law Review, 40*(3), 431–446. https://digitalcommons.law.wne.edu/lawreview/vol40/iss3/4

Bell, D. (1995). Who's afraid of critical race theory? *University of Illinois Law Review, 1995*(4), 893–910.

Bellamy, W., & Berry, R. Q., III. (2017). Mentoring for a lifetime: The perspective of a Black man who served as a mentor. *A Professing Education, 16*(2), 27–37.

Benjamin Banneker Association. (2017). *Implementing a social justice curriculum: Practices to support the participation and success of African-American students in mathematics.* https://bbamath.org/wp-content/uploads/2017/11/BBA-Social-Justice-Position-Paper_Final.pdf

Berry, R. Q., III. (2008). Access to upper-level mathematics: The stories of successful African American middle school boys. *Journal for Research in Mathematics Education, 39*(5), 464–488. https://doi.org/10.5951/jresematheduc.39.5.0464

Berry, R. Q., III., Ellis, M., & Hughes, S. (2014). Examining a history of failed reforms and recent stories of success: Mathematics education and Black learners of mathematics in the United States. *Race Ethnicity and Education, 17*(4), 540–568. https://doi.org/10.1080/13613324.2013.818534

Berry, R. Q., III, Thunder, K., & McClain, O. L. (2011). Counter narratives: Examining the mathematics and racial identities of Black boys who are successful with school mathematics. *Journal of African American Males in Education, 2*(1), 10–23.

Blair, R., Kirkman, E. E., & Maxwell, J. W. (2013). *Statistical abstract of undergraduate programs in the mathematical sciences in the United States: Fall 2010 CBMS survey.* American Mathematical Society.

Bonilla, Y., & Rosa, J. (2015). #Ferguson: Digital protest, hashtag ethnography, and the racial politics of social media in the United States. *American Ethnologist, 42*(2), 4–17. https://doi.org/10.1111/amet.12112

Borowski, E. J., & Borwein, J. M. (1991). *The HarperCollins dictionary of mathematics.* HarperCollins.

Borum, V., Hilton, A. A., & Walker, E. (2016). The role of Black colleges in the development of mathematicians. *Journal of Research Initiatives, 2*(1), Article 6. https://digitalcommons.uncfsu.edu/jri/vol2/iss1/6

Borum, V., & Walker, E. (2012). What makes the difference? Black women's undergraduate and graduate experiences in mathematics. *The Journal of Negro Education, 81*(4), 366–378. https://doi.org/10.7709/jnegroeducation.81.4.0366

Boutte, G., & Bryan, N. (2021). When will Black children be well? Interrupting anti-Black violence in early childhood classrooms and schools. *Contemporary Issues in Early Childhood, 22*(3), 232–243. https://doi.org/10.1177/1463949119890598

Bozeman, S. T., & Hughes, R. J. (2004). Improving the graduate school experience for women in mathematics: The EDGE program. *Journal of Women and Minorities in Science and Engineering, 10*(3), 243–253. https://dx.doi.org/10.1615/JWomenMinorScienEng.v10.i3.40

Branch, C. D. (2005). Variegated roots: The foundations of stepping. In T. L. Brown, G. S. Parks, & C. M. Phillips (Eds.), *African American fraternities and sororities: The legacy and the vision* (pp. 315–340). University Press of Kentucky.

Brawley, B. (2009). *History of Morehouse College.* Cosimo Classics. (Original work published 1917)

Bressoud, D. M. (2021). The strange role of calculus in the United States. *ZDM, 53*(3), 521–533. https://doi.org/10.1007/s11858-020-01188-0

Bressoud, D. M., Mesa, V., & Rasmussen, C. (Eds.). (2015). *Insights and recommendations from the MAA national study of college calculus.* Mathematical Association of America.

Brooms, D. R. (2017a). *Being Black, being male on campus: Understanding and confronting Black male collegiate experiences.* State University of New York Press.

Brooms, D. R. (2017b). Black otherfathering in the educational experiences of Black males in a single-sex urban high school. *Teachers College Record, 119*(12), 1–46.

Brown, A. L. (2018). From subhuman to human kind: Implicit bias, racial memory, and Black males in schools and society. *Peabody Journal of Education, 93*(1), 52–65. https://doi.org/10.1080/0161956X.2017.1403176

Bryan, N. (2021a). Remembering Tamir Rice and other Black boy victims: Imagining Black PlayCrit Literacies inside and outside urban literacy education. *Urban Education, 56*(5), 744–771. https://doi.org/10.1177/0042085920902250

Bryan, N. (2021b). *Toward a BlackBoyCrit pedagogy: Black boys, male teachers, and early childhood classroom practices.* Routledge.

Bullock, E. C. (2019). Mathematics curriculum reform as racial remediation: A historical counter-story. In J. Davis & C. C. Jett (Eds.), *Critical race theory in mathematics education* (pp. 75–97). Routledge.

Butler, M. (2013). Learning from service-learning. *PRIMUS, 23*(10), 881–892. https://doi.org/10.1080/10511970.2013.775978

Butts, C. O. (2006). I can do anything; I'm a Morehouse man. I could be involved in both religion and education. In J. H. Eaves (Ed.) *Speakers of the house: Morehouse men reflect on their journey to manhood* (pp. 55–61). Publishing Associates.

Carey, R. (2019). Am I smart enough? Will I make friends? And can I even afford it? Exploring the college-going dilemmas of Black and Latino adolescent boys. *American Journal of Education, 125*(3), 381–415.

Carson, C. (1997). Martin Luther King Jr.: The Morehouse years. *The Journal of Blacks in Higher Education, 15,* 121–125. https://doi.org/10.2307/2962714

Chapman, T. K. (2005). Expressions of "voice" in portraiture. *Qualitative Inquiry, 11*(1), 27–51. https://doi.org/10.1177/1077800404270840

Chatters, L. M., Taylor, R. J., & Jayakody, R. (1994). Fictive kinship relations in Black extended families. *Journal of Comparative Studies, 25*(3), 297–312. https://doi.org/10.3138/jcfs.25.3.297

Clark, L. M., Badertscher, E. M., & Napp, C. (2013). African American mathematics teachers as agents in their African American students' mathematics identity formation. *Teachers College Record, 115*(2), 1–36. https://eric.ed.gov/?id=EJ1018094

Collins, P. H. (2000). *Black feminist thought.* Routledge.

Cooper, C. W. (2009). Parent involvement, African American mothers, and the politics of educational care. *Equity & Excellence in Education, 42*(4), 379–394. https://doi.org/10.1080/10665680903228389

Cooper, D. A. (2000). Changing the face of mathematics Ph.D.'s: What we are learning at the University of Maryland. In M. E. Strutchens, M. L. Johnson, & W. F. Tate (Eds.), *Changing the faces of mathematics: Perspectives on African Americans* (pp. 179–192). National Council of Teachers of Mathematics.

Cooper, D. A. (2004). Recommendations for increasing the participation and success of Blacks in graduate mathematics study. *Notices of the AMS, 51*(5), 538–543.

Covington, M. (2017). If not us, then who? Exploring the role of HBCUs in increasing Black student engagement in study abroad. *College Student Affairs Leadership, 4*(1), Article 5. https://scholarworks.gvsu.edu/csal/vol4/iss1/5

Crenshaw, K. W. (1991). Mapping the margins: Intersectionality, identity politics, and violence against women of color. *Stanford Law Review, 43*(6), 1241–1299. https://doi.org/10.2307/1229039

Crosby, N. M. (2013). *Morehouse College: Department of mathematics, fall 2013.* Morehouse College.

Cunningham, J. (2021). "We made math!": Black parents as a guide for supporting Black children's mathematical identities. *Journal of Urban Mathematics Education, 14*(1), 24–44. https://doi.org/10.21423/jume-v14i1a414

Dahlke, R. M. (2011). *How to succeed in college mathematics: A comprehensive study and reference book for students and instructors* (2nd ed.). BergWay Publishing.

Dancy, T. E. (2012). *The brother code: Manhood and masculinity among African American males in college.* Information Age.

Dancy, T. E. (2014). (Un)doing hegemony in education: Disrupting school-to-prison pipelines for Black males. *Equity & Excellence in Education, 47*(4), 476–493. https://doi.org/10.1080/10665684.2014.959271

Dancy, T. E., Edwards, K. T., & Davis, J. E. (2018). Historically White universities and plantation politics: Anti-Blackness and higher education in the Black Lives Matter era. *Urban Education, 53*(2), 176–195. https://dx.doi.org/10.1177/004 2085918754328

Davis, J., Anderson, C., & Parker, W. (2019). Identifying and supporting Black male students in advanced mathematics courses throughout the K–12 pipeline. *Gifted Child Today, 42*(3), 140–149. https://doi.org/10.1177%2F1076217519842234

Davis, J., & Jett, C. C. (Eds.). (2019). *Critical race theory in mathematics education.* Routledge.

de Brito, A. S. (2013). Good hair. In A. Garrod, C. Gómez, & R. Kilkenny (Eds.), *Mixed: Multiracial college students tell their life stories* (pp. 19–29). Cornell University Press.

de Casanova, E. M., & Webb, C. L. (2017). A tale of two hoodies. *Men and Masculinities, 20*(1), 117–122. https://doi.org/10.1177%2F1097184X17696363

Delgado, R., & Stefancic, J. (2001). *Critical race theory: An introduction.* New York University Press.

Delpit, L. (2012). *"Multiplication is for White people": Raising expectations for other people's children.* The New Press.

Doan, I. (2019, May 20). Arlie Peters is one of the few tenured Black mathematicians. He wants to diversify his field. *The Chronicle.* www.dukechronicle.com /article/2019/05/duke-university-arlie-petters-black-math-professor-u-s-diversify -field

Dumas, M. J., & ross, k. m. (2016). "Be real Black for me": Imagining BlackCrit in education. *Urban Education, 51*(4), 415–442. https://doi.org/10.1177%2F0042085916628611

Dumbaugh, D. (2019). Rudy Lee Horne: The hidden figure of Hidden Figures, 1968–2017 (memorial tribute). *Notices of the AMS, 66*(2), 202–210. https://dx.doi.org/10.1090/noti1803

Eaves, J. H. (Ed.). (2006). *Speakers of the House: Morehouse men reflect on their journey to manhood*. Publishing Associates.

Eaves, J. H. (2009). *The Morehouse mystique: Lessons to develop Black men*. African American Images.

Ellington, R., Barber, J., Tannouri, A., Syafrida, S., & Nkwanta, A. (2021). The MSU Seminal Project: Incorporating principles of culturally responsive teaching in a pre-calculus course. *PRIMUS, 31*(3–5), 296–315. https://doi.org/10.1080/10511970.2020.1805661

Ellington, R., & Frederick, R. (2010). Black high achieving undergraduate mathematics majors discuss success and persistence in mathematics. *The Negro Educational Review, 61*(1–4), 61–84.

Elliott, K. C., Warshaw, J. B., & deGregory, C. A. (2019). Historically Black community colleges: A descriptive profile and call for context-based future research. *Community College Journal of Research & Practice, 43*(10–11), 770–784. https://doi.org/10.1080/10668926.2019.1600612

Ellis, J., Kelton, M. L., & Rasmussen, C. (2014). Student perceptions of pedagogy and associated persistence in calculus. *ZDM, 46*(4), 661–673. https://doi.org/10.1007/s11858-014-0577-z

Falconer, E. Z. (1996). The challenge of diversity. In N. Dean (Ed.), *African Americans in mathematics: DIMACS workshop* (pp. 169–182). American Mathematical Society. https://doi.org/10.1090/dimacs/034

Farinde-Wu, A., Allen-Handy, A., & Lewis, C. W. (Eds.). (2017). *Black female teachers: Diversifying the United States' teacher workforce*. Emerald Group Publishing.

Farley, J. (2012). Black mathematicians: The kind of problems they wish didn't need solving. *The Guardian*. www.theguardian.com/commentisfree/cifamerica/2012/apr/12/black-mathematicians-john-derbyshire-fields-medal

Favors, J. M. (2019). *Shelter in a time of storm: How Black colleges fostered generations of leadership and activism*. The University of North Carolina Press.

Figuero Charles, M. A. (2017). *Exponential genius: How African American male actuaries develop mathematical expertise*. [Doctoral dissertation, Texas A&M University]. https://hdl.handle.net/1969.1/165836

Ford, D. (2013). *Recruiting and retaining culturally different students in gifted education*. Prufrock Press.

Frank, T. J. (2019). Using critical race theory to unpack the Black mathematics teacher pipeline. In J. Davis & C. C. Jett (Eds.), *Critical race theory in mathematics education* (pp. 98–122). Routledge.

Frank, T. J., Powell, M. G., View, J. L., Lee, C., Bradley, J. A., & Williams, A. (2021). Exploring racialized factors to understand why Black mathematics teachers consider leaving the profession. *Educational Researcher, 50*(6), 381–391. https://doi.org/10.3102/0013189X21994498

Fries-Britt, S., Burt, B. A., & Franklin, K. (2012). Establishing critical relationships: How Black males persist in physics at HBCUs. In R. T. Palmer & J. L. Wood (Eds.), *Black men in college: Implications for HBCUs and beyond* (pp. 71–88). Routledge.

Fullilove, R. E., & Treisman, P. U. (1990). Mathematics achievement among African American undergraduates at the University of California, Berkeley: An evaluation of the mathematics workshop program. *The Journal of Negro Education, 59*(3), 463–478. https://doi.org/2295577

Garcia, G. A., Johnston, M. P., Garibay, J. C., Herrera, F. A., & Giraldo, L. G. (2011). When parties become racialized: Deconstructing racially themed parties. *Journal of Student Affairs Research and Practice, 48*(1), 5–21. https://doi.org/10.2202/1949-6605.6194

Gasman, M., Nguyen, T., Conrad, C. F., Lundberg, T., & Commodore, F. (2017). Black male success in STEM: A case study of Morehouse College. *Journal of Diversity in Higher Education, 10*(2), 181–200. https://dx.doi.org/10.1037/dhe0000013

Gasman, M., & Sullivan, L. W. (2012). *The Morehouse mystique: Becoming a doctor at the nation's newest African American medical school.* John Hopkins University Press.

Gay, G. (2018). *Culturally responsive teaching* (3rd ed.). Teachers College Press.

Gholson, M. L. (2016). Clean corners and algebra: A critical examination of the constructed invisibility of Black girls and women in mathematics. *The Journal of Negro Education, 85*(3), 290–301. https://doi.org/10.7709/jnegroeducation.85.3.0290

Graham, E., Higgins, R., Price, C., & Wilson, S. (2018). The mathematically gifted and Black website. *Notices of the AMS, 65*(2), 124–126. https://dx.doi.org/10.1090/noti1633

Greenlee, C. T. (2012, September 4). Football classics bring the HBCU experience—and their marching bands—to big-time arenas. *Diverse Issues in Higher Education.* http://diverseeducation.com/article/47775.

Grundy, S. (2012). "An air of expectancy": Class, crisis, and the making of manhood at a historically Black college for men. *The ANNALS of the American Academy of Political and Social Science, 642*(1), 43–60. https://dx.doi.org/10.1177/0002716212438203

Grundy, S. (2021). Lifting the veil on campus sexual assault: Morehouse College, hegemonic masculinity, and revealing racialized rape culture through the Du Boisian lens. *Social Problems, 68*(2), 226–249. https://doi.org/10.1093/socpro/spab001

Harcourt, G. (2009). Henry Louis Gates and racial profiling: What's the problem? *University of Chicago, Law & Economics.* Online Working Paper No. 482, 1–28. https://dx.doi.org/10.2139/ssrn.1474809

Harmon, A. (2019, February 18). For a Black mathematician, what it's like to be the "only one." https://www.nytimes.com/2019/02/18/us/edray-goins-black-mathematicians.html

Harper, S. R. (2015). Black male college achievers and resistant responses to racist stereotypes at predominately White colleges and universities. *Harvard Educational Review, 85*(4), 646–674. https://doi.org/10.17763/0017-8055.85.4.646

Harper, S. R., Davis, R. J., Jones, D. E., McGowan, B. L., Ingram, T. N., & Platt, C S. (2011). Race and racism in the experiences of Black male resident assistants at predominately White institutions. *Journal of College Student Development, 52*(2), 180–200. https://doi.org/10.1353/csd.2011.0025

Harper, S. R., & Harris, F., III. (2006). The role of Black fraternities in the African American male undergraduate experience. In M. Cuyjet (Ed.), *African American men in college* (p. 128–153). Jossey-Bass.

Harris, F., III., & Harper, S. R. (2014). Beyond bad behaving brothers: Productive performances of masculinities among college fraternity men. *International Journal of Qualitative Studies in Education, 27*(6), 703–723.

Hill, M. L. (2018). "Thank you, Black twitter": State violence, digital counterspaces, and pedagogies of resistance. *Urban Education, 53*(2), 286–302. https://doi.org/10.1177%2F0042085917747124

hooks, b. (2004). *We real cool: Black men and masculinity.* Routledge.

Hottinger, S. N. (2016). *Inventing the mathematician: Gender, race, and our cultural understanding of mathematics.* State University of New York Press.

Houston, J. L. (2000). *The history of the National Association of Mathematicians: The first thirty (30) years: 1969–1999.* National Association of Mathematicians.

Houston, J. L. (2019). A centennial year (2019) reflection on the life and contributions of mathematician David H. Blackwell (1919–2010). *Notices of the AMS, 66*(2), 221–226. https://www.ams.org/journals/notices/201902/rnoti-p221.pdf

Houston, J. L. (2021). The founding of the National Association of Mathematics. In O. Ortega, E. D. Lawrence, & E. H. Goins (Eds.), *The golden anniversary celebration of the National Association of Mathematics* (pp. 1–20). American Mathematical Society.

Houston, J. L. (n.d.) *Professor Claude B. Dansby legacy at Morehouse* [Poster]. Morehouse College.

Howard, J. (2019). Just playin': Black mixed-race boys and the injustices of boyhood. *Race Ethnicity and Education.* https://doi.org/10.1080/13613324.2019.1679760

Howard, T. C. (2014). *Black male(d): Peril and promise in the education of African American males.* Teachers College Press.

Hrabowski, F. A., Maton, K. I., & Grief, G. L. (1998). *Beating the odds: Raising academically successful African American males.* Oxford University Press.

Hufferd-Ackles, K., Fuson, K. C., & Sherin, M. G. (2004). Describing levels and components of a math-talk learning community. *Journal for Research in Mathematics Education, 35*(2), 81–116. https://doi.org/10.2307/30034933

Husband, T. (2012). "I don't see color": Challenging assumptions about discussing race with young children. *Early Childhood Education, 39*(6), 365–371. https://doi.org/10.1007/s10643-011-0458-9

Inniss, T. (2015). Importance of HBCUs in the development and nurturing of African American women mathematicians. In W. Pearson, L. M. Frehill, & C. L. McNeely (Eds.), *Advancing women in science: An international perspective* (pp. 191–194). Springer.

Inniss, T., Johnson, R. L., & Scott, S. (2022). Dr. Raymond L. Johnson: A mathematical journey and some reflections on African Americans in graduate mathematical sciences programs in the US. *Notices of the AMS, 69*(2), 232–238. https://doi.org/10.1090/noti2421

Jackson, A. (2016). From the AMS secretary: 2016 mathematics programs that make a difference. *Notices of the AMS, 63*(5), 552–554.

Jenkins, D. A., Tichavakunda, A. A., & Coles, J. A. (2021). The second ID: Critical race counterstories of campus police interactions with Black men at historically White institutions. *Race Ethnicity and Education, 24*(2), 149–166. https://doi.org/10.1080/13613324.2020.1753672

Jett, C. C. (2010). "Many are called, but few are chosen": The role of spirituality and religion in the educational outcomes of "chosen" African American male mathematics majors. *The Journal of Negro Education, 79*(3), 324–334. https://eric.ed.gov/?id=EJ943041

Jett, C. C. (2013a). Culturally responsive collegiate mathematics education: Implications for African American students. *Interdisciplinary Journal of Teaching and Learning, 3*(2), 102–116. https://eric.ed.gov/?id=EJ1063224

Jett, C. C. (2013b). HBCUs propel African American male mathematics majors. *Journal of African American Studies, 17*(2), 189–205. https://doi.org/10.1007/s12111-011-9194-x

Jett, C. C. (2016a). Building on our mathematical legacy of brilliance: A critical race reflective narrative. In B. L. McGowan, R. T. Palmer, J. L. Wood, & D. F. Hibbler (Eds.), *Black men in the academy: Narratives of resiliency, achievement, and success* (pp. 77–91). Palgrave Macmillan.

Jett, C. C. (2016b). Ivy League bound: A case study of a brilliant African American male mathematics major. *Spectrum: A Journal on Black Men, 4*(2), 83–97. https://doi:10.2979/spectrum.4.2.05

Jett, C. C. (2019a). Mathematical persistence among four African American male graduate students: A critical race analysis of their experiences. *Journal for Research in Mathematics Education, 50*(3), 311–340. https://doi.org/10.5951/jresematheduc.50.3.0311

Jett, C. C. (2019b). Using personal narratives to elucidate my CRT(ME) journey. In J. Davis & C. C. Jett (Eds.), *Critical race theory in mathematics education* (pp. 164–182). Routledge.

Jett, C. C. (2021). The qualms and quarrels with online undergraduate mathematics: The experiences of African American male STEM majors. *Investigations in Mathematics Learning, 13*(1), 18–28. https://doi.org/10.1080/19477503.2020.1827663

Jett, C. C. (2022a). "I have the highest GPA, but I can't be the valedictorian?": Two Black males' exclusionary valedictory experiences. *Race Ethnicity and Education, 25*(2), 290–308. https://doi.org/10.1080/13613324.2019.1599341

Jett, C. C. (2022b). "Third floor respect": A Black masculinist examination of Morehouse College's mathematics learning community. *The Journal of Higher Education, 93*(2), 248–272. https://doi.org/10.1080/00221546.2021.1971486

Jett, C. C., Savage, K, Ortiz, N. A., & China, E. J. (2021). Black male mathematics educators speak: Reflections from a symposium. *Journal of African American Males in Education, 12*(2), 1–16.

Jett, C. C., Stinson, D. W., & Williams, B. A. (2015). Communities for and with Black male students: Four strategies that can be effective in creating supportive learning environments. *Mathematics Teacher, 109*(4), 284–289. https://www.jstor.org/stable/10.5951/mathteacher.109.4.0284

Johnson, E., Keller, R., & Fukawa-Connelly, T. (2018). Results from a survey of abstract algebra instructors across the United States: Understanding the choice to (not) lecture. *International Journal of Research in Undergraduate Mathematics Education, 4*(2), 254–285. https://doi.org/10.1007/s40753-017-0058-1

Johnson, L., & Bryan, N. (2017). Using our voices, losing our bodies: Michael Brown, Trayvon Martin, and the spirit murders of Black male professors in the academy. *Race Ethnicity and Education, 20*(2), 163–177. https://doi:10.1080/13613324.2016.1248831

Johnson, M. L. (1984). Blacks in mathematics: A status report. *Journal for Research in Mathematics Education, 15*(2), 145–153. https://doi.org/10.2307/748890

Jones, S. M. (2019). *Women who count: Honoring African American women mathematicians.* American Mathematical Society.

Jones Williams, M. (2017). *Mathematically talented Black women of Spelman College, 1980s–2000s.* [Doctoral dissertation, Georgia State University]. https://scholarworks.gsu.edu/mse_diss/40/

Joseph, G. G. (1990). *The crest of the peacock: Non-European roots of mathematics.* Penguin Books.

Joseph, N. M., Hailu, M., & Boston, D. L. (2017). Black girls' and women's persistence in the P–20 mathematics pipeline: Two decades of children, youth, and adult education research. *Review of Research in Education, 41*(1), 203–227.

Joseph, R. L. (2011). Imagining Obama: Reading overtly and inferentially racist images of our 44th president, 2007–2008. *Communication Studies, 62*(4), 389–405. http://dx.doi.org/10.1080/10510974.2011.588074

Kafele, B. K. (2009). *Motivating Black males to achieve in school & in life.* ASCD.

Kedlaya, K. S., Poonen, B., & Vakil, R. (2002). *The William Lowell Putnam Mathematical Competition 1985–2000: Problems, solutions, and commentary.* Mathematical Association of America.

Kenschaft, P. C. (2005). *Change is possible: Stores of women and minorities in mathematics.* American Mathematical Society.

King, J. E., & Swartz, E. E. (2018). *Heritage knowledge in the curriculum: Retrieving an African episteme.* Routledge.

Kline, J. (2019, September 22). Billionaire makes good on promise to settle debt for Morehouse graduates. www.diverseeducation.com/article/155459/

Kurepa, A. (2019). The design and implementation of a mathematics learning community. *International Journal of Higher Education, 8*(3), 77–82. http://dx.doi.org/10.5430/ijhe.v8n3p77

Ladson-Billings, G. (2013). Critical race theory—What it is not! In M. Lynn & A. D. Dixson (Eds.), *Handbook of critical race theory in education* (pp. 34–47). Routledge.

Ladson-Billings, G., & Tate, W. (1995). Toward a critical race theory in education. *Teachers College Record, 97*(1), 47–68. https://www.tcrecord.org/Content.asp?ContentID=1410

Lawrence-Lightfoot, S., & Davis, J. H. (1997). *The art and science of portraiture.* Jossey-Bass.

Ledesma, M. C., & Calderón, D. (2015). Critical race theory in education: A review of past literature and a look to the future. *Qualitative Inquiry, 21*(3), 206–222. https://doi.org/10.1177%2F1077800414557825

Leonard, J., & Martin, D. B. (Eds.). (2013). *The brilliance of Black children in mathematics: Beyond the numbers and toward new discourse.* Information Age.

Lesane-Brown, C. L. (2006). A review of race socialization within Black families. *Developmental Review, 26*(4), 400–426. https://doi.org/10.1016/j.dr.2006.02.001

Levy, R., Laugesen, R., & Santosa, F. (2018). *BIG jobs guide: Business, industry, and government careers for mathematical scientists, statisticians, and operations researchers.* Society for Industrial and Applied Mathematics.

Lew, K., Fukawa-Connelly, T. P., Mejia-Ramos, J. P., & Weber, K. (2016). Lectures in advanced mathematics: Why students might not understand what the mathematics professor is trying to convey. *Journal for Research in Mathematics Education, 47*(2), 162–198. https://doi.org/10.5951/jresematheduc.47.2.0162

Leyva, L. (2021). Black women's counter-stories of resilience and within-group tensions in the White, patriarchal space of mathematics education. *Journal for Research in Mathematics Education, 52*(2), 117–151. http://dx.doi.org/10.5951/jresematheduc-2020-0027

Lorch, L. (1996). The painful path toward inclusiveness. In B. A. Case (Ed.), *A century of mathematical meetings* (pp. 83–94). American Mathematical Society.

Love, B. L. (2014). "I *see* Trayvon Martin": What teachers can learn from the tragic death of a young Black male. *The Urban Review, 46*(2), 292–306. https://doi.org/10.1007/s11256-013-0260-7

Lundy-Wagner, V., & Gasman, M. (2011). When gender issues are not just about women: Reconsidering male students at historically Black colleges and universities. *Teachers College Record, 113*(5), 934–969.

Maietta, R., Mihas, P., Swartout, K., Petruzzelli, J., & Hamilton, A. (2021). Sort and sift, think and shift: Let the data be your guide—An applied approach to working with, learning from, and privileging qualitative data. *The Qualitative Report, 26*(6), 2045–2060. https://doi.org/10.46743/2160-3715/2021.5013

Malcom, S. (2021, April 23–26). *Real analysis: Why isn't there more diversity in mathematics graduate education?* [Plenary]. AMS paraDIGMS (Virtual conference). https://www.imsi.institute/paradigms-spring-2021/

Malloy, C. E. (1997). Including African American students in the mathematics community. In J. Trentacosta & M. J. Kennedy (Eds.), *Multicultural and gender equity in the mathematics classroom: The gift of diversity* (pp. 23–33). National Council of Teachers of Mathematics.

Martin, D. B. (2000). *Mathematics success and failure among African-American youth: The roles of sociohistorical context, community forces, school influence, and individual agency.* Lawrence Erlbaum Associates.

Martin, D. B. (2009). Researching race in mathematics education. *Teachers College Record, 111*(2), 295–338. https://doi.org/10.5951/jresematheduc.44.1.0316

Martin, D. B. (2019). Equity, inclusion, and antiblackness in mathematics education. *Race Ethnicity and Education, 22*(4), 459–478. http://dx.doi.org/10.1080/13613324.2019.1592833

Martin, D. B., Groves Price, P., & Moore, R. (2019). Refusing systemic violence against Black children: Toward a Black liberatory mathematics education. In J. Davis & C. C. Jett (Eds.), *Critical race theory in mathematics education* (pp. 32–55). Routledge.

Massey, W. A. (2022). From CAARMS25 to CAARMS 2021 and beyond: Conferences for African-American researchers in the mathematical sciences. *Notices of the AMS, 69*(2), 261–268. https://doi.org/10.1090/noti2413

Mathematical Association of America. (n.d.). Mathematical Association of America. http://www.maa.org.

Matias, C. E. (2016). *Feeling White: Whiteness, emotionality, and education.* Sense Publishers.

Mays, B. E. (2003). *Born to rebel: An autobiography.* University of Georgia Press. (Original work published 1971)

McCluskey, A. T. (1989). Mary McLeod Bethune and the education of Black girls. *Sex Roles, 21*(1/2), 113–126. https://doi.org/10.1007/BF00289731

McCoy, M. L. (2005). Calls: An inquiry into their origin, meaning, and function. In T. L. Brown, G. S. Parks, & C. M. Phillips (Eds.), *African American fraternities and sororities: The legacy and the vision* (pp. 295–313). University Press of Kentucky.

McGee, E. O. (2014). When it comes to the mathematics experiences of Black pre-service teachers . . . race matters. *Teachers College Record, 116*(6), 1–50. https://journals.sagepub.com/doi/10.1177/016146811411600608

McGee, E. O. (2015). Robust and fragile mathematical identities: A framework for exploring racialized experiences and high achievement among Black college students. *Journal for Research in Mathematics Education, 46*(5), 599–625. https://doi:10.5951/jresematheduc.46.5.0599

McGee, E. O., & Martin, D. B. (2011). From the hood to being hooded: A case study of a Black male PhD. *Journal of African American Males in Education, 2*(1), 46–65. https://jaamejournal.scholasticahq.com/article/18412.pdf

McGee, E. O., & Spencer, M. B. (2015). Black parents as advocates, motivators, and teachers of mathematics. *The Journal of Negro Education, 84*(3), 473–490. https://doi.org/10.7709/jnegroeducation.84.3.0473

McKinney de Royston, M., Vakil, S., Nasir, N., ross, k. m., Givens, J., & Holman, A. (2017). "He's more like a 'brother' than a teacher": Politicized caring in a program for African American males. *Teachers College Record, 119*(4), 1–40. https://www.tcrecord.org/Content.asp?ContentId=21748

McKittrick, K. (2014). Mathematics Black life. *The Black Scholar: Journal of Black Studies and Research, 44*(2), 16–28. https://doi.org/10.1080/00064246.2014.11413684

Megginson, R. E. (2003). Yueh-Gin Gung and Dr. Charles Y. Hu award to Clarence F. Stephens for distinguished service to mathematics. *The American Mathematical Monthly, 110*(3), 177–180.

Milner, H. R., & Lomotey, K. (Eds.). (2021). *Handbook of urban education* (2nd ed.). Routledge.

Mobley, S. D., & Hall, L. (2020). (Re)defining queer and trans* student retention and "success" at historically Black colleges and universities. *Journal of College Student Retention: Research, Theory & Practice, 21*(4), 497–519. https://doi.org/10.1177%2F1521025119895512

Mobley, S. D., & Johnson, J. M. (2019). "No pumps allowed": The "problem" with gender expression and the Morehouse College "appropriate attire policy." *Journal of Homosexuality, 66*(7), 867–895. http://dx.doi.org/10.1080/0091836 9.2018.1486063

Mondisa, J. L., & Main, J. B. (2021). Mentors' perceptions of their African American undergraduate protégés' needs and challenges. *The Journal of Negro Education, 90*(2), 195–210. https://www.muse.jhu.edu/article/820492

Morehouse College. (2019, October 7). Oprah Winfrey announces $13 million gift to Morehouse College for Scholars Fund. *Inside* [Blog]. https://inside.morehouse.edu/news/news-inside/oprah-winfrey-announces-13-million-gift-to-morehouse-college-for-scholars-fund.html

Morehouse College. (n.d.). Morehouse College. https://www.morehouse.edu/

Moses, R. P., & Cobb, C. E. (2002). *Radical equations: Civil rights from Mississippi to the Algebra Project*. Beacon Press.

Mulcahy, C. (2017, January 4–7). *A century of mathematical excellence at Spelman College* [Conference session]. Joint Mathematics Meeting, Atlanta, GA. http://digitalcommons.auctr.edu/scpubs/13

Mutua, A. D. (Ed.). (2006). *Progressive Black masculinities*. Routledge.

Nasir, N. S. (2007). Identity, goals, and learning: The case of basketball mathematics. In N. S. Nasir & P. Cobb (Eds.), *Improving access to mathematics: Diversity and equity in the classroom* (pp. 132–145). Teachers College Press.

National Association of Mathematicians. (n.d.). Welcome to NAM! https://www.nam-math.org

National Council of Teachers of Mathematics. (2014). *Principles to action: Ensuring mathematics success for all*. Author.

National Research Council. (2013). *The mathematical sciences in 2025*. The National Academies Press.

National Science Foundation, National Center for Science and Engineering Statistics. (2017). *Women, minorities, and persons with disabilities in science and engineering: 2017* (Special Report NSF 17-310). Author.

Neal, M. A. (2013). *Looking for Leroy: Illegible Black masculinities*. New York University Press.

Noble, R. (2011). Mathematics self-efficacy and African American male students: An examination of two models of success. *Journal of African American Males in Education, 2*(2), 188–213.

Oeur, F. (2017). The respectable brotherhood: Young Black men in an all-boys charter high school. *Sociological Problems, 60*(6), 1063–1081. https://doi.org/10.1177/0731121417706071

O'Neil, C. (2016). *Weapons of math destruction: How big data increases inequality and threatens democracy*. Crown.

Owens, D., Lacey, K., Rawls, G., & Hobart-Quince, J. A. (2010). First-generation African American male college students: Implications for career counselors. *The Career Development Quarterly, 58*(4), 291–300. http://dx.doi.org/10.1002/j.2161-0045.2010.tb00179.x

Owens, E. W., Shelton, A. J., Bloom, C. M., & Cavil, J. K. (2012). The significance of HBCUs to the production of STEM graduates: Answering the call. *Educational Foundations, 26*(3/4), 33–47. https://eric.ed.gov/?id=EJ1000229

Paar, C., & Pelzl, J. (2009). *Understanding cryptography: A textbook for students and practitioners*. Springer.

Palmer, R. T., & Wood, J. L. (Eds.). (2012). *Black men in college: Implications for HBCUs and beyond*. Routledge.

Parks, G. S., & Brown, T. L. (2005). "In the fell clutch of circumstance": Pledging and the Black Greek experience. In T. L. Brown, G. S. Parks, & C. M. Phillips (Eds.), *African American fraternities and sororities: The legacy and the vision* (pp. 437–464). University Press of Kentucky.

Parshall, K. H. (2016). Mathematics and the politics of race: The case of William Claytor. *The American Mathematical Monthly, 123*(3), 214–240. http://dx.doi.org/10.4169/amer.math.monthly.123.3.214

Patton, L. D. (2014). Preserving respectability or blatant disrespect? A critical discourse analysis of the Morehouse appropriate attire policy and implications for intersectional approaches to examining campus policies. *International Journal of Qualitative Studies in Education, 27*(6), 724–746. http://dx.doi.org/10.1080/09518398.2014.901576

Patton, L. D., & Ward, L. W. (2016). Missing Black undergraduate women and the politics of disposability: A critical race feminist perspective. *The Journal of Negro Education, 85*(3), 330–349. https://www.jstor.org/stable/10.7709/jnegroeducation.85.3.0330

Pelzer, D. L. (2016). Creating a new narrative: Reframing Black masculinity for college men. *The Journal of Negro Education, 85*(1), 16–27. https://www.jstor.org/stable/10.7709/jnegroeducation.85.1.0016

Peretz, T. (2016). Why study men and masculinities? A theorized research review. *Graduate Journal of Social Science, 12*(3), 30–43.

Perry, T., Steele, C., & Hilliard, A., IIII. (2003). *Young, gifted, and Black: Promoting high achievement among African-American students*. Beacon Press.

Picker, S., & Berry, J. (2000). Investigating pupils' images of mathematicians. *Educational Studies in Mathematics, 43*(1), 65–94. http://dx.doi.org/10.1023/A:1017523230758

Pierre, P. A. (2015). A brief history of the collaborative minority engineering effort: A personal account. In J. B. Slaughter, Y. Tao, & W. Pearson, *Changing the face of engineering: The African American experience* (pp. 13–35). John Hopkins University Press.

Pittman, C. (2020). "Shopping while Black": Black consumers' management of racial stigma and racial profiling in retail settings. *Journal of Consumer Culture, 20*(1), 3–22. https://doi.org/10.1177/1469540517717777

Preissle, J., & Grant, L. (2004). Fieldwork traditions: Ethnography and participant observation. In K. deMarrais & S. D. Lapan (Eds.), *Foundations for research: Methods of inquiry in education and the social sciences* (pp. 161–180). Lawrence Erlbaum Associates.

Proffitt, W. A. (2022). From "problems" to "vulnerable resources": Reconceptualizing Black boys with and without disability labels in U.S. urban schools. *Urban Education, 57*(4), 686–713. https://doi.org/10.1177/0042085920972164

Quigley, M. W., & Mitchell, A. B. (2018). "What works": Applying critical race praxis to the design of educational and mentoring interventions for African American males. *Journal of African American Males in Education, 9*(2), 74–102.

Rasmussen, C., & Wawro, M. (2017). Post-calculus research in undergraduate mathematics education. In J. Cai (Ed.), *Compendium for research in mathematics education* (pp. 551–581). National Council of Teachers of Mathematics.

Reinholz, D. L. Rasmussen, C., & Nardi, E. (2020). Time for (research on) change in mathematics departments. *International Journal of Research in Undergraduate*

Mathematics Education, 6(2), 147–158. https://doi.org/10.1007/s40753-020 -00116-7

Reynolds, R. E., Howard, T. C., & Jones, T. K. (2015). Is this what educators really want? Transforming the discourse on Black fathers and their presence in schools. *Race Ethnicity and Education*, 18(1), 89–107. https://doi.org/10.1080 /13613324.2012.759931

Richards, D. A. R., & Awokoya, J. T. (2012). *Understanding HBCU retention and completion*. United Negro College Fund.

Richardson, R. (2007). *Black masculinity and the U.S. South: From Uncle Tom to gangsta*. University of Georgia Press.

Rizzo, C. (2017, February 10). The locations behind the true story of "Hidden Figures." https://www.travelandleisure.com/culture-design/tv-movies/hidden-figure -location-guide

Roberson, V. (2021, January 4). Virginia Union launches first national Center for the Study of HBCUs. https://hbcubuzz.com/2021/01/virginia-union-launches-first -national-center-for-the-study-of-hbcus/

Ross, L. C. (2000). *The divine nine: The history of African American fraternities and sororities*. Kensington Publishing.

Rousseau Anderson, C. (2020). The contrarieties of (mixed) race: The meaning of race from a multiracial perspective. In A. D. Dixson, G. Ladson-Billings, C. E. Suarez, W. T. Trent, & J. D. Anderson (Eds.), *Condition or process?: Researching race in education* (pp. 83–110). American Educational Research Association.

Rovaris, D. J. (2005). *Mays and Morehouse: How Benjamin E. Mays developed Morehouse College*. Beckham Publications Group.

Saldaña, J. (2013). *The coding manual for qualitative researchers* (2nd ed.). Sage.

Saxe, K., & Braddy, L. (2015). *A common vision for undergraduate mathematical sciences programs in 2025*. Mathematical Association of America.

Schumacher, C. S., & Siegel, M. J. (2015). *2015 CUPM curriculum guide to majors in the mathematical sciences*. Mathematical Association of America.

Scott, J., Trujillo, T., & Rivera, M. D. (2016). Reframing Teach for America: A conceptual framework for the next generation of scholarship. *Education Policy Analysis Archives*, 24(12), 1–28.

Seymour, E., & Hunter, A. (Eds.). (2019). *Talking about leaving revisited: Persistence, relocation, and loss in undergraduate STEM education*. Springer.

Shetterly, M. L. (2016). *Hidden figures: The American dream and the untold story of the Black women mathematicians who helped win the space race*. HarperCollins Publishers.

Sidbury, C. K., Johnson, J. S., & Burton, R. Q. (2015). Spelman's dual-degree engineering program: A path for engineering diversification. In J. B. Slaughter, Y. Tao, & W. Pearson, *Changing the face of engineering: The African American experience* (pp. 335–353). John Hopkins University Press.

Siddle Walker, V. (1996). *Their highest potential: An African American school community in the segregated South*. University of North Carolina Press.

Slack, M. (2013, May 19). President Obama delivers the commencement address at Morehouse College. *White House Blog*. https://obamawhitehouse.archives.gov /blog/2013/05/19/president-obama-delivers-commencement-address-morehouse -college

Smith, W. A., Allen, W. R., & Danley, L. L. (2007). "Assume the position . . . you fit the description": Psychosocial experiences and racial battle fatigue among African American male college students. *American Behavioral Scientist, 51*(4) 551–578. https://doi:10.1177/0002764207307742

Smith, W. A., Mustaffa, J. B., Jones, C. M., Curry, T. J., & Allen, W. R. (2016). "You make me wanna holler and throw up my hands!": Campus culture, Black misandric microaggressions, and racial battle fatigue. *International Journal of Qualitative Studies in Education, 29*(9), 1189–1209. https://doi.org/10.1080/09518398.2016.1214296

Smith, W. M., Voigt, M., Ström, A., Webb, D. C., & Martin, W. G. (Eds.). (2021). *Transformational change efforts: Student engagement in mathematics through an institutional network for active learning.* American Mathematical Society.

Smitherman, G. (2000). *Black talk: Words and phrases from the hood to the amen corner.* Houghton Mifflin.

Solórzano, D. G., & Yosso, T. J. (2002). Critical race methodology: Counterstorytelling as an analytical framework for education research. *Qualitative Inquiry, 8*(1), 23–44. https://doi.org/10.1177%2F107780040200800103

Stiff, L. B., & Harvey, W. B. (1988). On the education of Black children in mathematics. *Journal of Black Studies, 19*(2), 190–203. https://doi.org/10.1177/002193478801900206

Stinson, D. W. (2013). Negotiating the "White male math myth": African American male students and success in school mathematics. *Journal for Research in Mathematics Education, 44*(1), 69–99. https://doi.org/10.5951/jresematheduc.44.1.0069

Stinson, D. W., Jett, C. C., & Williams, B. (2013). Counterstories from mathematically successful African American male students. In J. Leonard & D. B. Martin (Eds.), *The brilliance of Black children in mathematics: Beyond the numbers and toward new discourse* (pp. 221–245). Information Age.

Strayhorn, T. (2019). *College students' sense of belonging: A key to educational success for all students* (2nd ed.). Routledge.

Strutchens, M. E. (2000). Confronting beliefs and stereotypes that impede the mathematical empowerment of African American students. In M. E. Strutchens, M. L. Johnson, & W. F. Tate (Eds.), *Changing the faces of mathematics: Perspectives on African Americans* (pp. 7–14). National Council of Teachers of Mathematics.

Sturner, K. K., Bishop, P., & Lenhart, S. M. (2017). Developing collaboration skills in team undergraduate research experiences. *PRIMUS, 27*(3), 370–388. https://doi.org/10.1080/10511970.2016.1188432

Tate, W. F. (1995). School mathematics and African American students: Thinking seriously about opportunity-to-learn standards. *Educational Administration Quarterly, 31*(3), 424–448. https://doi.org/10.1177%2F0013161X95031003006

Taylor, E. V. (2013). The mathematics of tithing: A study of religious giving and mathematical development. *Mind, Culture, and Activity, 20,* 132–149. http://dx.doi.org/10.1080/10749039.2012.691595

Thompson, G. L. (2003). No parent left behind: Strengthening ties between educators and African American parents/guardians. *The Urban Review, 35*(1), 7–23. https://doi.org/10.1023/A:1022589405679

Thompson, G. L. (2008). *What African American parents want educators to know.* Rowman & Littlefield Education.

Thompson, R. C., Monroe-White, T., Xavier, J., Howell, C., Moore, M. R., & Haynes, J. K. (2016). Preparation of underrepresented males for scientific careers: A study of the Dr. John H. Hopps Jr. defense research scholars program at Morehouse College. *CBE—Life Sciences Education, 15*(3), 1–13. https://doi .org/10.1187/cbe.15-12-0263

Toldson, I. A. (2019). *No BS (bad stats): Black people need people who believe in Black people enough not to believe every bad thing they hear about Black people.* Brill Sense.

Trawick, C., Monroe-White, T., Tola, J. A., Clayton, J. P., & Haynes, J. K. (2020). K–12 DREAMS to teach program at Morehouse College: Challenges and opportunities creating the next generation of African American male STEM teachers. *Journal of College Science Teaching, 49*(5), 68–75.

Urschel, J., & Thomas, L. (2019). *Mind and matter: A life in math and football.* Penguin Press.

U.S. Bureau of Labor Statistics. (2022). *Occupational employment and wage statistics: Major occupational groups as a percentage of total employment, May 2021.* https://www.bls.gov/oes/2021/may/largest3.htm

U.S. Department of Education, Institute of Education Sciences, National Center for Education Statistics. (2019). *Annual reports and information staff.* http://nces .ed.gov/annuals/

U.S. Office of the Press Secretary. (2014, February 27). *Remarks by the president on "My Brother's Keeper" initiative* [Transcript]. https://www.whitehouse.gov/the -press-office/2014/02/27/remarks-president-my-brothers-keeper-initiative

Walker, E. N. (2012). *Building mathematics learning communities: Improving outcomes in urban high schools.* Teachers College Press.

Walker, E. N. (2014). *Beyond Banneker: Black mathematicians and the paths to excellence.* State University of New York Press.

Walker, E. N. (2016). The importance of communities for mathematics learning and socialization. *Journal of Urban Mathematics Education, 9*(2), 5–10. https://doi .org/10.21423/jume-v9i2a315

Watkins, W. H. (2001). *The White architects of Black education: Ideology and power in America, 1865–1954.* Teachers College Press.

Wei, X., Lenz, K. B., & Blackorby, J. (2013). Math growth trajectories of students with disabilities: Disability category, gender, racial, and socioeconomic status differences from ages 7 to 17. *Remedial and Special Education, 34*(3), 154–165. https://doi.org/10.1177%2F0741932512448253

Whitaker, T. R., & Snell, C. L. (2016). Parenting while powerless: Consequences of "the talk." *Journal of Human Behavior in the Social Environment, 26*(3–4), 303–309. https://doi.org/10.1080/10911359.2015.1127736

White, A. M., & Peretz, T. (2010). Emotions and redefining Black masculinity: Movement narratives of two profeminist organizers. *Men and Masculinities, 12*(4), 403–424.

Williams, K. L., & Davis, B. L. (2019). *Public and private investments and divestments in historically Black colleges and universities.* American Council on Education.

Williams, S. (1997). *Mathematicians of the African diaspora.* http://www.math .buffalo.edu/mad/index.html

Williams, T. (2018). *Power in numbers: The rebel women of mathematics*. Race Point Publishing.

Wolcott, H. F. (2008). *Ethnography: A way of seeing* (2nd ed.). AltaMira Press.

Wright, B. L., & Counsell, S. L. (2018). *The brilliance of Black boys: Cultivating school success in the early grades*. Teachers College Press.

Zaslavsky, C. (1999). *Africa counts: Number and pattern in African cultures* (3rd ed.). Lawrence Hill Books.

Zhoa, C., & Kuh, G. (2004). Adding value: Learning communities and student engagement. *Research in Higher Education, 45*(2), 115–138. https://doi.org/10.1023/B:RIHE.0000015692.88534.de

Index

About the Author

Christopher C. Jett, PhD, is an Associate Professor of Mathematics Education in the College of Education & Human Development at Georgia State University. Prior to this, he spent a decade as a professor in the Department of Computing and Mathematics at the University of West Georgia. As one of the nation's foremost scholars regarding Black men's math experiences, his work has been published in *The Journal of Negro Education,* the *Journal of African American Studies,* the *Journal for Research in Mathematics Education,* and *The Journal of Higher Education.* He also coedited *Critical Race Theory in Mathematics Education* (Routledge, 2019).

Dr. Jett has a distinguished record of research, teaching, service, and leadership in math education. He received NSF's Faculty Early Career Development (CAREER) award, the 2019 Early Career Award from the Association of Mathematics Teacher Educators (AMTE), and a Presidential Early Career Award for Scientists and Engineers (PECASE). In addition, he was appointed to the U.S. National Commission on Mathematics Instruction in 2021, a council under the auspices of the National Academy of Sciences—National Research Council.

Dr. Jett received a bachelor's degree in mathematics and a master's degree in the mathematical sciences from Tennessee State University as well as his doctoral degree in mathematics education from Georgia State University. With longstanding interests in race-related work, he takes great pride in conducting research and teaching math. On a personal note, he enjoys singing in his church choir, mentoring via the 100 Black Men of America, Inc., and playing spades.